Medical Eponyms: Who *Was* Coudé?

Medical Eponyms: Who *Was* Coudé?

JOHN A. LOURIE, BM, PhD, FRCS

Professor of Human Biology
University of Papua New Guinea
Sometime Senior Registrar
Nuffield Orthopaedic Centre
and John Radcliffe Hospital,
Oxford

Churchill Livingstone ▥

EDINBURGH LONDON MELBOURNE AND NEW YORK 1986

CHURCHILL LIVINGSTON
Medical Division of Longman Group UK Limited

Distributed in the United States of America by
Churchill Livingstone Inc., 1560 Broadway, New York,
N.Y. 10036, and by associated companies, branches
and representatives throughout the world.

First published 1982 (Pitman Publishing Ltd)
  Reprinted 1983
  Reprinted 1984
  Reprinted 1986 (Churchill Livingstone)

ISBN 0-443-03802-3

British Library Cataloguing in Publication Data
Lourie, J. A.
  Medical eponyms: who was Coudé?
  1. Medicine—Glossaries, vocabularies, etc.
  I. Title
  603   R121

Printed at The Bath Press, Avon

For Lucinda, Sara and David

Contents

Foreword

Everyone—at least every right-thinking person—loves eponyms. Who would deprive Magellan of his Straits or Everest of his Mount? Eponyms are not vestigial remains—they are human memoranda, breathing life and warmth into their context. The vocabulary of doctors would be so much poorer without Cushing's syndrome, Colles' fracture or Still's disease. There may be dreary pedants who would prefer adult hyperadrenocorticism, a transverse fracture of the lower radius and juvenile polyarthritis with splenomegaly and lymphadenopathy. But even they might jib at the jargon resulting from dehumanising Cheyne-Stokes respiration or Syme's amputation.

Eponyms have their uses. As students beginning Anatomy we used to ask each other over coffee (once the Times Crossword was completed), 'what of Fallopius' . . . or 'Malpighi' . . . 'and where?' Very instructive: and more recently I heard a Fellowship examiner pounce on a candidate who mentioned a Mr So-and-So (a somewhat doddery contemporary), to ask whether he was alive or dead; the laughter which greeted the reply 'Well, sir, about half and half', guaranteed a pass.

John Lourie has had the charming idea of collecting the more popular eponyms and adding pithily entertaining potted biographies of the originators (eponants? eponites? eponauts?). His researches have been extensive and rewarding. When, in 1968, Mercer Rang published his 'Anthology of Orthopaedics', which had a similar flavour, I bought 25 copies; one for my bedside and 24 to be used as small Christmas presents. I expect other surgeons did the same and, like me, only regret buying so few. I forecast a similar well-merited response to this present book.

A. Graham Apley, FRCS

Introduction

It will be evident to any serious medical historian that I
have leaned heavily in the compilation of this little
dictionary on a number of excellent reference sources:
these are listed in the Bibliography, which is by no
means exhaustive. The interested reader is referred to
these books, which contain a wealth of fascinating
material to which I have pleasure in acknowledging a
great debt.

It is well known that the names attached to diseases or
syndromes, tests, operations and instruments, and
anatomical features, are in many instances quite unfair
with respect to precedence. For this reason, if no other,
many deplore the perpetuation of personalities by
medical eponyms. It is also undeniable that an
eponymous title conveys no scientific information. On
the other hand, I would agree with Jessie Dobson (1962)
that 'the eponym tends to serve as a mnemonic, since it
arouses the interest of the student in the historical side of
his studies'. In any event, there seems little doubt that,
rightly or wrongly, most of the names listed here are in
everyday use, and are here to stay, and one might
perhaps forgive the examiner who looked askance at the
candidate who knew all about paralysis agitans, but had
never heard of Parkinson.

The sum of our present medical knowledge is built on
the multitude of contributions, large and small, of
individuals over the centuries. We can take heart from
the fact that these pages show that they include the
obscure, the poor, the very young, and even the mad, as
well as the rich and the famous and the successful in the
eyes of the world. Somehow, the recorded foibles of
some of our more colourful predecessors do seem to
help one remember better the details of the condition to
which their name has been attached.

The length of each biographical note is not intended

to bear any relation to the importance of the individual's contribution; indeed those apparently dismissed in a few lines are in many cases the truly great, about whom, however, much more eloquent and comprehensive information is readily available elsewhere.

If this book serves no other purpose, I hope at least that it will help to remind us what we can easily forget in this era of high technology: that medicine is people.

Oxford, April 1981

My thanks are due to Mrs Gill McGinn for her help with typing the manuscript, and to my family for putting up with me.

Abbreviations

The following abbreviations are used in the text:

★	Individual also listed in his or her own right
Barts	St Bartholemew's Hospital, London
(C)	Contemporary
D.	Year of description
FRCP	Fellow of the Royal College of Physicians
FRCS	Fellow of the Royal College of Surgeons
FRS	Fellow of the Royal Society
GMC	General Medical Council
MRC	Medical Research Council
P.	Professor
U.	University
UCH	University College Hospital, London

Medical Eponyms

A

ABBOTT, William Osler (1902–1943)
Miller–Abbott Tube: See *Miller*. D. 1934. (Sometimes called Abbott–Rawson tube.)

Assistant P. of Medicine, U. of Pennsylvania, Philadelphia.

ACHILLES
Achilles Tendon: Calcaneal tendon.

Greek hero, son of Peleus and Thetis, said to have been held by one heel when dipped in the River Styx by his mother, becoming invulnerable wherever the water had touched him. He was finally killed by Paris who wounded him fatally in the heel.

ADAMKIEWICZ, Albert (1850–1921)
Arteries of Adamkiewicz: Vessels supplying the spinal cord. D. 1882.

He studied in Königsberg, Breslau and Würzburg, becoming P. of Pathology in Cracow, then Vienna.

ADAMS, Robert (1791–1875)
Stokes–Adams Attacks: See *Stokes*. D. 1827. (D. 1846 by Stokes, 1761 by Morgagni★, and 1691 by Gerbezius.)

He founded the Peter Street and Carmichael Schools of Medicine in Dublin, was appointed Regius P. of Surgery in Dublin aged 70, and became Surgeon to Queen Victoria. He was President of the Royal

College of Surgeons of Ireland three times. He suffered from gout and wrote a classic paper on it (1857), but died of a heart attack.

ADDIS, Thomas (1881–1949)
Addis Count: Cellular and protein analysis of urine to diagnose renal pathology. D. 1925.

San Francisco physician.

ADDISON, Sir Christopher (1869–1951)
1. *Transpyloric Plane of Addison*: Transverse line midway between the suprasternal notch and the symphysis pubis, at the level of the pylorus and of the L1/2 intervertebral disc. D. 1899.
2. *Addison's Point*: The mid-epigastric point.

He studied at Barts, taught anatomy at Sheffield as Tutor, then Lecturer from 1894 to 1896, becoming FRCS in 1895, and was appointed the first Arthur Jackson P. of Anatomy in Sheffield the same year, aged 26. From 1901 to 1907 he was Lecturer in Anatomy and Dean of the Charing Cross Hospital Medical School, and from 1907 to 1913, Lecturer in Anatomy at Barts. Meanwhile he was elected MP for Hoxton (Shoreditch) in London's East End, and from 1918 to 1921 was Britain's first Minister of Health, under Lloyd George.

ADDISON Thomas (1793–1860)
1. *Addison's Anaemia*: Pernicious anaemia ('of Addison–Biermer') due to Vitamin B_{12} deficiency. D. 1849.
2. *Addison's Disease*: Adrenal insufficiency, classically due to TB of adrenals. D. 1849.

Born in Long Benton, Northumberland, the son of a grocer of Cumbrian yeoman stock, he qualified both at Edinburgh (1815) and at Guy's (1819), where he took down all his lecture notes in Latin. He founded the skin department while on the staff at Guy's: he was appointed Assistant Physician in 1824, Lecturer on Materia Medica in 1827, and Physician in 1837, and was a colleague of Bright★ and close friend of Robert Todd.★ The Founder of Endocrinology, he was the first to show that the adrenals were essential to life. Elected FRCP in 1838, he was an abrasive personality, said to be happier in the post-mortem room than in the wards. He married a widow with two children at 52, became a depressive, and died in

Brighton of a head injury after falling from a height, perhaps intentionally . His death was marked by only one obituary.

ADIE, William John (1886–1935)
Holmes–Adie Syndrome. (Pupil). See *Holmes.* D. 1931 (independently of Holmes).

Australian–born, he studied at Edinburgh, and became a neurologist in the First World War, surviving the retreat from Mons. He was later on the staffs of the Royal Northern, Royal London Ophthalmic, and Mount Vernon Hospitals, and the National Hospital for Nervous Diseases. A kindly and approachable man, he died of a coronary at 48.

ADSON, Alfred Washington (1887–1951)
1. *Adson's Forceps.*
2. *Adson's Syndrome*: Adult amaurotic familial idiocy.

P. of Neurosurgery, Mayo★ Clinic. He described several indications for sympathectomy including chronic arthritis (1930) and Hirschsprung's★ Disease (1933) and the operation of total parotidectomy with preservation of the facial nerve (1923).

ALBERS-SCHÖNBERG, Heinrich Ernst (1865–1921)
Albers-Schönberg Disease: Osteopetrosis, or 'marble-bone disease'. D. 1904.

Originally a surgeon, he became P. of Radiology, Hamburg. One of the first to use therapeutic X-rays to treat uterine cancer, he was himself one of the first 'X-ray martyrs' to die from excessive unprotected exposure to radiation.

ALBRIGHT, Fuller (1900–1969)
1. *Albright's Syndrome (1)*: Polyostotic fibrous dysplasia, precocious puberty, and café-au-lait skin patches. D. 1937.
2. *Albright's Syndrome (2)*: Pseudopseudohypo-parathyroidism. D. 1952.

P. of Medicine, Harvard University.

ALCOCK, Benjamin (b. 1801)
Alcock's Canal: Canal for the internal pudendal vessels and nerve in the ischio-rectal fossa. D. 1836.

A Scholar of Trinity College Dublin, he became in 1837 P. of Anatomy, Physiology and Pathology at

the new St Cecilia Street School of the Apothecaries'
Hall, Dublin, and in 1849, the first P. of Anatomy at
Queen's College, Cork. In 1853 he was asked to
resign by the Lord Lieutenant because of
'irregularities' in the working of the Anatomy Acts;
in 1855 he was dismissed, despite a petition to Queen
Victoria. He went to America and was never heard of
again.

ALDRICH, Robert Anderson (b. 1917)
1. *Wiskott-Aldrich Syndrome*: See *Wiskott*.
2. *Aldrich Syndrome*: Eczema, otitis media, bloody
diarrhoea, and thrombocytopenia in childhood
inherited as a sex-linked recessive.

He studied at Amherst College and Northwestern
U., Chicago, and became P. of Paediatrics and
Preventive Medicine, Denver, Colorado.

ALZHEIMER, Alois (1864–1915)
Alzheimer's Disease: A form of pre-senile dementia.
D. 1906.

Born in Bavaria, the son of a notary, he studied
medicine in Berlin, Würzburg and Tübingen, from
1882 to 1887. He worked closely with Nissl★ at
Frankfurt, and was at first a clinical neurologist. He
then turned to pathology, describing characteristic
microscopical changes in the brains of patients dying
with progressive dementia. Kraepelin employed him
at his clinic in Heidelberg in 1902, and in Munich in
1903. He became Privatdozent in 1904 and
Extraordinarius in 1908. In 1912 he was appointed P.
of Psychiatry, Breslau, and had a heart attack on the
train going there. He married the widow of a banker
treated for syphilis by his great friend Erb★, and died
of rheumatic endocarditis at 52.

ANDERSON, James Christie (C)
Anderson–Hynes Pyeloplasty: Reconstruction of renal
pelvis in hydronephrosis.

Surgeon, United Sheffield Hospitals.

ANDERSON, Roger (1891–1971)
Anderson Splint: Method of treating lower limb
fractures using the well leg for counter-traction. D.
1932.

Orthopaedic surgeon in Seattle, Washington, who
popularised external fixation. ('Roger Anderson
apparatus').

ANDREWS, Henry Russell (1871–1942)
Brandt-Andrews Manoeuvre: see *Brandt*.

Born in Highgate, London, the son of a vicar, he
qualified from the London Hospital in 1894,
returning there as Honorary Consultant Obstetrician
and Gynaecologist after postgraduate study in Berlin
and Vienna. He was a good teacher and swift
operator with a large private practice; he helped
found the British College of Obstetrics and
Gynaecology. He married late in life and retired
happily at 55 to a manor-house in Sussex.

ANGSTRÖM, Anders Jonas (1814–1874)
Angström: Unit of wave-length, 10^{-7} mm. D. 1853.

P. of Physics, Uppsala, Sweden, who discovered the
spectrum of haemoglobin in 1855. He discovered the
presence of hydrogen in the sun's atmosphere in
1862, and received the Rumford Medal of the Royal
Society in 1872.

APERT, Eugène (1868–1940)
Apert's Syndrome: Acrosphenosyndactylia: mental
retardation with a pointed head and syndactyly. D.
1923.

Paediatrician in Paris.

APLEY, Alan Graham (C)
Apley's Grinding Test: In a meniscal tear pain is
produced by compressing the joint surfaces with the
knee flexed and the patient prone.

Consulting Orthopaedic Surgeon, St Thomas's
Hospital, London, and Emeritus Orthopaedic
Surgeon, Rowley Bristow Orthopaedic Hospital,
Pyrford, Surrey.

ARGYLL ROBERTSON, See *Robertson*.

ARMSTRONG, Arthur Riley (C)
King-Armstrong Unit: See *King*.

Director of Laboratories, Hamilton Health
Association, Hamilton, Ontario, Canada. He was
previously at the Banting Institute, U. of Toronto.

ARNETH, Joseph (1873–1955)
Arneth Count: Proportion of segmented leucocytes in
a blood smear, presented graphically. A 'shift to the

left' indicates an increase in segmented forms. D. 1904.

German physician.

ARNOLD, Friedrich (1803–1890)
1. *Arnold's Nerve*: Auricular branch of the vagus. D. 1834.
2. *Arnold's Ganglion*: Otic ganglion.

He studied at Heidelberg, and was successively P. of Anatomy at Zürich (1835), Freiburg (1840), Tübingen (1845) and Heidelberg (1852), where he died.

ARNOLD, Julius A. (1835–1915)
Arnold–Chiari Malformation: Hind-brain anomaly in which the roof of the 4th ventricle lies below the level of the foramen magnum and causes CSF outflow obstruction and hydrocephalus. D. 1894.

P. of Pathological Anatomy, Heidelberg.

ARRHENIUS, Svante August (1859–1927)
Doctrine of Arrhenius: The rate of a reaction depends upon temperature.

Born in Vik, Sweden, he was the son of a surveyor who was Supervisor of Uppsala U., where Svante studied mathematics, chemistry and physics. He only received a 4th class for his doctoral thesis on the electrolytic theory of dissociation in Stockholm in 1884, but was soon recognised and worked in Riga, Leipzig, Würzburg (with Nernst*), Graz, and Amsterdam. In 1895 he became P. of Physics in Stockholm, and Rector of the U. from 1896 to 1905. In 1903 he won the Nobel Prize for Chemistry, and became Director of Physical Chemistry at the Nobel Institute. He also received the Davy Medal, the Faraday Medal, and the first Willard Gibbs Medal, and became a foreign FRS in 1911. He married his best pupil in 1894.

ARTHUS, Nicholas Maurice (1862–1945)
Arthus Phenomenon: Immediate (Type III) hypersensitivity reaction with gangrene and ulceration at the site of a second injection of e.g. horse serum. D. 1903.

French physiologist and bacteriologist. He

demonstrated the importance of calcium in blood clotting in 1890.

ASCHHEIM, Selmar (1878–1965)
Aschheim–Zondek Pregnancy Test: Injection of pregnancy urine into mice. D. 1927.

Director of Laboratories, Women's Hospital, Berlin; Honorary P. of Gynaecology, U. of Berlin.

ASCHOFF, Karl Albert Ludwig (1866–1942)
1. *Aschoff's Node*: The atrio-ventricular node (also called the Node of Tawara★). D. 1906.
2. *Aschoff's Nodules*: Roughened inflammatory swellings on heart valves in rheumatic carditis. D. 1904.

Pathologist at the U. of Marburg, later P. of Pathology and Freiburg and then Berlin. He introduced the concept of the reticulo-endothelial system.

AUERBACH, Leopold (1828–1897)
Auerbach's Plexus: Myenteric plexus in gut wall. D. 1862.

In 1872 he became P. of Neuropathology at Breslau, where he was born and died.

AVOGADRO, Amadeo (1776–1856)
Avogadro's Hypothesis (or Law): Equal volumes of all gases at the same temperature and pressure contain the same number of molecules. D. 1811.

P. of Mathematical Physics, Turin. He was the first to demonstrate that the molecules of many elements contain more than one atom.

AXENFELD, Karl Theodor Paul Polykarpus (1867–1930)
Morax–Axenfeld Bacillus: See *Morax*.

Ophthalmologist in Heidelberg.

B

BABBITT, Isaac (1799–1862)
Babbitt's Metal: Alloy of tin, copper and antimony, used in dental fillings.

American engineer and designer who also invented the computer ('Babbitt's Machine').

BABCOCK, William Wayne (1872–1963)
Babcock's Tissue-holding Forceps

Philadelphia surgeon. Several operations (for varicose veins, hernia, spina bifida and aortic aneurysm) also bear his name.

BABINSKI, Joseph François Felix (1857–1932)
Babinski's Sign: Extensor plantar response to stroking the sole in upper motor neurone lesions of the pyramidal tract. D. 1896. (E. Remak had noted the sign 3 years before, but did not grasp its diagnostic significance.)

Born in Paris, the son of Polish political refugees, in 1884 he qualified MD Paris with a thesis on multiple sclerosis. He was a pupil of and Assistant to Charcot★ at the Salpêtrière, and Head of the Neurological Clinic at the Hôpital La Pitié from 1890 to 1927, but failed the competitive examination for Full Professor, so did not succeed Charcot. A famous gourmet, he developed Parkinson's★ Disease in old age, but wrote 288 papers over 48 years, including descriptions of the pupillary reflex (1900) and acromegaly with a pituitary tumour (1900), and in 1922 he localised clinically the first spinal cord tumour to be removed in France.

von BAER, Karl, Ernst (1792–1876)
von Baer's Law: Early phases in animals' life-histories resemble each other more than later phases.

'The Father of Modern Embryology' was born in Estonia, and became successively P. of Zoology at Dorpat, Königsberg and St Petersburg (1834–1867), where he was a convenor of the first Congress of Anthropologists, in 1861. He was the first to describe the three embryonic germ layers (1828), and discovered the mammalian ovum (1827) and the notochord.

BAINBRIDGE, Francis Arthur (1874–1921)
Bainbridge Reflex: Increased venous pressure with increased heart-rate. D. 1914.

Physiologist, U. of Durham College of Medicine.

BAKER, William Morrant (1838–1896)
Baker's Cyst: Popliteal cyst; a pressure diverticulum

behind the knee commonly associated with osteoarthrosis. D. 1877.

The son of a solicitor, he obtained the FRCS at 25, but took another 18 years to get on the staff at Barts as Full Surgeon. Meanwhile he was out-patient assistant, casualty surgeon, physician-in-charge of the skin department, anatomy lecturer, and assistant to Paget★ in his private practice. He invented the rubber tracheostomy tube (1877) and married his anaesthetist's sister. He died of locomotor ataxia.

BAKEŠ, Jaroslav (1871–1930)
Bakeš Dilator: Olive-tipped instrument for dilating the common bile duct and sphincter of Oddi★. D. 1928

Chief Surgeon to the County Hospital, Brno, Czechoslovakia.

BALL, Sir Charles Bent (1851–1916)
Anal Valves of Ball: Remnants of fusion of proctodaeum with post-allantoic gut. (Previously D. by Morgagni★.)

Born in Dublin, he became Regius P. of Surgery there, a Member of the GMC, and Surgeon to the King in Ireland. He described operations for rectal prolapse and hernia, and sensory neurectomy for pruritus ani. In 1900 he became an honorary FRCS, in 1903 was knighted, and in 1911 was made a baronet. He died in Dublin.

BANCROFT, Joseph (1836–1894)
Wuchereria bancroftii: See *Wucherer*. D. 1878. (Also called *Filaria bancroftii*.)

The son of a famous London physiologist, he became Surgeon to the General Hospital, Brisbane, Australia.

BANKART, Arthur Sydney Blundell (1879–1951)
1. *Bankart Lesion*: Separation of the anterior part of the glenoid labrum in recurrent shoulder dislocation.
2. *Bankart Procedure*: Operative reattachment of the above-mentioned labral detachment. (He first performed this operation in 1923, on one of his former house-surgeons.) Perthes★ had in fact performed a similar procedure in 1906.

The son of an Exeter surgeon, he studied at Guy's, and was the first surgical registrar at the Royal

National Orthopaedic Hospital, where he was later on the staff. He was Surgeon to Maida Vale Hospital for Nervous Diseases from 1911 to 1933, and during the First World War worked closely with Robert Jones★ and Girdlestone★. In 1920 he was also appointed as the first Orthopaedic Surgeon to the Middlesex Hospital, where he stayed until 1946. He was President of the British Orthopaedic Association in 1932–1933.

BANTI, Guido (1852–1925)
Banti's Syndrome: Hepatomegaly, splenomegaly and thrombocytopenia. D. 1882.

Pathologist and physician in Florence, Italy.

BÁRÁNY, Robert (1876–1936)
Bárány Noise Machine: ENT instrument for aural testing.

Born and trained in Vienna, he worked as a neurologist in Frankfurt, Heidelberg and Paris, before returning to Vienna where he worked in Politzer's★ Ear Clinic, especially on vestibular disorders, becoming Privatdozent in 1908 and then P. Extraordinarius. During the First World War in the Austrian Army he was taken prisoner by the Russians, and in 1914 Prince Karl of Sweden had to persuade the Tsar to release him to travel to Stockholm to receive the Nobel Prize. In 1917 he became P. of Otology in Uppsala, and was a noted humanitarian and pacifist.

BARLOW, Sir Thomas (1845–1945)
Barlow's Disease: Infantile scurvy. D. 1882. (First noted with the introduction of prepared infant feeds, and given Barlow's name by Heubner in Germany in 1892.)

He studied at Manchester and University College, London, and was Physician to Charing Cross Hospital (1876) and UCH (1880–1910), and was also on the Staff of Great Ormond Street Hospital for Sick Children. He was Physician to Queen Victoria, Edward VII and George V; was knighted in 1900; and became President of the Royal College of Physicians from 1910 to 1914. He also described the subcutaneous nodules of rheumatic fever in 1881.

BARLOW, Thomas G. (C)
Barlow's Test: Modifications of Ortolani's★ Test for congenital dislocation of the hip.

Orthopaedic Surgeon, Hope Hospital, Manchester.

BARR, Murray Llewellyn (b. 1908)
Barr Body: Sex chromatin body. D. 1949.

The son of a Canadian farmer of Ulster extraction, he qualified MD at the U. of Western Ontario (1933) where he subsequently became Head of the Department of Anatomy in the Health Sciences Center.

BARRÉ, Jean Alexandre (1880–1967)
Guillain–Barré Syndrome: See *Guillain*.

Born in Nantes, where he studied medicine, he was Babinski's★ houseman in Paris, and wrote a thesis on tabetic osteoarthropathy. During the First World War he was at the Neurological Centre of the 6th Army, whose Director was Guillain★. Together they wrote a textbook on war-time neurological practice: Barré received the Légion d'Honneur. In 1919 he became P. of Neurology in Strasbourg. He wrote over 800 papers, and was President of the Société de Neurologie in 1937. During the Second World War his Department was removed to Clermont-Ferrand; he then returned to Strasbourg, and died following a stroke.

BARRETT, Norman Rupert (1903–1979)
Barrett's Ulcer: Oesophageal ulceration with stricture. D. 1950.

Born in Adelaide, South Australia, he was educated in England at Eton (he hit a 'six' in the Eton–Harrow match at Lords) and Trinity College, Cambridge, and became Thoracic Surgeon to St Thomas's and the Brompton Hospitals, London.

BARTHOLIN, Caspar Secundus (1655–1738)
Bartholin's Glands: Greater vestibular glands. D. 1677.

One of a distinguished Copenhagen family of theologians, physicians, physicists, orientalists and writers, his father Thomas (1616–1680) was an anatomist and P. of Mathematics, who discovered the adrenal medulla, the thoracic duct, and the lymphatic system. His grandfather Caspar Primus, the brother-in-law of Ole Worm★, was P. of Medicine at

Copenhagen for 52 years, and five of his seven sons became Professors there, while his daughter founded a dynasty of doctors. At 13, Bartholin edited his father's book on the anatomy of the swan; at 16 became a medical student; at 19 P. of Philosophy, and then of Medicine, Anatomy and Physics, at the U. of Copenhagen. In 1703 he turned to politics, eventually becoming Procurator-General and Deputy for Finances, and in 1731 he became a baronet.

BARTON, John Rhea (1794–1871)
Barton's Fracture: Fracture of articular margin of distal radius with anterior and proximal displacement. D. 1838.

Born in Pennsylvania, the son of a judge, he studied under Dr Physick, 'The father of American surgery', who was himself a pupil of John Hunter★. An ambidextrous surgeon, he practised in Philadelphia; he performed the first hip arthroplasty (1826) and was the first to wire a fractured patella (but the patient died of sepsis).

von BASEDOW, Carl Adolphe (1799–1854)
Jod-Basedow Thyrotoxicosis: (Jod is German for iodine.) Secondary thyrotoxicosis due to prophylactic iodine administration. D. 1840.

General practitioner, Mersburg, Germany.

BASSINI, Edoardo (1844–1924)
Bassini Repair: Inguinal herniorrhaphy by suture of the conjoint tendon to the inguinal ligament. D. 1889.

He studied in Turin under Antonio Carle (who also taught Galeazzi★ and who was a pupil of Billroth★) and became P. of Surgery at the U. of Padua.

BATSON, Oscar Vivian (b. 1894)
Vertebral Veins of Batson: Plexus of anastomotic channels which may be responsible for blood-borne spread of metastases from prostatic carcinoma to the lower vertebral and pelvic bones. D. 1940.

Anatomist in Philadelphia who perfected vein injection techniques.

BATTLE, William Henry (1855–1936)
1. *Battle's Sign*: Discolouration of post-auricular skin in middle cranial fossa fracture. D. 1890.
2. *Battle's Incision*: Muscle-cutting incision for

appendicectomy. D. 1895. (Also called Jaboulay's★ incision.)

Surgeon to St Thomas's Hospital, London.

BAZIN, Pierre Antoine Ernest (1807–1878)
Bazin's Disease: Erythema induratum with localised areas of fat necrosis which may ulcerate, occurring particularly in adolescent girls with plump legs and a tendency to chilblains. D. 1861.

Dermatologist, Hôpital St Louis, Paris. A pioneer of parasitology in skin conditions.

BEHÇET, Halushi (1889–1948)
Behçet's Syndrome: Ulceration of oro-pharynx and genitalia with arthralgia; probably auto-immune. D. 1937.

Turkish dermatologist.

BELL, Sir Charles (1774–1842)
1. *Bell's Palsy*: 'Idiopathic' lower motor neurone facial palsy. D. 1821.
2. *Long Thoracic Nerve of Bell*: Nerve to serratus anterior. D. 1821.
3. *Bell-Magendie Law*: Anterior spinal nerve roots are motor; posterior are sensory. D. 1811.

Born in Edinburgh, the son of a clergyman who died when Charles was 4, he was educated to the age of 14 by his mother, who taught him to draw. He studied medicine in Edinburgh, became FRCSE in 1799, and ran an anatomy school there with his brother John. After a feud between John and the medical faculty, he went to London in 1804 to teach artists and medical students at William Hunter's★ Great Windmill St Anatomy School (where the Lyric Theatre now stands). In 1807 he became P. of Anatomy at the Royal Academy, and in 1812 became the sole proprietor of the Windmill St School, and also became Surgeon to the Middlesex Hospital (whose medical school he founded), and later P. of Surgery at UCH. In 1815 he ran a military hospital in Brussels after Waterloo; in 1825 he became P. of Anatomy and Surgery at the Royal College of Surgeons; in 1826, became FRS; in 1831, was knighted; and from 1835 to 1842 was P. of Surgery at Edinburgh. He died in Worcestershire of a heart attack, two days after arriving there for a rest, saying 'London is a good place to live in, but not to die in.' A kind, cheerful man, he so lacked greed that he died almost bankrupt, and his widow was supported by the State.

BELLINI, Lorenzo (1643–1704)
Ducts of Bellini: Orifices of kidney tubules. D. 1662.

Born in Florence, he was an anatomist and physician, who also described the taste buds. At 21 he became P. of Philosophy and Anatomy at Pisa, a post he held for 30 years.

BENCE JONES, Henry (1818–1873)
Bence Jones Protein: Low molecular-weight heat-labile protein found in the urine of patients with multiple myeloma. D. 1848.

Physician to St George's Hospital, London.

BENEDICT, Stanley Rossiter (1884–1936)
Benedict's Test (and Reagent): Semi-quantitative test for glycosuria. The reagent is based on Fehling's★ solution. D. 1915.

Physiological chemist, Cornell U., New York.

BENNETT, Edward Halloran (1837–1907)
Bennett's Fracture: Intra-articular fracture-subluxation of the base of the first metacarpal. D. 1886.

The son of the Recorder of Cork, Ireland, he qualified in medicine at Trinity College, Dublin, and became an anatomist. Later he became P. of Surgery at Trinity College, succeeding Robert Smith★, and then President of the Royal College of Surgeons of Ireland. A great collector of bone pathology, he is remembered as an honest man and a fine teacher, but was inclined to be blunt to the point of rudeness.

BERKEFELD, Wilhelm (1836–1897)
Berkefeld Filter: Bacterial filter.

German manufacturer and chemist, who owned the mine at Kieselgühr, Hanover, where the earth was mined for the production of this filter by Nordtmeyer, in 1891.

BERRY, Sir James (1860–1946)
Berry Aneurysm: Vascular anomaly, commonly on the Circle of Willis★, whose rupture may be the cause of a subarachnoid haemorrhage.

Canadian surgeon.

BETZ, Vladimir Aleksandrovich (1834–1894)
Betz Cells: Large pyramidal cells of the motor cortex.
D. 1874.

P. of Anatomy, Kiev, Ukraine, from 1868 to 1889.

BIEDL, Arthur (1869–1933)
Laurence–Moon–Biedl Syndrome: See *Laurence*. D.
1922.

P. of Physiology, German U., Prague. An
endocrinologist who in 1910 demonstrated the
adrenal cortex to be essential for life.

BIELSCHOWSKY, Max (1869–1940)
Bielschowsky's Stain: Ammoniacal silver stain for
nerve tissue. D. 1904.

Born in Breslau, the son of a merchant, he studied
there and in Berlin and Munich (MD 1893), worked
with Edinger★ and Weigert★ in Frankfurt, and then
moved to the Neurobiology laboratory at the U. of
Berlin. In 1933 he was dismissed by the Nazis, and
worked in Amsterdam, Utrecht and Madrid, and
then in London where he died of a stroke.

BIER, August Karl Gustav (1861–1949)
Bier's Block: Ischaemic arm block for regional
anaesthesia. D. 1908.

Berlin surgeon who pioneered spinal anaesthesia
(using cocaine) and wrote extensively on medical
philosophy and Hippocratic doctrine. He described
an osteoplastic amputation of the leg, and a method
of treatment of acute limb infections by venous
congestion produced by proximal constriction with a
rubber band.

BIGELOW, Henry Jacob (1818–1890)
1. *Y-Shaped Ligament of Bigelow*: Ilio–femoral
ligament of the hip-joint; the strongest ligament in
the body. D. 1869.
2. *Bigelow's Evacuator*: Instrument for removing
fragmented bladder calculi after litholapaxy. D. 1878.

Born in Boston, Massachusetts, the son of a doctor,
he studied in France and at Harvard (MD 1841). In
1846 he became surgeon to Massachusetts General
Hospital, and from 1849 to 1882 was P. of Surgery at
Harvard U. Medical School. Primarily a urologist,
and pioneer of litholapaxy, he was also the first to

resect the head of the femur (1852) – an operation later known as Girdlestone's★ procedure.

BILHARZ, Theodor Maximilian (1825–1862)
Bilharzia: Schistosomiasis. D. 1852.

German physician and comparative anatomist who became P. of Zoology in Cairo.

BILLROTH, Christian Albert Theodore (1829–1894)
Billroth Gastrectomy: ('Billroth I') Subtotal gastrectomy – excision of the pyloric part of the stomach with end-to-end anastomosis of the remaining stomach to the duodenum. D. 1881.

Born in Bergen in Rügen, Prussia, he studied in Griefswald, Göttingen and Berlin. He was Assistant at Langenbeck's★ Clinic from 1853 to 1860, and is considered 'the father of modern abdominal surgery', and was a pioneer of Listerian★ antisepsis in Europe. He founded the Vienna School of Surgery, was the first to resect the oesophagus (1872), and to perform total laryngectomy (1873), and gastrectomy (1881) successfully. In 1860 he became P. of Surgery in Zürich, and in 1867 in Vienna. Among many others, he taught Mikulicz★, Murphy★, and Rutherford Morison★. He was also a talented musician and a friend of Brahms.

BINET, Alfred (1857–1911)
Stanford–Binet Test: Standardised intelligence test. D. 1914 by Binet, later modified at Stanford U., California.

French physiologist and psychologist, who, with Th. Simon (1873–1961) in 1905–1908 developed a scale of tests to determine feeble-mindedness, and to classify adults by 'mental age'.

BITOT, Pierre A. (1822–1888)
Bitot's Spots: Keratinized areas on the conjunctivae in Vitamin A deficiency. D. 1863.

Physician in Bordeaux, France.

BITTNER, John Joseph (b. 1904)
Bittner Factor: Transmissible factor of mouse mammary carcinoma. D. 1936.

Pathologist, Bar Harbor, Maine, USA.

BLALOCK, Alfred (1899–1964)
Blalock's Operation: Subclavian to pulmonary artery
shunt for Fallot's★ Tetralogy. D. 1945.

Emeritus P. of Surgery, Johns Hopkins U.,
Baltimore.

BLANDIN, Philippe Frédéric (1798–1849)
Glands of Blandin and Nühn: Minor salivary glands in
tongue. D. 1826.

Anatomist, and Surgeon to Hôtel-Dieu, Paris; later
P. of Surgery.

BLOODGOOD, Joseph Colt (1867–1935)
1. *Bloodgood's Operation*: Reconstruction of the
posterior wall of the inguinal canal with a flap of
rectus sheath. D. 1918.
2 *Blue-domed Cyst of Bloodgood*: Solitary cyst of
breast. D. 1921.

Surgeon to Johns Hopkins Hospital, Baltimore. He
gave the first accurate description of osteoclastoma
(1910).

BLOUNT, Walter Putnam (b. 1900)
Blount's Disease: Osteochondrosis of medial aspect of
upper tibial epiphysis causing tibia vara. D. 1937.
(Previously D. by Erlacher in 1922.)

Orthopaedic Surgeon, Milwaukee, Wisconsin. He
also made important contributions to the brace
treatment of scoliosis.

BLUMER, George (1858–1940)
Rectal Shelf of Blumer: Indentation of anterior rectal
wall due to extra-rectal mass. D. 1909.

Emeritus P. of Medicine, Yale U., New Haven,
Connecticut.

BOAS, Ismar Isidor (1858–1938)
Boas's Sign: Hyperaesthesia over right 9th to 11th ribs
posteriorly in acute cholecystitis.

Berlin physician who founded the first specialist
gastro-enterological polyclinic in Germany. His
name is given to various tests for gastric acid, now
superseded.

BOCHDALEK, Victor Alexander (1801–1883)
Foramen of Bochdalek: Congenital hiatus in left
postero-lateral part of diaphragm due to persistence

of pleuro-peritoneal canal, through which herniation may occur.

P. of Anatomy, Prague, from 1845 to 1871.

BOECK, Caesar Peter Moeller (1845–1917)
Boeck's Sarcoidosis: Local tissue response and lymphadenopathy possibly due to tubercle bacilli. D. 1899.

P. of Dermatology, Oslo.

BÖHLER, Lorenz (b. 1885)
Böhler Iron, Böhler Frame, Böhler Splint: Various orthopaedic appliances.

He trained in Vienna and in 1914 studied general surgery at the Mayo★ Clinic, later becoming an orthopaedic surgeon, and Director of the Accident Hospital in Vienna. In 1926 he became Consulting Surgeon for Traumatology to the Insurance Company for Accidents, and later P. of Surgery, U. of Vienna.

BONNEY, William Francis Victor (1872–1953)
1. *Bonney's Blue*: Skin marking ink.
2. *Bonney Test*: Elevation of the bladder neck reduces the urine loss in stress incontinence.

Born in Chelsea, London, the son of a GP, he studied first at Barts, then at the Middlesex and became gynaecologist there in 1908. He was also on the staffs of the Royal Masonic Hospital, the Chelsea Hospital for Women, and the Postgraduate Medical School. He was the only gynaecologist of his day ever elected to the Council of the Royal College of Surgeons, and was the first Honorary Fellow of the Australasian College of Surgeons. Internationally famous as a highly skilled operator, he pioneered conservative gynaecology, but also radical pelvic surgery for cancer. He went to art school so that he could himself illustrate his *Textbook of Operative Gynaecology*; he was also a devoted admirer of Rudyard Kipling, and Vice-President of the Kipling Society.

BORDET, Jules Jean Baptiste Vincent (1870–1961)
1. *Bordetella pertussis*: Organism causing whooping cough. D. 1906 (with Gengou★).
2. *Bordet–Gengou Medium*: Bacterial culture medium.
3. *Bordet–Gengou Phenomenon*: Complement fixation. D. 1900.

Born in Soignies, Belgium, he studied in Brussels, and went to work at the Pasteur★ Institute in Paris in 1894; he was an assistant in Metchnikoff's★ laboratory until 1901 when he founded the Pasteur Institute in Brussels. In 1907 he became Honorary P. of Bacteriology in Brussels, and in 1916 a foreign FRS. A pioneer of complement fixation and immunology, he received the Nobel Prize in 1919. He was the first to demonstrate bacterial cytolysis, in 1898.

BORNHOLM
Bornholm Disease: Epidemic pleurodynia ('Devil's Grip'). D. and named 1930, by Ejnar Sylvest, a Danish physician.

The first well-documented epidemic was on Bornholm Island, off the coast of Denmark in the Baltic Sea, though the disease was first seen in Iceland by J. C. Finsen in 1856, and described by Daae in Norway in 1872.

BORREL, Amédée (1867–1936)
Borrelia: A genus of spirochaetal bacteria including the causative organism of relapsing fever.

Bacteriologist in Strasbourg.

BOWEN, John Templeton (1857–1941)
Bowen's Disease: Intradermal pre-cancerous skin lesion. D. 1912.

P. of Dermatology, Harvard U., Boston.

BOWMAN, Sir William Paget (Bt.) (1816–1892)
1. *Bowman's Capsule*: Area surrounding the glomerulus in the kidney. D. 1842.
2. *Bowman's Membrane*: Anterior 'elastic' membrane of the cornea.

Born in Cheshire, as a youth he injured his hand playing with gunpowder, and while watching it heal he decided to become a doctor. He first became Surgeon to Birmingham General Hospital, then went to London in 1837. In 1841 he was elected FRS and in 1842 won the Royal Medal of the Royal Society for his account of the function of the Malpighian★ body in the kidney; he evolved the filtration theory of urine formation (described, however, 36 years earlier, in 1806, in Japan by Soteki Fuseya (1747–1811)). He also discovered the basement membrane of the cornea, and has been called the 'Father of Histology'. In 1844

he became FRCS, and in 1846 Surgeon to Moorfields
Eye Hospital; he was the first to use the
ophthalmoscope (invented by von Helmholtz*
in 1851), was the first in England to treat
glaucoma by iridectomy (1862), and was the first
President of the Royal Ophthalmological
Society. A tranquil and religious man, he was
from 1848 to 1856 P. of Anatomy and
Physiology at King's College Hospital, London.

BOYLE, Henry Edmund Gaskin (1875–1941)
Boyle's Apparatus: Continuous-flow anaesthetic
machine. D. 1917.

Anaesthetist to Barts.

BOYLE, Robert (1627–1691)
Boyle's Law: The pressure of a gas is inversely
proportional to the volume which it occupies. D.
1662. (14 years later Marriotte discovered the law
independently in France.)

'The seventh son of the earl of Cork and the Father of
Modern Chemistry' travelled through Europe for his
health as a young man, became a scientist, an
opponent of the 'iatrochemical school', and one of the
founders of the Royal Society. In 1675 he wrote the
first English treatise on electricity, and in Oxford
with Willis*, Lower*, and Sir Christopher Wren,
experimented with intravenous infusions in animals.

BRAILLE, Louis (1809–1852)
Braille: A system of raised dots for reading by touch
by the blind.

A Frenchman, himself blinded at the age of 3 in an
accident, he was a teacher of the blind in Paris, and
introduced the system (originally proposed by
Captain Charles Barbier in 1820) in 1829–1830.

BRAILSFORD, James Frederick (1888–1961)
Morquio–Brailsford Disease: See *Morquio*.

Director of Radiology, U. of Birmingham.

BRANDT, Thure (1819–1895)
Brandt–Andrews Manoeuvre: Expression of placenta in
3rd stage of labour by traction and abdominal
pressure. D. 1868.

Obstetrician and gynaecologist in Stockholm. He
invented a system of uterine gymnastic exercises for
prolapse.

BRAUN, Gustav August (1829–1911)
Braun's Hook: Instrument for fetal decapitation. D. 1861.

Gynaecologist in Vienna.

BRAXTON-HICKS, John (1825–1897)
Braxton-Hicks Contractions: Intermittent uterine contractions prior to the onset of labour. D. 1871.

Gynaecologist to Guy's Hospital, London. He introduced podalic version by manipulation in obstructed labour (1860).

BRIGHT, Richard (1789–1858)
Bright's Disease: Acute post-streptococcal haemorrhagic glomerulo-nephritis. D. 1836.

Born in Bristol, the son of a banker, he studied in Edinburgh (MD 1813) and Guy's, and wrote an account of the natural history of Iceland after a student expedition there. In 1814 he travelled through Europe, returning through Belgium a fortnight after Waterloo, and visited the wounded in hospital in Brussels. In 1820 he became Assistant Physician to Guy's Hospital, and in 1824 Full Physician (until 1843). He was elected FRCP in 1832, and gave the Gulstonian Lectures in 1833 on renal disease. A colleague of Thomas Addison★ and Thomas Hodgkin★ – 'The Great Men of Guy's' – Bright was a kindly, happy man, and one of the leading physicians of the day, who first distinguished renal from cardiac dropsy, and described 'Jacksonian'★ epilepsy in 1836, status lymphaticus in 1838, and appendicitis in 1839. He collected engravings and was himself a talented artist and travelled widely as an amateur botanist, geologist, and naturalist. He died in London, at his house in Savile Row.

BRILL, Nathan Edwin (1860–1925)
1. *Brill–Symmers Disease*: Giant follicular lymphoblastoma; a relatively benign form of lymphoma. D. 1925. (D. 1927 by Symmers.)
2. *Brill's Disease*: Recurrent typhus. D. 1910.

Physician in New York.

BRITTAIN, Herbert Alfred (1904–1954)
Brittain's Arthrodesis of the Hip: Extra-articular ischio-femoral arthrodesis.

Born in Southern Ireland, he trained in Dublin and became Orthopaedic Surgeon to the Norfolk and Norwich Hospital. Calvé★ stimulated his development of the arthrodesis which bears his name. He was Hunterian Professor in 1940, and was a keen sportsman and hunter.

BROCA, Pierre Paul (1824–1880)
  1. *Broca's Area*: Area parolfactoria; the speech area in the cerebral cortex. D. 1861.
  2. *Broca's Point, Line, etc.*: Various anthropometric landmarks.

Born at Ste Foy-la-Grande, near Bordeaux (where Gratiolet★ was also born), he was the son of a doctor and Napoleonic surgeon of Huguenot extraction. He married the daughter of J. G. A. Lugol★, and became Surgeon to the Hôpital Necker, Paris, and P. of Clinical Surgery. He was also Director of the Anthropological Laboratories, founder of the first Anthropological Society of France and of the *Revue d'Anthropologie*, and a Member of the Academie des Sciences and the Senate of the Republic. A pioneer of neurosurgical operations, he also invented many anthropometric instruments. He described muscular dystrophy before Duchenne★, and rickets as a nutritional disorder before Virchow★. He wrote over 500 papers and died in Paris of a coronary. His two sons became P. of Paediatric Surgery and P. of Medical Physics.

BRODIE, Sir Benjamin Collins (1783–1862)
  1. *Brodie's Abscess*: Chronic osteomyelitis with no acute stage. D. 1832.
  2. *Brodie–Trendelenburg★ Test*: For competence of sapheno–femoral valve. D. 1846. (D. by Trendelenburg★ in 1890).
  3. *Sero-cystic Disease of Brodie*: Cystosarcoma phylloides, a rapidly growing fibro–adenoma of the breast. D. 1840.

The son of a clergyman, he was born in Winterslow, Wiltshire, studied at St George's under James Wilson and Everard Home, and then became an anatomy demonstrator and lecturer there, and at the Windmill St School. Then he was successively Assistant Surgeon to St George's (1808); Fellow of the Royal Society (1810); Copley medal-holder of the Royal Society, for physiological research (1811); and Full Surgeon to St George's (1822). One of the original Fellows of the Royal College of Surgeons, he introduced the FRCS examination, was made a baronet (1843), and was President of the College in 1844. In 1858 he was President of the Royal Society, but resigned in 1861 on account of failing eyesight. Brodie was also Surgeon to George IV, Sergeant Surgeon to William IV, and the first President of the GMC. Henry Gray★ dedicated the first edition of *Gray's Anatomy* to him (1858). He died at Brome Park, Surrey.

BROWN, Robert (1773–1858)
Brownian Movement: Movement of minute particles in a liquid due to thermal activity. D. 1828.

English botanist, who gave the first description of the cell nucleus, in 1831.

BROWNE, Denis John Wolko (1892–1967)
Denis Browne Splints: For club foot: D. 1934.

This second-generation Australian became the 'Father of paediatric surgery in the English-speaking world'. He came to England with the Australian forces fighting in Europe in the First World War, going on to the staff of the Great Ormond Street Hospital for Sick Children, London. Apart from his many contributions to general and orthopaedic surgery (club foot and congenital dislocation of the hip) he designed a better bicycle seat, a personal inflatable lumbar corset, and a new grip for a tennis racquet, with which he himself played at Wimbledon.

BROWN-SÉQUARD, Charles Edouard (1818–1894)
Brown-Séquard Syndrome: Hemicompression of spinal cord, causing ipsilateral motor weakness, loss of vibration sense and proprioception, and contralateral loss of pain and temperature sense. D. 1851.

Born in Mauritius, the son of a Frenchwoman and an Irish–American pirate, he went to Paris as a would-be playwright, then studied medicine, was Trousseau's★ assistant, and performed many experiments on himself, which included swallowing a sponge on the end of a string and pulling it back to study the gastric juice. In great poverty, he also experimented on frogs and rabbits in his own flat, and, having become involved in revolutionary politics, went to America, armed only with a letter from his friend Broca★. He earned his living teaching French, giving lectures and delivering babies, then went to Mauritius to deal with a cholera outbreak. Later, he was successively P. at the Medical College of Virginia; on the staff of the National Hospital, Queen Square, London (1860) (where he persuaded Hughlings Jackson★ to be a neurologist); P. of Medicine at Harvard; and finally succeeded Claude Bernard on his death in 1878 as P. of Medicine at the Collège de France in Paris. One of the founders of endocrinology, he was the first to show the adrenals were essential to life (1856).

BRUCE, Major-General Sir David (1855–1931)
Brucellosis: Undulant fever; Malta fever. Infectious disease due to bacteria of the genus *Brucella*. D. 1887 (while serving in Malta with the RAMC).

Born in Melbourne, Australia, of Scottish parents, he left school at 14 and qualified in Edinburgh at 26. He became a British Army surgeon in 1883, rose through the ranks, was elected FRS, and was Head of the Malta Fever Commission from 1904 to 1906. He was knighted in 1908. In South Africa the farmers called him 'Bruce of Natal' as he identified the trypanosome causing cattle plague; he also demonstrated that the tse-tse fly was the vector of sleeping-sickness to man, with research in Zululand and Uganda. Devoted to his wife, who stayed with him throughout the siege of Ladysmith in the Boer War, he died during her funeral.

BRUCH, Carl Wilhelm Ludwig (1819–1884)
Bruch's Membrane: Lamina vitrea of the choroid. D. 1844.

P. of Anatomy in Basle, then Giessen.

BRUNNER, Johann Konrad (1653–1727)
Brunner's Glands: Secretory glands in the duodenal mucosa. D. 1687. (Previously D. by J. J. Wepfer, his father-in-law.)

Born in Diessenhofen, Switzerland, he studied in Paris under Duverney; became P. of Anatomy at Heidelberg aged 34, then at Strasbourg. He described the 'Crypts of Lieberkühn'★ in 1715, when Lieberkühn was 4.

BRUNSCHWIG, Alexander (1901–1969)
Brunschwig's Operation: Radical pelvic evisceration for advanced cancer.

He studied and practised surgery in Chicago, and later became Gynaecologist to the Memorial Hospital for the Treatment of Cancer, New York. He also described a radical hysterectomy with pelvic lymph node excision for cancer of the cervix; and duodenopancreatectomy (D. 1937) also bears his name.

BRUSHFIELD, Thomas (1858–1937)
Brushfield's Spots: Pigmented spots on the iris in Down's★ Syndrome. D. 1924.

London physician.

BRYANT, Thomas (1828–1914)
Bryant's Triangle: A surface marking about the hip to assess if shortening is above or below the level of the greater trochanter. D. 1876.

He became FRCS in 1853, was Surgeon to Guy's Hospital, London from 1857 to 1888, President of the Royal College of Surgeons from 1890 to 1892, and in 1893 became Surgeon Extraordinary to Queen Victoria. His father was a friend of Astley Cooper★.

BUCK, Gurdon (1807–1877)
1. *Buck's Fascia*: Superficial layer of the superficial fascia of the abdominal wall. (= Camper's★ Fascia). D. 1848.
2. *Buck's Extensions*: Skin traction for femoral fractures, developed in the American Civil War. D. 1860.

Buck's forebears came to England with William the Conqueror, and to America with the Pilgrim Fathers. He studied in New York, Paris, Berlin and Vienna, and became one of the foremost general and plastic surgeons at the New York Hospital.

BUCKY, Gustav P. (1880–1963)
Bucky Grid: Diaphragm used in radiography to achieve improved contrast and definition. D. 1913.

German physician and radiologist who emigrated to the USA and practised in St Louis.

BUDD, George (1808–1882)
Budd–Chiari Syndrome: Hepatomegaly and cirrhosis due to portal vein occlusion. D. 1845. (D. 1842 by Rokitansky, and D. 1898 by Chiari★.)

P. of Medicine, King's College Hospital, London.

BUERGER, Leo (1879–1943)
1. *Buerger's Disease*: Thrombo-angiitis obliterans; a progressive juvenile obliterative arteritis, usually affecting smokers. D. 1908.
2. *Buerger's Position*: Head-up, to promote vasodilatation by hydrostatic pressure.
3. *Buerger's Exercises*: Repeated raising and lowering of the leg. D. 1910.

Born in Vienna, he came to the USA aged 1, trained at City College of New York and Columbia Medical School, and was Surgical Pathologist to Mount Sinai Hospital, then P. of Urology at the Polyclinic Medical School, New York. He designed an improved cystoscope, and went to Los Angeles as P. of Urology at the College of Medical Evangelists. An egoist addicted to expensive cars, he was not re-employed at Mount Sinai when he subsequently returned to New York.

BULL, Sir Graham MacGregor (C)
Bull's Regime: No-protein, no-mineral, low-fluid diet in acute renal failure.

He studied medicine in Cape Town (MD 1947), later becoming P. of Medicine at Queen's U., Belfast, then Director of the Clinical Research Centre of the Medical Research Council, London, and is now retired in Hampstead.

BUNNELL, Sterling (1882–1957)
Bunnell Suture: For tendon repair. D. 1918.

Born in San Francisco, he studied at the U. of California and practised privately in San Francisco. In the 1920s he piloted his own plane to visit patients and to operate in other cities. He is remembered above all as a hand surgeon, but also described positive-pressure anaesthesia for thoracic surgery in 1923, and an operation for cleft palate. His famous *Surgery of the Hand* was first published in 1944, and he made enormous contributions to the care of war-time hand injuries. A keen hunter and fisherman and enthusiast for wild-life, he made a film of the brown bears in Alaska, and kept two alligators in his garden.

BUNNELL, Walls Willard (1902–1966)
Paul–Bunnell Test: See *Paul*.

American physician.

BUNSEN, Robert Wilhelm Eberhard (1811–1899)
Bunsen Burner: Laboratory bench gas-burner.

Born in Göttingen, the 4th son of the P. of Modern
Languages, he studied there and later became
Privatdozent at the U. of Göttingen (1833). In 1838
he became P. of Chemistry at Marburg, and in 1852
at Heidelberg, where he remained until his retirement
at the age of 78. He was a devoted teacher, research
worker, and traveller, and never married. He
introduced spectrum analysis in 1859, and mainly
contributed to inorganic chemistry and geology. He
was elected a foreign FRS in 1858, and received the
Copley Medal in 1860, and the first Davy Medal
(with Kirchoff) in 1877. The Royal Society of Arts
awarded him the Albert Medal in 1898.

BURDACH, Karl Friedrich (1776–1847)
Burdach's Column: Postero-lateral column of spinal
cord. D. 1819.

P. of Anatomy and Physiology, Königsberg.

BURKITT, Denis Parsons (b. 1911)
Burkitt's Lymphoma: Malignant lymphoma of
sub-Saharan Africa, associated with a specific climatic
environment.

Formerly Senior Surgeon, Mulago Hospital,
Kampala, Uganda; now Member of the External
Scientific Staff, Medical Research Council, London.
He was elected FRS in 1972.

BURNS, Allan (1781–1813)
Burns' Space: Suprasternal fossa.

Anatomy lecturer at his brother John's private school
in Glasgow, where he was born, and died.

BURTON, Henry (1799–1849)
Burton's Line: Discolouration of gums in lead
poisoning (due to the sulphide). D. 1840.

In 1828 he became Assistant Physician to St Thomas's
Hospital, London; in 1837, Lecturer in Materia
Medica; and in 1849 was appointed Dean of the
Medical School, but he died of cholera 3 weeks later.

C

CAFFEY, John (1895–1966)
Caffey's Syndrome: Infantile cortical hyperostosis,

involving several bones simultaneously. (The differential diagnosis includes 'battered baby' syndrome.)

P. Emeritus of Radiology, College of Physicians and Surgeons, Columbia U., New York, and Visiting P. of Radiology to the Children's Hospital, Pittsburgh, Pennsylvania. His standard textbook on paediatric X-ray diagnosis is now in its 7th edition.

CALDWELL, George Walter (1834–1918)
Caldwell–Luc Operation: Radical antrostomy. D. 1893.

ENT surgeon in New York, later in San Francisco and Los Angeles.

CALMETTE, Léon Charles Albert (1863–1933)
Bacille Calmette–Guérin: Attenuated live strain of bovine TB used as a prophylactic antituberculous vaccine (BCG). D. 1908.

Born in Nice of Breton parents, he wanted to be a sailor, but nearly died in a school typhoid epidemic in Clermont-Ferrand, so he became a doctor instead. A pupil of Pasteur★ in Paris, he did eventually enter the naval and colonial service as a surgeon, and worked in the French Congo, then in St Pierre and Miquelon, then became the first Director of the Pasteur Institute, Saigon. He introduced anti-snakebite serum, and in 1895 founded the Lille Institute of Hygiene. In 1917 he became Sub-Director of the Pasteur Institute in Paris. A cheerful man, his enthusiasm for BCG blinded him to shortcomings in his statistics, despite the deaths from TB of 72 out of 251 children in Lübeck, Germany, who had been vaccinated with BCG contaminated by virulent bacilli.

CALVÉ, Jacques (1875–1954)
1. *Calvé's Disease*: 'Osteochondritis' of vertebral body, now believed to be due to eosinophilic granuloma. D. 1925.
2. *Calvé–Legg–Perthes Disease*: See *Perthes*. D. 1910 (July) by Calvé. (D. in the same year in February by Legg and in October by Perthes.)

Orthopaedic surgeon with a special interest in paraplegia, and a great friend of Robert Jones★. He married an American, and raised money from America to build the Fondation Franco-Américaine

Hospital in Berck-Plage, France, and an associated trade school; he was its first Surgical Director.

CAMPER, Pieter (Petrus) (1722–1789)
Camper's Fascia: Superficial layer of the superficial fascia of the abdominal wall. (Called Buck's★ Fascia in the USA.) D. 1801.

Born in Leyden, Holland, he became renowned as a physician, comparative anatomist, palaeontologist, anthropologist and artist, and was a great teacher. He discovered that the bones of birds contain air. In 1749 he was P. of Philosophy, Medicine and Surgery in Francker; from 1755 to 1761, P. of Medicine in Amsterdam; and from 1763 to 1773, P. of Medicine, Anatomy, Surgery and Botany in Gröningen. He died in The Hague.

CARABELLI, Elder von Lunkaszprie George (1787–1842)
Carabelli's Cusp: Inconstant extra tubercle on upper first molar tooth.

Born in Pest, Hungary, he became P. of Dental Surgery in Vienna, where he died.

CARREL, Alexis (1873–1944)
Carrel-Dakin Solution: See *Dakin*.

Born in Lyon, where he studied medicine, he was deeply impressed by the assassination of Sadi Carnot, the French President, in 1894, who was stabbed: the knife severed the portal vein, and Carrel then devoted himself to experimental vascular surgery, for which he was awarded the 1912 Nobel Prize. He learned his fine suturing technique from a renowned embroidress in Lyon, who taught him while he was an intern; he also had almost obsessionally high standards of asepsis. In 1904 he emigrated to Canada, working in Montreal, then Chicago and later in New York, where at the Rockefeller Institute he devised the first germ-free pump oxygenator with Charles Lindbergh, the engineer and aviator. In 1907 he wrote of possible renal homotransplants from accident victim donors, having performed several successful transplants of hearts, lungs and kidneys in dogs in 1905–1907.

CASAL, Gaspar (1679–1759)
Casal's Necklace: Pigmented area around the neck in pellagra.

Spanish physician who gave the first description of pellagra in 1735 (and appreciated its relation to a maize diet). By the time this was published, however, (posthumously in 1762), F. Thièry had published a description in *Mal de la Rosa* in 1755.

CASONI, Tomaso (1880–1933)
Casoni Test: Intradermal test for hydatid disease. D. 1912.

Italian physician at the Ospedale Coloniale Vittorio Emanuele III, Tripoli.

CELESTIN, Louis Roger (C)
Celestin Tube: Tube inserted past inoperable oesophageal cancer to relieve dysphagia.

Studied at UCH (MB 1951). Now Consultant General Surgeon, Frenchay Hospital, Bristol. He developed the tube while a senior registrar at Bristol Royal Infirmary.

CELSIUS, Anders (1701–1744)
Celsius Scale of Temperature: Centigrade.

Swedish astronomer and scientist, who described his thermometer to the Swedish Academy in 1742. The term centigrade was applied by the French after the introduction of metrication.

CELSUS, Aulus Aurelius Cornelius (53 B.C.–A.D. 7)
Celsus' 4 Cardinal Signs of Inflammation: Redness, swelling, heat and tenderness.

Roman encyclopaedist and medical writer.

CHAGAS, Carlos (1879–1934)
1. *Chagas' Disease*: South American trypanosomiasis, caused by *T. cruzi*.★ D. 1909.
2. *Chagasia*: An anopheline sub-species discovered by Cruz.★

Brazilian scientist and physician, who worked at Cruz's Institute in Rio de Janeiro.

CHAMBERLEN, Peter (1601–1683)
Chamberlen's Forceps: The original obstetric forceps.

Member of a Huguenot family who fled to England

in 1569. The invention of the forceps (in about 1670) was kept secret for about a century.

CHANCE, C. Q.
Chance Fracture: Vertebral fracture caused by acute flexion, with horizontal splitting of spinous process and neural arch. D. 1948.

Radiologist to Derbyshire Royal Infirmary, Derby.

CHAPUT, Henri (1857–1919)
Tubercle of Chaput: Bony projection on lateral aspect of distal tibia.

French surgeon; he was the first to perform urinary diversion by ureterosigmoidostomy.

CHARCOT, Jean-Martin (1825–1893)
1. *Charcot's Joints*: Neuropathic joints, classically in syphilis.
2. *Maladie de Charcot*: Motor neurone disease. D. 1865.
3. *Charcot–Marie–Tooth Disease*: Peroneal type of progressive muscular atrophy. D. 1886, with Marie. (D. 1886 independently by Tooth.)
4. *Charcot's Biliary Fever*: Intermittent hepatic fever of suppurative cholangitis. D. 1876.
5. *Charcot–Leyden Crystals*: Found where eosinophilic leucocytes are fragmenting.
6. *Charcot's Artery*: Lenticulo-striate artery; 'the artery of cerebral haemorrhage'.

The son of a Paris coachbuilder, he studied in Paris and became an intern at the Salpêtrière Hospital (Louis XIII's former gunpowder store) at 23, and superintendent physician at 37. He immediately began to describe and classify the conditions seen among the 5000–8000 indigent patients there, and in 1872 he became P. of Pathological Anatomy, and in 1882, P. of Nervous Diseases. This was the first Chair in Neurology in the world, created especially for him. He was the first to describe many neurological diseases, including amyotrophic lateral sclerosis (1865), and also intermittent claudication and hysteria, and he made the distinction between gout and rheumatoid arthritis, and between multiple sclerosis and Parkinson's★ Disease. He gave world-famous lecture-demonstrations on a floodlit stage every Tuesday and Friday morning, and lived in style, patronised the arts (he was himself a talented caricaturist) and kept two pet monkeys. His pupils included Babinski★, Marie★ and Freud★, and his son Jean-Baptiste was also a neurologist (and an Antarctic explorer, who led the search for Amundsen). He was succeeded as P. of Neurology at the Salpêtrière, at the age of 65, by Dejerine★. Babinski noted that many of the hysterical patients at the Salpêtrière lost their symptoms after the death of Charcot, of pulmonary oedema, while on holiday.

CHARNLEY, Sir John (C)
1. *Charnley Total Hip Replacement*: A design of low-friction arthroplasty.
2. *Charnley Compression Arthrodesis*: Technique for knee and ankle fusions using external compression device.
3. Many other orthopaedic operations and instruments bear his name.

He studied at Manchester (MB 1935), became Consultant Orthopaedic Surgeon to King Edward VII Hospital, Midhurst, Surrey; Honorary Orthopaedic Surgeon (formerly Director, and Founder), Centre for Hip Surgery, Wrightington Hospital, Wigan; and is Emeritus P. of Orthopaedics, U. of Manchester. He has also been awarded the CBE and is the only orthopaedic surgeon to have been elected FRS.

CHARRIÈRE, Joseph François Bernard (1803–1876)
Charrière Scale: 'French' scale of measurement of urinary catheters.

Surgical instrument-maker in Paris, who also designed one of the first ether inhalers, in 1847.

CHASSAIGNAC, Charles Marie Edouard (1804–1879)
Tubercle of Chassaignac: Prominence on the transverse process of C6 against which the common carotid artery may be compressed. D. 1834.

Born in Nantes, he came to Paris and was elected P. of Anatomy and Surgery. He died at Versailles.

CHEYNE, John (1777–1836)
Cheyne–Stokes Respiration: Cyclical periods of apnoea in severe alkalosis. D. 1818. (D. 1854 by Stokes.)

Born in Leith, Scotland, the son and grandson of doctors, he was apprenticed to his GP father, but took 12 years to qualify, attending Sir Charles Bell's★ courses in Edinburgh. In 1811 he became Physician to the Meath Hospital, Dublin; in 1813, was the first P. of Medicine at the Royal College of Surgeons of Ireland (where he was succeeded in 1828 by the father of William Stokes★); and in 1820 became Physician-General to the Forces in Ireland. He retired to England on account of ill-health in 1831.

CHEYNE, Sir William Watson (1852–1932)
Watson Cheyne Probe: Fine surgical probe.

Born in Fetlar, Shetland, he studied in Aberdeen and Edinburgh, where he met Lister★ and followed him to King's College Hospital, London. Here he became P. of Surgery, and also made many contributions to bacteriology. He also became President of the Royal College of Surgeons, and a baronet, and retired to Shetland.

von CHIARI, Hans (1851–1916)
1. *Arnold–Chiari Malformation*: See *Arnold.*
2. *Budd–Chiari Syndrome*: See *Budd.* D. 1898.

Viennese pathologist who became P. of Pathological Anatomy at Strasbourg, then at Prague, and made important contributions to laryngology and rhinology.

CHOPART, François R. (1743–1795)
Chopart's Amputation: Mid-tarsal amputation through Chopart's joint (the talo-navicular/calcaneo-cuboid articulation). Named for Chopart by his pupil Laffiteau in 1792.

P. of Surgery, Paris. He was also a pioneer urologist, and noted physiologist and pathologist. He died of cholera.

CHRISTIAN, Henry Asbury (1876–1951)
Hand–Schüller–Christian Disease: See *Hand.* D. 1919, in a collection of papers dedicated to Osler★. (D. 1893 by Hand, and 1915 by Schüller.)

P. of Medicine, Harvard.

CHRISTMAS, Mr
Christmas Disease: Bleeding disorder due to Factor IX deficiency.

Named after the patient in whom this deficiency was first detected.

CHVOSTEK, František, Sr (1835–1884)
Chvostek's Sign: Hyperexcitability on percussion of facial nerve in hypocalcaemic tetany. D. 1876.

Physician at Josefsakademie, Vienna. His son Franz (b. 1864) also worked in Vienna and described the bone lesions in parathyroid disease, and wrote on tetanus and myasthenia gravis.

CLARKE, Jacob Augustus Lockhart (1817–1880)
Clarke's Column: Dorso-lateral tract in the spinal cord. D. 1851.

Physician and Neurologist to the Hospital for Epilepsy and Paralysis, London. He was elected FRS in 1854.

CLELAND, John (1835–1925)
Cleland's Ligaments: Cutaneous ligaments of the digits: prolongations of the interdigital ligaments along the sides of the digits. D. 1867.

Born in Perth, Scotland, he was elected FRS in 1872, and from 1878 to 1909 was P. of Anatomy in Glasgow. Cleland and Mackay's *Textbook of Human Anatomy* (Glasgow, 1896) was one of the first to be illustrated with photographs. He retired to Kent, where he died.

CLOQUET, Baron Jules Germain (1790–1883)
Gland of Cloquet: Lymph-gland in the apex of the femoral canal. D. 1817 (in his thesis).

The son of the Inspector–General of Commercial Ports of French Morocco, he joined the Army, but was discharged on the grounds of ill-health (he went on to live to 92). From 1831 to 1858 he was P. of Surgical Pathology at the Hôpital St Louis, Paris (his elder brother Hippolyte was P. of Anatomy). He performed a mastectomy under hypnosis in 1829, became Surgeon to Napoleon III, and was President of the French Academy of Medicine for the last 20 years of his life. He had a farm in Provence where he grew rare plants, and was a close friend of Gustave Flaubert, the author of *Madame Bovary*.

CLUTTON, Henry Hugh (1850–1909)
Clutton's Joints: Chronic synovitis of the knee seen in congenital syphilis. D. 1886.

Surgeon to St Thomas's Hospital, London.

COCK, Edward (1805–1892)
Cock's Peculiar Tumour: Ulceration of an infected sebaceous cyst, which resembles an epithelioma.

Surgeon to Guy's Hospital, London, who described perineal urethrotomy in 1866.

COCKETT, Frank Bernard (C)
Cockett and Dodd Operation: Sub-fascial ligation for varicose veins.

Studied at St Thomas's (MB 1940); now Surgeon to St Thomas's Hospital, London, and King Edward VII Hospital for Officers.

CODMAN, Ernest Amory (1869–1940)
Codman's Triangle: Periosteal elevation adjacent to osteogenic sarcoma.

Surgeon, Massachusetts General Hospital, Boston. With his fellow-student Cushing★ he devised the first anaesthetic record sheet and in 1934 coined the term 'frozen shoulder'.

COLLES, Abraham (1773–1843)
1. *Colles Fracture*: Of distal radius, with dorsal and radial displacement and angulation. D. 1814. (Formerly believed to be a wrist dislocation.)
2. *Colles Fascia*: Deep layer of superficial fascia of the abdominal wall, and perineal fascia. D. 1811.

He was born in Kilkenny, Ireland, where his father owned a marble quarry. As a boy, he found an anatomy book in a field where it had been swept by a flood, and decided to become a surgeon. He studied at Dublin U. and qualified in 1795, working so hard that his landlady pleaded with him to rest 'lest he read himself into his coffin'. In 1797 he became MD Edinburgh, then walked to London, where he worked with Astley Cooper★. In 1799 he was appointed to the staff of Dr Steevens Hospital, Dublin; in 1802 became President of the Irish College of Surgeons (at 29), and from 1804 to 1836 was P. of Anatomy and Surgery in Dublin, where over 300 students would attend his lectures. He was the first to ligate the innominate artery, and wrote books on surgical anatomy in 1811, club foot in 1818, and venereal disease in 1837. He had one of the largest private practices in Dublin, but refused a baronetcy in 1839. Of his 10 children, the eldest son became President of the Royal College of Surgeons of Ireland in 1863. When Colles died in Dublin, his post-mortem was performed by his successor, Robert

Smith★, remembered eponymously for the 'reversed Colles fracture'.

COLLINS, Edward Treacher (1862–1932)
Treacher Collins Syndrome: Incomplete mandibulo-facial dystostosis, with deformities of the eyelids and maxilla. D. 1900. (D. previously by G. A. Berry in 1888.) Sometimes referred to as Collins–Franceschetti★ Syndrome.

Surgeon to the Royal Ophthalmic Hospital, Moorfields, London.

COLONNA, Paul Crenshaw (1892–1966)
Colonna Operation: Acetabuloplasty for late treatment of congenital hip dislocation. D. 1932.

Born in Norfolk, Virginia, he studied at Johns Hopkins and from 1921 to 1937 worked at the Hospital for The Ruptured and Crippled in New York. From 1935 to 1937 he was Clinical P. of Orthopaedic Surgery at the College of Physicians and Surgeons of Columbia U., then P. of Orthopaedics at Oklahoma (1937) and finally in Philadelphia (1942), where he worked continuously (though nominally retired in 1958), seeing patients on the wards until the day before he died.

CONN, Jerome William (b. 1907)
Conn's Syndrome: Primary aldosteronism. D. 1955.

Formerly Director of the Division of Metabolism and Endocrinology, U. of Michigan, Ann Arbor; in 1974 he became Emeritus P., U. of Michigan, and is also Distinguished Physician of the Veteran's Administration (only the 7th such appointment in the USA). He worked at a desk 30 ft long, and wrote over 300 papers.

COOLEY, Thomas Benton (1871–1945)
Cooley's Anaemia: Thalassaemia major. D. 1927

P. of Paediatrics, Wayne U. College of Medicine, Detroit.

COOMBS, Robin Royston Amos (b. 1921)
Coombs Test: Antiglobulin test to detect Rhesus antibody on the surface of red cells.

Quick P. of Biology, and Fellow of Corpus Christi College, Cambridge. He obtained a PhD from

Cambridge and MRCVS from Edinburgh, and is a FRS.

COOPER, Sir Astley Paston (1768–1841)
1. *Ligament of Astley Cooper*: Upper part of the pectineal fascia. D. 1804.
2. *Cooper's Fascia*: Covering of the spermatic cord. D. 1804.
3. *Cooper's Ligaments*: Skin attachments of the breast. D. 1840.

'The most famous English surgeon of his generation' was born in Norfolk, the son of a clergyman. He studied in Edinburgh, Paris, and at St Thomas's and Guy's in London (where he was a pupil of John Hunter★). His grandfather had been a surgeon at Norwich and his uncle was a surgeon at Guy's. He became Surgeon to St Thomas's and Guy's himself in 1800, then P. at Surgeons' Hall, and was in 1819 President of the Royal Medical and Chirurgical Society, and of the Royal College of Surgeons in 1827 and 1836–1837. Elected FRS in 1802, he was one of the first to amputate at the hip (1824), perform myringotomy (1801), and ligate the common carotid (1808) and external iliac arteries for aneurysm, and the abdominal aorta in 1817. In 1821 he received a baronetcy and 1000 guineas for removing an infected wen from the head of George IV at Brighton. He was in current parlance a 'workaholic', working from 6 a.m. till late at night, dictating notes in his carriage as he did his rounds. He was buried in Guy's Hospital and his statue is in St Paul's.

CORRIGAN, Sir Dominic John, Bt. (1802–1880)
Corrigan's Pulse: 'Waterhammer' or 'collapsing' pulse in aortic incompetence. D. 1832.

Born in Dublin, he qualified MD in Edinburgh in 1825, returning to be Physician to Jervis Street Hospital, Dublin, and was the city's most popular doctor: his consulting rooms had a secret door through which he could escape from the eager queue of patients. In 1843 he became MRCS, in 1854 Honorary Fellow of the College of Physicians of Ireland; in 1866 he was made a baronet; and in 1870 became Queen Victoria's physician in Ireland. He wrote a book on the lives of the great physicians, and died in Dublin of cerebral haemorrhage.

CORTI, Marquis Alfonso (1822–1888)
Organ of Corti: Spiral structure in the cochlea of the inner ear. D. 1851.

Italian anatomist and histologist born in Sardinia who worked in Vienna, Würzburg and Turin, mainly on descriptions of the ear and the structure of the retina. He never held an academic post.

Da COSTA, Jacob Mendes (1833–1900)
Da Costa's Syndrome: Effort syndrome; 'disorderly action of the heart'; a functional cardiac irregularity. D. 1871.

Philadelphia surgeon who identified this condition in American Civil War soldiers. It was again recognised in the First World War, as 'neurocirculatory asthenia'. He also described 'phantom tumours' of the abdomen.

COTTON, Frederic Jay C. (1869–1938)
Cotton's Fracture: (1) Trimalleolar ankle fracture. D. 1910. (2) 'Fender Fracture', with comminution of the lateral tibial condyle. D. 1929.

Surgeon in Boston, USA, who was also a pioneer of endotracheal anaesthesia, and contributed mainly to orthopaedic and traumatic surgery.

COUDÉ
See p. 207.

COUNCILMAN, William Thomas (1854–1933)
Councilman Bodies: Acidophilic structures seen in viral hepatitis.

Born in Pikesville, Maryland, he studied pathology in the USA and Germany, where he was a pupil of Julius Cohnheim (1839–1884) who was himself Virchow's★ most distinguished pupil. He introduced the term 'amoebic dysentery' in 1891. He was Associate P. of Pathology at Johns Hopkins U. from 1886 to 1891, and Shattuck P. of Pathological Anatomy at Harvard Medical School from 1892 to 1922. He died at York Village, Maine.

COURVOISIER, Ludwig Georg (1843–1918)
Courvoisier's Law: If in the presence of jaundice the gall–bladder is palpable, the obstruction is unlikely to be due to stone. D. 1890.

Born in Basle, Switzerland, the son of a merchant and grandson of an English clergyman, he spent his childhood in Malta and almost died of typhus before starting medical school. He studied at Göttingen and Basle (MD 1868), then worked in London and Vienna. He was a military surgeon during the Franco–Prussian War, returning to be P. of Surgery at Basle, where he founded biliary surgery. He was also an enthusiastic natural historian, and wrote 21 papers on entomology.

COUVELAIRE, Alexandre (1873–1948)
Couvelaire Uterus: Placental separation with disruption of uterine muscle.

Paris obstetrician.

COWPER, William (1666–1709)
Cowper's Glands: Bulbo-urethral glands. D. 1700. (These had been described in 1684 by Jean Méry (1645–1722), Paris anatomist and Surgeon to the Queen of France.)

Born in Hampshire, he set up as a London surgeon, was elected FRS in 1698, and wrote prolifically and stylishly, though plagiarising almost all his writings and anatomical engravings from the sources of others, to which he never gave acknowledgement.

CREDÉ, Karl Sigmund Franz (1819–1892)
Credé's Manoeuvre: External uterine pressure to expel the placenta. D. 1860. (This had been described in 1767 by John Harrie, and had been used for many centuries by the American Indians.)

Born in Berlin, he became Director of the obstetric and gynaecological wards at the Charité Hospital in 1852, then founded the gynaecology clinic at Leipzig, where he became P. of Obstetrics. He introduced the use of silver nitrate eye-drops to prevent ophthalmia neonatorum (1884).

CREUTZFELD, Hans Gerhard (1885–1964)
Jakob-Creutzfeld Syndrome: See *Jakob*. D. 1920. (D. 1921 by Jakob.)

Psychiatrist in Spielmeyer's Institute, Munich.

Van CREVELD, Simon (b. 1894)
Ellis–Van Creveld Syndrome: See *Ellis*.

Dutch paediatrician.

CRIGLER, John F. (Jr) (b. 1919)
Crigler-Najjar Syndrome: Congential
hyperbilirubinaemia. D. 1952.

Educated at Duke U. and Johns Hopkins; he is now
Associate P. of Pediatrics, Harvard Medical School,
and Boston Children's Hospital.

CROHN, Burrill Bernard (b. 1884)
Crohn's Disease: Regional ileitis. D. 1932. (Morgagni★
also described the condition in 1769.)

Born in New York, he studied at City College of
New York and Columbia U., and was from 1925 to
1969 Chief of Gastroenterology at Mount Sinai
Hospital, New York, and later Emeritus P. of
Medicine.

CROUZON, Octave (1874–1938)
Crouzon's Disease: Cranio–facial dysostosis. D. 1912.

Neurologist in Paris.

CRUTCHFIELD, William Gayle (b. 1900)
Crutchfield's Tongs: Apparatus for applying skeletal
traction to skull for dislocation of the cervical spine.
D. 1933.

Neurosurgeon in Richmond, Virginia, USA.

CRUVEILHIER, Jean (1791–1874)
Cruveilhier's Ulcer: Simple gastric ulcer. D. 1829.

Born in Limoges, the son of an Army surgeon, he
at first intended to be a priest, but at his mother's
insistence went to Paris, becoming Dupuytren's★
registrar, and eventually the first P. of Pathology,
the Chair having been founded by his former chief.
Along the way he had been variously P. of
Medicine in Paris, P. of Operative Surgery in
Montpelier, a GP in Limoges (where he retired to
avoid the siege of Paris), and P. of Anatomy in
Paris, where he was also President of the
Anatomical Society (succeeding Laennec★) for over
40 years. A form of progressive muscular atrophy
also bears his name, and he described multiple
sclerosis before Charcot★ (1835) and also gave
descriptions of hypertrophic pyloric stenosis and
colonic diverticula.

CRUZ, Oswaldo (1872–1917)
Trypanosoma cruzi: Causative parasite of Chagas'★
Disease.

Director of Public Health, Rio de Janeiro, Brazil
(1903); founder (in 1901) of the Institute to which
the citizens of Rio gave his name in 1908; reformer
of the Brazilian Sanitary Service; and responsible for
the elimination of yellow fever from Rio in 1909. He
discovered a sub-species of anopheles, named
Chagasia★ after his co-worker.

CULLEN, Thomas Stephen (1868–1953)
Cullen's Sign: Bluish discolouration of lower
abdominal wall skin in pancreatitis and
intra-abdominal haemorrhage. (First described in
a case of ruptured ectopic pregnancy in 1919,
in a collection of papers dedicated to William
Osler★.)

P. of Gynaecology, Johns Hopkins U., Baltimore.
He wrote a classic textbook on *Cancer of the Uterus*.
(1900).

CURIE, Pierre and   Marie Sklodowska (Pierre:
1859–1906; Marie: 1867–1934).
Curie, millicurie: Units of radiation.

Pierre was Chief of Laboratories of the School of
Physics and Chemistry of the City of Paris, and
later P. of Physics at the Sorbonne. Marie was born
in Warsaw, the youngest of five children of a
teacher. She worked for 5 years from the age of 17
as a governess to save enough to come to Paris and
study. She was Pierre's pupil, married him in 1895,
and succeeded him as P. of Physics (the first
woman in this post) after his death. (He was run
over and killed by a carriage in a Paris street.)
Together, they discovered radium (1898) and
polonium while experimenting with uranium in a
laboratory converted from a shed. Tiny quantities
of radium were isolated from several tons of
pitchblende and in 1903 they received the Nobel
Prize jointly with Antoine Henri Becquerel
(1852–1908), P. of Physics at the Ecole
Polytechnique, Paris, who had discovered the
radioactivity of uranium in 1896. Continuing
Pierre's work after his death, Marie became
Director of the Radium Institute at the U. of Paris,
received the Nobel Prize again in 1911 (the only
woman ever to receive it twice), and in 1921 was
presented with a gram of radium by the President

of the USA. Long exposure to radiation led to her death from pernicious anaemia.

CURLING, Thomas Blizard (1811–1888)
Curling Ulcer: Peptic ulcer associated with severe burns. D. 1842.

The nephew of Sir William Blizard, Surgeon to the London Hospital, Curling was elected to the surgical staff at the age of 22. He was the first to describe the physiological effects of thyroid deficiency (1850). He resigned his post in 1869 and became President of the Royal College of Surgeons in 1873.

CURSCHMANN, Heinrich (1846–1910)
Curschmann's Spirals: Mucinous coils found in the sputum of asthmatics. D. 1882.

P. of Internal Medicine, Leipzig. On his death he was succeeded by von Strümpell.★

CUSHING, Harvey Williams (1869–1939)
1. *Cushing's Syndrome*: Adult hyperadrenocorticism. D. 1932.
2. *Cushing's Clips*: Silver haemostatic clips applied to cerebral vessels.

'The Founder of Neurosurgery' was a 4th-generation doctor, and son of the P. of Obstetrics and Gynaecology at Western Reserve U. School of Medicine, Cleveland, Ohio. He trained at Yale and Harvard, and interned at Massachusetts General Hospital; then worked for Halsted★ at Johns Hopkins Hospital in Baltimore. With his fellow-student Ernest Codman★ he designed the first anaesthetic record sheet. In 1900–1901 he travelled through Europe with his friend William Osler★ whom he met at Johns Hopkins, and who taught him clinical neurology; his biography of Osler won him the Pulitzer Prize in 1925. He worked with Kocher★ in Bern, and returned to set up as a neurosurgeon at Johns Hopkins, and in 1910 he successfully removed a large intracranial meningioma from Major-General Leonard Wood, a US Army Chief-of-Staff (who went on to serve throughout the First World War and became Governor of the Philippines). In 1912 he became Moseley P. of Surgery at Harvard, and Surgeon-in-Chief to the Peter Bent Brigham Hospital, Boston. From 1933 to 1939 he was Sterling P. of Neurology at Yale, and Director of Studies in the History of Medicine: his own collection of rare books formed the nucleus of the Yale Medical Historical Library. He was Senior Consultant Neurosurgeon to the American Expeditionary Force in France in 1917, and did much experimental work on pituitary pathology, describing the gland as 'the conductor of the endocrine orchestra'. A tall man with great personal charm, he nevertheless could be tyrannical if his meticulous surgical technique was not followed in theatre. An inveterate cigarette smoker, he died of a coronary at 70.

CUVIER, Baron Georges Léopold Chrétien Frédéric Dagobert (1769–1832)
Duct of Cuvier: Vessel joining the cardinal veins in the embryo. D. 1805.

Born in Montbéliard, he became Lecturer in Comparative Anatomy in Paris in 1800, and in 1802 Instructor-General in Education, and then P. of Natural History. Primarily a zoologist and palaeontologist, he was considered the most eminent naturalist of his day. He set up the world's first Chair of Pathological Anatomy (at the French U. of Strasbourg) in 1819, whose first incumbent, J. F. Lobstein (1777–1835) coined the term 'pathogenesis'. He was raised to the peerage in 1831.

D

DAKIN, Henry Drysdale (1880–1952)
Dakin's Solution: Dilute sodium hypochlorite antiseptic solution. D. 1915.

New York chemist. The solution, sometimes called Carrel★–Dakin Solution, was promoted as an antiseptic for cleansing infected wounds in the First World War.

DALTON, John (1766–1844)
Daltonism: Colour blindness. D. 1794.

Chemist and physicist, born in Cumberland of Quaker stock, who was at first a teacher in a village school, then taught mathematics privately in Manchester, and at the Royal Institution, and discovered the Atomic Theory. Colour-blind himself, it was said that he 'could not tell a laurel leaf from a stick of red sealing-wax'.

DANCE, Jean Baptiste Hippolyte (1797–1832)
Signe de Dance: Emptiness in the right iliac fossa in intussusception. D. 1826.

Physician to the Hôpital Cochin, Paris. He described tetany in 1831.

DANLOS, Henri Alexandre (1844–1932)
Ehlers–Danlos Syndrome. See *Ehlers*. D. 1908. (D. 1901 by Ehlers.)

Dermatologist in Paris. In 1901 he was the first to use radium to treat lupus erythematosus.

DARIER, Ferdinand Jean (1856–1938)
Darier's Disease: Pseudoxanthoma elasticum. D. 1896. His name is also given to follicular keratosis. (D. 1889, in his thesis.)

Paris dermatologist, who also gave classic descriptions of sarcoid (1904) and acanthosis nigricans (1893).

DARROW, Daniel Cady (1895–1965)
Darrow's Solution: Potassium-containing fluid for intravenous therapy. (122 mEq/l sodium; 104 mEq/l chloride; 35 mEq/l potassium; 53 mEq/l lactate.)

Paediatrician, New Haven, Connecticut, then P. of Pediatrics, Duke U. School of Medicine, Durham, North Carolina, USA.

DARWIN, Charles Robert (1809–1882)
1. *Darwinism*: Theory of evolution by natural selection. (D. 1859, in *The Origin of Species*.)
2. *Darwin's Tubercle*: Prominence on the helix of the ear. (Thomas Woolner (1825–1892), the sculptor and poet, drew Darwin's attention to it.)

Born in Shrewsbury, he was the son of a doctor, and grandson of the famous physician Erasmus Darwin (1751–1802). His maternal grandfather was the potter Josiah Wedgewood. He began to study medicine in Edinburgh in 1825, but turned to botany, and joined HMS *Beagle* as naturalist on a 5-year voyage (1831–1835). On his return, he lived almost as a recluse at Down House, Downe, Kent, where he spent 20 years writing *The Origin of Species*. All 1250 copies were sold out on the day the first edition was published in 1859. He was elected FRS in 1839.

Down House, where he died, was left to the Royal
College of Surgeons.

DAVIS, John Staige (1824–1885)
Davis's Gag: Instrument to maintain jaw opening in
intra-oral operations, e.g. tonsillectomy.

Surgeon in Baltimore, USA, who was the first to
specialise in plastic surgery, and described the 'small
deep graft' which also bears his name.

DEAVER, John Blair (1855–1931)
Deaver Retractor: Broad abdominal retractor.

Philadelphia anatomist and surgeon, known as one of
the most skilful operators of his time. His name is
sometimes associated with the fat-free windows in
the mesentery. He described a paramedian incision
for appendicectomy (1895).

DEJERINE, Joseph Jules (1849–1917)
1. *Landouzy-Dejerine Dystrophy*: See *Landouzy*.
2. *Dejerine-Klumpke Paralysis*: See *Klumpke*.

French neurologist and psychiatrist born in Geneva,
the son of a carriage proprietor, who studied in Paris
(MD 1879) and was successively Chef de Clinique at
the Bicêtre Hospital (1882–1901), P. of the History of
Medicine and Clinical Medicine in Paris (1901), and
Chef de Clinique at the Salpêtrière (1911–1917), and
P. of Neurology, succeeding Charcot★. He married
his student Auguste Klumpke★ in 1890. The name
Dejerine has no accents.

DELPHI
Delphic Nodes: Pre-tracheal lymph nodes.

The Oracle of Apollo at Delphi in Greek mythology
gave equivocal answers, and these nodes were
similarly thought to be of uncertain significance.

DENONVILLIERS, Charles Pierre (1808–1872)
Fascia of Denonvilliers: Recto-vesical fascia. D. 1836.

P. of Anatomy, Paris, later succeeding Malgaigne★ as
P. of Surgery.

De PEZZER, Oscar Michel Benvenuto (1853–1917)
De Pezzer Catheter: Urinary catheter.

Assistant Surgeon in the Department of Urology,
Hôpital Necker, Paris.

DERCUM, François Xavier (1856–1931)
Dercum's Disease: Multiple painful lipomata (Adiposis dolorosa). D. 1888.

P. of Neurology, Jefferson Medical College, Philadelphia, USA.

DESCEMET, Jean (1732–1810)
Descemet's Membrane: Posterior limiting membrane of the cornea. D. 1785. (Possibly previously D. by Benedict Duddell, an English oculist.)

P. of Anatomy and Surgery in Paris.

DESJARDINS, Abel
Desjardins Forceps: Instrument for holding gall-stones.

Formerly Consulting Surgeon, Dispensaire Henri de Rothschild, Paris. He made a study of pancreatitis.

DICK, George Frederick (1881–1967) and Gladys Rowena (1881–1963)
Dick Test: Subcutaneous injection of erythrogenic toxin as test for scarlet fever. D. 1924.

American physicians who identified streptococci as the cause of scarlet fever in 1923.

Di GEORGE, Angelo Mario (b. 1921)
Di George's Syndrome: Congenital absence of thymus associated with normal immunoglobulin levels. D. 1965.

Director of Clinical Research Centre and P. of Pediatrics, Temple U. Medical School, Philadelphia.

DODD, Harold (C)
Cockett and Dodd Operation: See *Cockett*.

Surgeon to the Royal Homeopathic Hospital, London.

DÖDERLEIN, Albert Siegmund Gustav (1860–1941)
Döderlein's Bacillus: *Lactobacillus acidophilus*; a Gram*-positive micro-organism found in the vagina.

German obstetrician and gynaecologist; a pioneer in the use of radiation to treat uterine cancer.

DONATH, Julius (1870–1950)
Donath–Landsteiner Syndrome: Paroxysmal cold haemoglobinuria. D. 1904.

German pathologist and immunologist.

DONNAN, Frederick George (1870–1956)
Donnan Equilibrium: Theorem governing the
distribution of ions across a semi-permeable
membrane. D. 1911. (Sometimes called the
Gibbs–Donnan equilibrium, as Josiah Willard Gibbs
(1839–1903), P. of Mathematical Physics at Yale had
predicted it 40 years before.)

The son of a Belfast merchant, he was born in
Ceylon, and studied in Belfast, Leipzig and Berlin.
He then lectured in chemistry at University College,
London, and in 1904 became P. of Physical
Chemistry in Liverpool, and in 1913 in London. He
was elected FRS in 1911, never married, lost his
London house in the Blitz, and retired to live with his
sisters in Kent, where he died.

DONOVAN, Lt Col. Charles (1863–1951)
1. *Leishman-Donovan Bodies*: See *Leishman*.
2. *Donovan Body*: Gram★-negative rod of *Donovania
granulomatosis*, seen in the cytoplasm of large
mononuclear tissue cells in cases of granuloma
venereum. D. 1905.

He studied medicine in Ireland and entered the Indian
Medical Service, becoming successively Second
Physician at the Government General Hospital,
Madras; Civil Superintendent of Royapettah
Hospital; and P. of Physiology at Madras College.
Leishman★ had discovered the bodies in 1900, but
both described them in 1903. Donovan resigned from
the Army at 57, and spent his last 30 years quietly at
Bourton-on-the-Water in the English Cotswolds.

DOPPLER, Christian Johann (1803–1853)
Doppler Effect: Relationship of apparent wavelength
to relative movement of source and receptor.

Austrian physicist and mathematician.

DORMIA, Enrico (C)
Dormia Basket: Instrument for cystoscopic removal of
stones from the lower ureter.

Assistant P. of Urology, Milan.

DORSET, Marion (1872–1935)
Dorset Egg: Medium for cultivating TB bacillus. D.
1902.

American bacteriologist and veterinary pathologist,

who worked in the Bureau of Animal Industry of the Department of Agriculture.

DOUGLAS, Claude Gordon (1882–1963)
Douglas Bag: Container for collection of expired air. D. 1911.

A pioneer of respiratory physiology: a pupil and co-worker of J. S. Haldane★ at Oxford.

DOUGLAS, James (1675–1742)
Pouch of Douglas: Recto-uterine pouch of peritoneum. D. 1730.

Born in Scotland, he went to London as an anatomist and male midwife, becoming Physician to Queen Caroline, the wife of George II. He was elected FRS in 1706 (three of his brothers were also Fellows), and Honorary FRCP in 1721. He wrote extensively on comparative myology, and died in Red Lion Square, London, leaving 557 volumes of Horace. He had greatly encouraged the Hunter★ brothers when they came to London.

DOVER, Thomas (1660–1742)
Dover's Powder: Sedative mixture of 10% opium, 10% ipecacuanha, and 80% lactose. D. 1733.

Born in Warwickshire (his father had been a Royalist cavalry officer in the Civil War, and his grandfather had been President of Corpus Christi College, Oxford – and had been dismissed for fraud), he studied at both Oxford and Cambridge (MB 1687), and then under Thomas Sydenham★ in London, who also treated him for smallpox (with a diet of oil of vitriol and 12 pints of beer a day). He survived, later pioneering inoculation against smallpox, and became a GP in Bristol. Many of his patients were rich slave-traders, but he treated the poor free, though he himself in 1708 forsook medicine to lead the most successful pirate expedition in British history, plundering the Spanish cities of Ecuador and Chile. In 1709 he rescued a shipwrecked Scottish sailor, Alexander Selkirk, from the island of Juan Fernandez off the coast of Chile, where he had lived alone for 4 years. Dover returned to England in 1711 with a vast booty, and resumed medical practice, mainly consulting in a London coffee-house in the Strand. Meanwhile Daniel Defoe wrote *Robinson Crusoe*, based on the story of Alexander Selkirk.

DOWN, John Langdon Haydon (1828–1896)
Down's Syndrome: Mongolism (Group G trisomy). D.
1866.

Born in Cornwall, the son of an apothecary, he
started working with his father. He studied medicine
at the London Hospital Medical College, becoming
Medical Superintendent at Earlswood Asylum for
Idiots, Redhill, then Assistant Physician to the
London Hospital. In 1868 he became FRCP, and
went into private practice in Harley Street. He
founded Normansfield Mental Hospital, naming it
after his friend Norman Wilkinson; three generations
of Downs were Physician–Superintendents there.
Remembered as a charming, gentle man, he
incidentally described Fröhlich's* Syndrome 40 years
before Fröhlich.

DRAGER, Glenn A. (1917–1967)
Shy-Drager Syndrome: See *Shy*.

Neurologist at the National Institute of Neurological
Diseases and Blindness, Bethesda, Maryland; later at
Baylor U. College of Medicine, Houston, Texas.

DRESSLER, William (1890–1969)
Dressler's Syndrome: Post-infarction pericarditis and
pneumonitis. D. 1955.

Cardiologist, Maimonides Hospital, New York.
(Dressler's Disease, an intermittent haemoglobinuria
(D. 1854) is ascribed to a Würzburg physician of the
same name.)

DUBIN, Isadore Nathan (b. 1913)
Dubin–Johnson Syndrome: Hyperbilirubinaemia in
young people associated with hepatic pigment
deposition. D. 1954.

Born in Montreal, he studied at McGill, and is now
P. of Pathology. Medical College of Pennsylvania,
Philadelphia.

Du BOIS, Delafield (1882–1959)
Du Bois Formula: For estimation of body surface area
from height and weight. D. 1915.

New York physiologist.

DUCHENNE, Guillaume Benjamin Amand
(1806–1875)
1. *Erb-Duchenne Palsy*: See *Erb*. D. 1855. (D. 1874 by
Erb.)

2. *Duchenne-type muscular dystrophy*:
Pseudo-hypertrophic progressive muscular
dystrophy. D. 1849. (Previously D. by Broca★.)

Descended from a family of fishermen and
sea-captains, he was born in Boulogne and studied at
Douai and Paris, and after qualifying practised in
Boulogne from 1831 to 1842, before returning to
Paris after his wife had died in childbirth, and her
family had alienated his son from him. He never held
a hospital or university post, but was one of the first
to specialise in neurology, wandering through the
wards of the Paris hospitals looking for clinical
material. He was a pioneer of the use of
electrodiagnostic methods, and the founder of
electrotherapy. He gave the first descriptions of
progressive bulbar palsy (1860) and locomotor ataxia
(1858). In 1862 his son joined him as a neurologist in
Paris, but died of typhoid 9 years later; in another 4
years Duchenne himself succumbed to a stroke.

DUCREY, Augusto (1860–1940)
Ducrey's Bacillus: *Haemophilus ducreyii*, the causative
organism of soft chancre. D. 1889.

P. of Dermatology in Pisa, then Rome.

DUKES, Cuthbert Esquire (b. 1890)
Dukes Classification: System of grading the extent of
spread of carcinoma of the rectum. D. 1932.

Pathologist, St Mark's Hospital, London.

DUNLOP, John (b. 1876)
Dunlop Traction: Traction-elevation for
supracondylar fractures of humerus. D. 1939.

Orthopaedic surgeon, Pasadena, California. He
described an index finger-to-thumb transfer in 1923.

DUNN, Naughton (1884–1939)
Naughton Dunn's Arthrodesis: Triple fusion, of
subtalar and mid-tarsal joints.

Surgeon to the Royal Cripples' Hospital,
Birmingham. He studied at Aberdeen, and had been
houseman and private assistant to Robert Jones★ in
Liverpool. He worked with Jones at Shepherd's Bush
Military Hospital during the First World War, and

was later on the Staff of the Orthopaedic Hospital at Oswestry, and Lecturer in Orthopaedics at Liverpool U. He was President of the British Orthopaedic Association just before he died.

DUPUYTREN, Baron Guillaume (1777–1835)
1. *Dupuytren's Contracture*: Palmar fibromatosis. D. 1831. (The condition had been recognised by Astley Cooper★ in 1822, and by Henry Cline in 1808.)
2. *Dupuytren's Fracture*: Ankle fracture with complete diastasis of the tibiofibular syndesmosis and upward displacement of the talus. D. 1816.

The son of a poor advocate in southern France, he was kidnapped at the age of 3 by a rich woman from Toulouse, and again at the age of 12 by a cavalry officer, who took him to Paris, where, in great poverty, he studied medicine at the Collège de la Manche. It was said that he used fat from the dissecting room cadavers for oil for his lamp. At 18 he became Prosector; in 1802 Surgeon to the Hôtel-Dieu; in 1812 P. of Operative Surgery; and in 1813 Surgeon-in-Chief at the Hôtel-Dieu, where he had 100 of the 250 beds. His Assistant was Méniére★. A cold, rude, ambitious and arrogant man, he earned such epithets as 'the brigand of the Hôtel-Dieu', and 'the Napoleon of Surgery'. But he was a bold operator, and, among many feats, excised the mandible in 1812, was the first to excise the cervix for cancer, and described Langer's★ Lines (1832) before Langer. He saw 10,000 private patients a year, and was Surgeon to Louis XVIII and Charles X during the restoration of the Bourbon monarchy, offering to lend the latter a million francs in exile. He left 200,000 francs to found a Chair of Pathological Anatomy, first occupied by Cruveilhier★. In 1833 he had a stroke, and died 2 years later in Paris, rich and famous, but surely unloved, 'first among surgeons; last among men'.

DWYER, Allan Frederick (1920–1975)
Dwyer Fusion: Anterior spinal fusion using staples, screws and a tension cable.

Born and trained in Sydney, he became Orthopaedic Surgeon to the Mater Hospital, Sydney, was awarded the OBE in 1974, and was politically active, becoming State President of the Democratic Labour Party.

DWYER, Frederick Charles (C)
Dwyer Osteotomy: Calcaneal osteotomy for club foot.

He qualified in Cape Town in 1931, then came to England, becoming Orthopaedic Surgeon to Sefton General Hospital and Alder Hey Children's Hospital, Liverpool.

E

EBSTEIN, Wilhelm (1836–1912)
1. *Pel–Ebstein Fever*: See *Pel*. D. 1887.
2. *Ebstein's Anomaly*: Deformity of tricuspid valve.

P. of Medicine, Göttingen. He followed in the tradition of the great German pathologists (Virchow★, Zenker★, Weigert★, von Recklinghausen★) with descriptions of degenerations, in his case urates in gout.

EDINGER, Ludwig (1855–1918)
Edinger–Westphal Nucleus: Nucleus accessorius of the oculomotor nerve concerned with accommodation. D. 1885.

He was born at Worms, the son of a textile merchant, and was given a microscope for his 14th birthday, which led to his interest in biology. He studied under Arnold★ and Bunsen★ at Heidelberg, but was a poor student and was nearly failed by Schwann★ in his final examinations. But Leyden's★ clinical neurology lectures influenced him, and the only book he took for holiday reading was Leyden's on comparative histology. He worked with Waldeyer★ in Strasbourg and was also Kussmaul's★ assistant there, and learned pathology from von Recklinghausen★. He went to Giessen in 1879 as neurology lecturer; at that time an unknown physicist called Röntgen★ was working there. In 1881 he visited Ehrlich★, Wernicke★ and Westphal★ in Berlin, Erb★ and von Strümpell★ in Leipzig, and Charcot★ in Paris, and in 1883 set up as a neurologist in Frankfurt. For 20 years he worked closely with Weigert★, whose myelin stain was so important to Edinger's neuropathological investigations. He built up a Neurological Institute in Frankfurt, and in 1914 became P. of Neurology at the Goethe U. there. He was also an accomplished artist, and an effective hypnotist, and when he died of a heart attack after an operation, the autopsy he had requested revealed several unusual features of his brain, including very large occipital lobes.

EGGERS, George William Nordholtz (1896–1963)
Eggers Plates: Bone fixation plates.

P. of Orthopaedic Surgery, U. of Texas, Galveston.

EHLERS, Edvard (1863–1937)
Ehlers–Danlos Syndrome: Various types of congenital collagen disorder resulting in hyperelasticity of skin and connective tissue; 'cutis laxa'. D. 1901. (D. 1908 by Danlos.)

Dermatologist in Berlin.

EHRLICH, Paul (1854–1915)
Ehrlich's Reaction: Red colour resulting from the action of diazotised sulphanilic acid and ammonia on urobilinogen. D. 1882.

Born in Strehlen, Silesia (Weigert★ was his cousin), he studied in Breslau and Strasbourg. He first worked in Berlin on TB; contracting the disease himself in 1887, he spent 3 years in Egypt recuperating, then returned to Koch's★ Institute for Infectious Diseases in Berlin in 1890 to work on immunity. In 1896 he founded the Institute for Serum Studies at Steiglitz, in 1889 the Institute for Experimental Therapy at Frankfurt, and in 1907 the Georg Speyer Haus for Chemotherapy. Ehrlich was a towering figure of the early years of chemotherapy, always searching for the 'magic bullet', a completely specific antibacterial agent. His discoveries included the staining methods which distinguished the three types of polymorphonuclear leucocytes, the fuschsin acid-fast stain for tubercle bacilli (1882), and Salvarsan (arsenobenzol), or Compound 606 for the treatment of syphilis (1910). It was the 606th arsenical compound he and his Japanese co-worker Sacachiro Hata had tested. In 1908 he shared the Nobel Prize with Elie Metchnikoff★ of the Pasteur★ Institute, Paris, for his work on immunity.

EINTHOVEN, Willem (1860–1927)
Einthoven's Triangle: Mathematic model of standard ECG leads.

P. of Physiology, Leiden, Holland, who designed the first effective electrocardiograph in 1903, a delicate string galvanometer with silver-coated quartz fibre. He received the 1924 Nobel Prize for his discovery.

EISENMENGER, Victor (1864–1932)
Eisenmenger Complex: Ventricular septal defect with over-riding aorta and right ventricular hypertrophy. D. 1897.

German physician.

ELLIS, Richard White Bernhard (1902–1966)
Ellis–van Creveld Syndrome: Hereditary multiple chondro-ectodermal abnormalities, including dwarfism, polydactyly, and heart disease.

Paediatrician in Edinburgh.

ELLISON, Edwin Horner (1918–1970)
Zollinger–Ellison Syndrome: See *Zollinger*.

Associate P. of Surgery, Ohio State U., Columbus, Ohio.

ERB, Wilhelm (1840–1921)
Erb's Palsy: Upper limb paralysis due to traction injury of upper roots of brachial plexus – classically a birth injury – producing the 'waiter's tip' position of the limb. D. 1874. (Sometimes called Erb–Duchenne★ palsy; D. 1855 by Duchenne.)

The son of a Bavarian forester, he studied at Heidelberg, Erlangen and Munich (MD 1864). In 1880 he became P. of Medicine at Leipzig, and in 1883 at Heidelberg (succeeding Friedreich★, who had taught him as a student). Erb was an obsessional workaholic, brusque and offensive to many; he pioneered electrodiagnosis, introducing galvanic★ and faradic stimulation; described myasthenia gravis in 1878; classified the muscular dystrophies in 1891; and introduced the term 'tendon reflex' for the knee-jerk, which had first been described by Westphal★. He wrote 273 papers, and ranks as Germany's greatest neurologist, as Charcot★ was to France. He lost a son killed on the first day of the First World War, and he himself died at 80 of pneumonia, caught during a rare moment of relaxation, listening to Beethoven's 'Eroica' at a concert.

ESCHERICH, Theodor (1857–1911)
Escherichia coli: Common Gram★-negative rod; a bowel commensal. D. 1886.

Born in Munich, he was a paediatrician there, then P. of Paediatrics in Graz, then Vienna (where von Pirquet★ was his registrar). He discovered the organism during a study of the bacterial flora of the suckling infant.

von ESMARCH, Johann Friedrich August (1823–1908)
Esmarch Bandage: Elastic bandage applied tightly to exsanguinate a limb prior to the application of a tourniquet. D. 1869 (but previously used by G. Silvestri of Padua in 1862).

Born in Schleswig-Holstein (then a province of Denmark), the son of a doctor, he studied at Kiel and Göttingen (MD 1848) where he became Assistant to Langenbeck★. He married the daughter of Stromeyer, the P. of Surgery at Kiel, and then (1857) became Professor himself. He organised the resistance against Denmark in his native province, and was taken prisoner during the ensuing war with Germany. Esmarch became a famous war surgeon, writing books on bullet-wounds and battlefield first-aid (in which he described (1885) an apparatus for the transfusion of defibrinated blood). He introduced the first 'First Aid Package' in 1870, and his bandage was widely used to control haemorrhage and to provide a bloodless field for amputations during the Franco-Prussian War. In 1871 he became Surgeon-General to the German Army, and in 1873 married (for the second time) a Princess of Schleswig-Holstein, thereby becoming an uncle-by-marriage of Kaiser Wilhelm II. His son was a well-known bacteriologist.

EUSTACHI, Bartolomeo (?1513–1574)
1. *Eustachian Tube*: The auditory tube, through which the tympanic cavity communicates with the nasopharynx. D. 1562 (and named for Eustachi a century later by Valsalva★).
2. *Eustachian Valve*: Valve of the inferior vena cava.

Born of noble parents in San Severino de Mariano, Italy, he became a physician in 1539, and performed anatomical researches in Rome. In 1547 he became physician to the Pope, and in 1549, P. of Anatomy in Rome. At first he was a Galenist★, but later enthusiastically supported the new school of anatomy. He discovered the thoracic duct, and was the first to show that the secondary dentition did not arise from the roots of the deciduous teeth. He discovered the abducent nerve, described the adrenals, and gave the first correct picture of the uterus. In 1552 he produced the first anatomical plates on copper, which were lost for 160 years in the Vatican, and were only published in 1714.

EVANS, Dillwyn (1910–1974)
Dillwyn Evans Procedure: Lateral wedge tarsectomy and medial release for club foot.

Orthopaedic surgeon in Cardiff, Wales. He visited Brazil as P. of Orthopaedics. His career was curtailed by a severe stroke at 62 which prevented him operating, and which led to his death.

EWING, James (1866–1943)
Ewing's Sarcoma: Malignant bone tumour of adolescents. D. 1922.

P. of Pathology, Cornell U. Medical College, New York.

F

FABRICIUS, Hieronymus (Girolamo Fabrizi of Aquapendente) (1533–1619)
Bursa of Fabricius: Organ in fowl analogous to human thymus, associated with cell-mediated immunity. D. 1621.

Born in Aquapendente, Italy, he studied under Fallopio★ at Padua from 1550, succeeding him as P. of Surgery in 1565, and as P. of Anatomy in 1571. He taught William Harvey★, and demonstrated the valves in the veins (1574), but believed they carried blood away from the heart. (Canano had first described the valves in 1541.) He built an anatomy theatre in Padua in 1594, which still survives. Fabricius was the greatest surgeon of the Italian Renaissance, describing techniques for tracheostomy, pleural tapping, and urethral surgery. He invented braces for torticollis and scoliosis, and prostheses for amputees. He died rich and famous on his estate near Padua, leaving his niece a fortune of 200,000 ducats.

FAHRENHEIT, Gabriel Daniel (1686–1736)
Fahrenheit Scale: Temperature scale with freezing-point at 32°, boiling-point at 212°. D. 1709.

German physicist and scientist, born in Danzig, who later lived in Holland. He devised the first mercury thermometer in 1714 (instead of using spirits of wine), and took for the zero of his scale the lowest temperature observed at Danzig in the winter of 1709 ($-32°F$), by mixing snow and sal ammoniac.

FALLOPIO, Gabriele (1523–1563)
Fallopian Tubes: Oviducts. D. 1561.

Born in Modena, Italy, he studied theology, then medicine at Ferrara and Pisa. He was the favourite pupil of Vesalius★ whom he later succeeded (1551) as P. of Surgery and Anatomy at Padua, where he was also P. of Botany, and in charge of the botanical gardens. He was a fearless opponent of Galen's★ teaching, and the most illustrious of Italy's new school of anatomists in the sixteenth century, who 'taught all of Europe for a century-and-a-half'. He discovered the bony labyrinth of the ear, and the trigeminal, auditory and glossopharyngeal nerves, gave the first description of the chorda tympani and 'Poupart's'★ ligament, named the vagina and the placenta, and gave classic descriptions of the clitoris and the deep artery of the penis.

FALLOT, Etienne-Louis Arthur (1850–1911)
Fallot's Tetralogy: Ventricular septal defect, over-riding aorta, pulmonary stenosis, and right ventricular hypertrophy. D. 1888.

P. of Hygiene and Legal Medicine, Marseilles. Niels Stensen★ had described the tetralogy two centuries earlier, but Fallot was the first to correlate the clinical with the pathological findings. He refused to have any obituary written on his death.

FANCONI, Guido (b. 1892)
Fanconi Syndrome: Osteomalacia, renal glycosuria, amino-aciduria, phosphaturia, and cystine deposition. D. 1936. (D. 1933 by Guido De Toni; sometimes referred to as De Toni–Fanconi Syndrome.)

Emeritus P. of Paediatrics, U. of Zürich.

Von FEHLING, Hermann Christian (1812–1885)
Fehling's Solution: Copper-containing solution which is reduced in an alkaline medium; it is the basis of Benedict's★ semi-quantitative test for sugar. D. 1848.

P. of Chemistry, Stuttgart; chiefly an organic chemist.

FEIL, André (b. 1884)
Klippel-Feil Syndrome: See *Klippel*.

French neurologist.

FELIX, Arthur (1887–1956)
Weil–Felix Reaction: See *Weil*.

Prague bacteriologist, who never qualified in
medicine, but entered bacteriology as a form of war
work. After the First World War he went to Palestine
as Director of a bacteriological laboratory in Tel
Aviv. He did extensive work on the Widal★ reaction,
and described the Vi antigens of the typhoid bacillus
in 1934, while working in London.

FELTY, Augustus Roi (1895–1963)
Felty's Syndrome: Splenomegaly, lymphadenopathy
and leucopenia. D. 1924.

Physician, Hartford Hospital, Connecticut.

FERGUSSON, Sir William (Bt.) (1808–1877)
Fergusson's Lion Forceps: Instrument originally used in
excision of the upper jaw.

The son of the Laird of Lochmaben, he studied at
Edinburgh (where his dissections are still in the
Museum of the Royal College of Surgeons) under
Robert Knox, the Anatomy Professor who was
forced to resign over the Burke and Hare murders.
He became Licenciate of the Royal College of
Surgeons of Edinburgh aged 20, and a Fellow the
following year, Surgeon to the Dispensary in 1831,
and succeeded the great Robert Liston as Surgeon to
Edinburgh Royal Infirmary in 1839. In 1840 he
became P. of Surgery at King's College Hospital,
London (still aged only 32), in 1855 Surgeon
Extraordinary to Queen Victoria, and a baronet in
1866. In 1870 he was President of the Royal College
of Surgeons. He was a surgeon 'of lightning speed'
who demanded total silence during an operation: it is
recorded that he performed 134 operations for cleft
palate with only five failures, and 400 for harelip with
three failures. He died at 69 of Bright's★ Disease.

FEULGEN, Robert (1884–1955)
Feulgen Reaction: Aniline test for nucleic acid. D.
1924.

Physiologist and chemist in Giessen, Germany.

FICK, Adolph Eugen (1829–1901)
Fick Principle: Cardiac output equals oxygen uptake

divided by arterial/mixed venous oxygen difference. D. 1870.

Physiologist and physician in Würzburg and Braunschweig, Germany, who also introduced the myotonograph, the cosine lever, and an improved thermopile.

FILDES, Sir Paul Gordon (b. 1882)
McIntosh–Fildes Jar: See *McIntosh*.

Bacteriologist in London.

FINKELSTEIN, Harry (1865–1939)
Finkelstein Test: Pain on the radial border of the wrist on rapid ulnar deviation of the hand with the thumb clenched in the palm, indicative of de Quervain's★ tenosynovitis. D. 1930.

Emeritus Surgeon, Hospital for Joint Diseases, New York.

FINNEY, John Miller Turpin (1863–1942)
Finney Pyloroplasty: Inverted 'U' incision to give a wide gastro-duodenal anastomosis. D. 1902. He studied at Princeton and Harvard and became Surgeon to Johns Hopkins Hospital, Baltimore.

FLACK, Martin William (1882–1931)
Sino-atrial Node of Keith and Flack: See *Keith*.

Physiologist, later Director of Medical Research, Royal Air Force Medical Service.

FLEISCHER, Bruno Richard (1848–1904)
Kayser-Fleischer Rings: See *Kayser*.

Physician who practised in Munich, Berlin and Erlangen, and also described 'march haemoglobinuria'.

FLEXNER, Simon (1863–1946)
Flexner's Dysentery: Bacillary dysentery due to *Shigella★ flexneri*. D. 1900.

Born in Louisville, Kentucky, he studied there, and at Harvard, Yale and Johns Hopkins. He became P. of Pathological Anatomy at Johns Hopkins Medical School, and then in the U. of Pennsylvania. In 1903 he became the first Director of the Rockefeller Institute for Medical Research, New York. He

pioneered research into venoms, epidemic
meningitis, polio and encephalitis lethargica.

FLINT, Austin (1812–1886)
Austin Flint Murmur: Diastolic murmur in severe
aortic incompetence. D. 1862.

Physician to Bellevue Hospital Medical School, New
York, and founder of Buffalo Medical College.
Coming from a long line of doctors, he was one of
the foremost physicians of his day in New York; his
Principles and Practice of Medicine was a standard
textbook for many years.

FOGARTY, Thomas J. (C)
Fogarty Catheter: Inflatable balloon embolectomy
catheter.

Surgeon, U. of Oregon Medical School, Portland,
Oregon. He designed the catheter while a medical
student.

FOLEY, Frederic Eugene Basil (1891–1966)
Foley Catheter: Self-retaining urinary catheter.

Urologist to the Miller and Ancker Hospitals, St
Paul, Minnesota. He also described methods of
ureterolithotomy and pyeloplasty.

FONTANA, Abbé Felice Gaspar Ferdinand
(1730–1805)
Space of Fontana: Space at the irido-corneal angle. D.
1787.

Born in the village of Pomarolo in the Trentino in
Italy, he was at school in Verona and Parma, then
studied in Padua, Bologna and Rome, principally for
the Church, but was never ordained, though he
always dressed as a lay abbot. Principally a
physiologist and naturalist, he became P. of
Physiology at Pisa in 1765, and was later appointed
by the Grand Duke of Tuscany to found Florence's
Museum of Natural History. He was the first to
describe the kidney tubules, the axon cylinder, and
the nerve sheath, and to recognise the cell as a
uniform body with a spot at its centre. He performed
experiments on spinal reflex activity on the heads and
bodies of decapitated criminals; he also wrote a
treatise on viper venom. He supported the
Revolution in France and so was imprisoned by
Austria, but Napoleon freed him to return to

Florence, where he died at 75, and is buried in Santa Croce.

FOREL, Auguste Henri (1848–1931)
Decussation of Forel: Decussation of tracts in the mesencephalon. D. 1872.

Born in Morges, on the shores of Lake Geneva, he was an authority on ants as a medical student at Zürich. He failed his cantonal qualifying examination in Lausanne for political reasons, and in 1878 set off on an expedition to Colombia, but had to return when his travelling companion (whose daughter he later married) died in the Virgin Islands on the way. He became Director of the Burghölzi Asylum and P. of Psychiatry in Zürich in 1879. He retired to Vaud in 1898 to write about ants, philosophy, and sexual problems, and to crusade for socialism and against alcohol; he had a stroke in 1912 but learned to write with his left hand, remaining active until his death at 83.

FORSSMAN, John (1868–1947)
Forssman Antigen: Heterophile antigen producing sheep red cell haemolysin. D. 1929.

Swedish pathologist and physician.

FOUCHET, André (b. 1894)
Fouchet's Test: Test for bilirubinaemia by the addition of trichloracetic acid and ferric chloride. D. 1917.

French chemist and physician.

FOURNIER, Jean Alfred (1832–1914)
Fournier's Gangrene: Fulminating streptococcal inflammation of the scrotum and lower abdominal skin.

P. of Dermatology, Paris. He founded the skin and venereal disease clinics at the Hôpital St Louis, wrote a book on *Syphilis and Marriage* (1890), and was the first to recognise the relation of syphilis to tabes dorsalis and GPI.

FOWLER, Edson Brady (1865–1942)
Fowler's Procedure: Osteotomy of metatarsal heads.

Surgeon in Evanston, Illinois, who in 1934 described a method of fracture fixation employing cow's horn.

FOWLER, George Ryerson (1848–1906)
Fowler's Position: Head-up position. D. 1900,
originally for the treatment of peritonitis, to allow
drainage into the pelvis.

Surgeon in Brooklyn, New York.

FRANCESCHETTI, Adolphe (1896–1968)
Collins–Franceschetti Syndrome: See *Collins*.

P. of Ophthalmology, U. of Geneva, Switzerland.

FREI, Wilhelm Siegmund (1885–1943)
Frei Test: Intradermal test for lymphogranuloma
venereum. D. 1925.

He practised in Breslau, then became P. of
Dermatology at the State Hospital, Spandau, Berlin.
He fled the Nazi regime and settled in New York.

FREIBERG, Albert Henry (1869–1940)
Freiberg's Disease: Osteochondritis of the head of the
2nd metatarsal. D. 1914. (Also called Köhler's★
Second Disease: D. 1900 by Köhler.)

Born in Cincinatti, Ohio, he studied there and in
Würzburg, Strasbourg, Berlin and Vienna, and
became P. of Orthopaedic Surgery to the General
Hospital in Cincinatti, where he remained, apart
from a term as orthopaedic surgeon to Walter Reed
Military Hospital during the First World War, where
he was succeeded by Keller★. He was President of the
American Orthopaedic Association in 1910–1911.

FREUD, Sigmund (1856–1939)
Freudian Theory: Repressed reactions to childhood
psychological traumas (especially sexual) are
manifested in adulthood as hysterical symptoms.

Viennese neurologist and psychiatrist, the founder of
psycho-analysis (1895). He studied in Paris with
Charcot★ in 1885. He described the origin and central
course of the auditory nerve (1886).

FREUND, Jules Thomas (1891–1960)
Freund's Adjuvant: Emulsion containing antigen
which induces antibody formation. D. 1942.

Hungarian-born bacteriologist who emigrated to
America, and worked in New York.

FREY, Lucja (1889–1944)
Frey's Syndrome: 'Auriculo-temporal syndrome':

cutaneous hyperaesthesia and sweating, instead of salivation, in response to food, resulting from regeneration of nerve fibres with inappropriate connections following damage to the auriculo-temporal nerve. D. 1923.

Warsaw neurologist; she was killed by the Nazis during the German occupation of Poland.

Von FREY, Max (1852–1932)
Von Frey's Hairs: Stiff hairs used in sensory testing. D. 1896.

Physiologist in Würzburg, who investigated the nature of 'referred pain'.

FRIDERICHSEN, Carl (b. 1886)
Waterhouse–Friderichsen Syndrome: See *Waterhouse*. D. 1918. (D. 1911 by Waterhouse and in 1901 by Sir Ernest Gordon Graham Little (b. 1867), a London physician.)

Director of Children's Department, Sundby Hospital, Copenhagen, Denmark.

FRIEDLÄNDER, Carl (1847–1887)
Friedländer's Bacillus: Organism now known as *Klebsiella★ pneumoniae*. D. 1882.

Born in Brieg, Silesia, he studied in Breslau, Würzburg, Zürich and Berlin, and was Assistant to Heidenhain★ and von Recklinghausen★. He became Pathologist to the Friederichshain Hospital, Berlin, and Editor of *Friedländer's Journal*, in which Gram★ first published details of his stain. An early student of bacteriology, he himself died at 40 of pulmonary TB.

FRIEDREICH, Nikolaus (1825–1882)
Friedreich's Ataxia: Progressive spino-cerebellar ataxia. D. 1863.

Born in Würzburg, he studied there (where his father and grandfather had been P. of Medicine) and at 31 succeeded Virchow★ as P. of Pathological Anatomy. After 1 year he went to Heidelberg as P. of Pathology and Therapy, and among his pupils were Erb★ (who later succeeded him) and Kussmaul★. He was a skilful clinical neurologist and teacher, as well as pathologist, but inclined to be obsessional about his

work and paranoid to any opposition. He died in
Heidelberg of a ruptured aortic aneurysm.

FRÖHLICH, Alfred (1871–1953)
Fröhlich's Syndrome: Adiposogenital dystrophy; a
condition of pituitary dysfunction in children,
characterised by obesity and sexual infantilism, which
can be caused by a craniopharyngioma, when patients
may develop bitemporal hemianopia from upward
pressure on the optic chiasma. D. 1901. (Down* had
described the condition 40 years before.)

P. of Pharmacology, U. of Vienna, who also
practised as a neurologist.

FROIN, Georges (1874–1932)
Froin's Syndrome: Block to CSF circulation (e.g. due
to congenital stenosis of the Aqueduct of Sylvius*)
which becomes yellow, and may clot spontaneously.
D. 1903.

Neurologist in Paris.

FROMENT, Jules (1878–1946)
Froment's Sign: Test of adductor pollicis function for
integrity of the ulnar nerve. D. 1915.

Neurologist, and P. of Clinical Medicine, Lyon,
France. He had qualified in 1906 with a thesis on
thyrotoxicosis, and in the First World War worked
on nerve injuries at Rennes, and later with Babinski*
in Paris. After the War he ran a Red Cross Hospital in
Lyon, and in 1926 was nearly killed by a deranged
patient.

G

GABRIEL, William Bashall (b. 1893)
Gabriel's Syringe: Instrument for injecting
haemorrhoids, originally described in 1929 for
injecting anaesthetic solutions in oil for pruritus ani
and anal fissure.

Surgeon to St Mark's and Royal Northern Hospitals,
London. He also described a one-stage
perineo-abdominal excision of the rectum in 1934.

GAERTNER, Hermann Treschow (1785–1827)
Gaertner's Duct: Unobliterated distal end of the
mesonephric duct. The duct may in fact have first

been described by his younger brother Benjamin, and was probably recognised 100 years before by Malpighi★.

A Dane, he was born in St Thomas, West Indies (then a Danish possession), studied in Copenhagen, and became a Surgeon in the Norwegian Army. He visited London and Edinburgh in 1811–1812.

GALEAZZI, Ricardo (1866–1952)
Galeazzi Fracture-dislocation: Fracture of radius with distal radio-ulnar joint dislocation. D. 1934.

Director of the Orthopaedic Clinic, Milan, for 35 years. He had been taught by Antonio Carle (who had also taught Bassini★), himself a pupil of Billroth★. Galeazzi was a pioneer of cineplastic amputation, and also a prolific writer. At one time he reviewed 12,000 cases of congenital dislocation of the hip.

GALEN, Claudius (Clarissimus) (A.D. 130–200)
Great Vein of Galen: Great cerebral vein, formed by the union of the two internal cerebral veins (Veins of Galen).

The son of an architect, he was born at Pergamum in Asia Minor, studying there, and at Smyrna, Corinth and Alexandria. He became Surgeon to the Gladiators at Pergamum, then went to Rome in A.D. 164 where he owned a chemist's shop near the Forum, and became the City's top physician, treating three Emperors, including Marcus Aurelius at Venice (for colic after over-indulgence in cheese). Galen showed the arteries contained blood, gave the first description of the cranial nerves and the lymphatic system, and showed that division of the spinal cord produced paraplegia. Though he never dissected the human body, his teachings were regarded as infallible for the next 15 centuries. It is not known with certainty where Galen died.

GALLIE, William Edward (1882–1959)
Gallie Needle: Large-eyed needle used for suture with strips of fascia lata. D. 1921.

P. of Surgery, U. of Toronto. He inspired a devoted following of trainees, who formed the 'Gallie Club' (though they privately referred to themselves as 'galley-slaves'); and was awarded the Gold Medal of the Royal College of Surgeons of England on his 75th birthday.

GALVANI, Luigi (1737–1798)
Galvanic Stimulation: Stimulation of an excitable tissue with current of low intensity and long duration. D. 1791.

P. of Anatomy, Bologna. Also a physicist and a physiologist, his chance observation that electric current caused the muscle of a skinned frog's leg to contract formed the basis of the science of 'animal electricity' (1786). He had also noticed that frogs hung from an iron fence by brass hooks through their spinal cords exhibited contractions; this also led him to discover the electrolytic potentials of dissimilar metals.

GAMGEE, Joseph Samson (1828–1886)
Gamgee Dressing: Absorbent wool-and-gauze dressing material. (It was a household word in the late nineteenth century.) D. 1880.

The son of an Italian-born veterinary surgeon who practised in London and Edinburgh, he himself first qualified as a vet, then MRCS in 1854. In 1855 he became Surgeon to the Italian Legation in Britain, and in 1857 Surgeon to Queen's Hospital, Birmingham. During the Crimean War he was Surgeon to a base hospital in Malta. His brother Arthur was P. of Physiology at Manchester and a FRS; his son Leonard Parker (1868–1956) became a Surgeon in Leamington.

GANSER, Sigbert Joseph Maria (1853–1931)
Ganser's Ganglion: Nucleus interpeduncularis.

Psychiatrist in Dresden and München. He was a student of von Gudden, the neuropathologist who was killed by drowning by the mad King Ludwig II of Bavaria.

GARDEN, Robert Symon (C)
Garden Grades: Classification of subcapital fractures of the femoral neck.

He studied at Aberdeen (MD 1934) and is now Honorary Consultant Orthopaedic Surgeon to the Royal Infirmary, Preston, Lancashire.

GARRÉ, Carl (1857–1928)
Sclerosing Osteomyelitis of Garré: Subacute bone infection, usually in tibia or femur, sterile on culture. D. 1893.

Born in St Gallen, Switzerland, he studied in Zürich, Leipzig and Bern, and taught surgery in Basle, Tübingen, Rostock and Bonn. He did extensive bacteriological work on wound and bone infections, and nearly killed himself by inoculating himself with cultures of staphylococcus experimentally.

GASSER, Johann Laurentius (Ludwig) (1723–1765)
Gasserian Ganglion: Semilunar ganglion of trigeminal nerve, lying in Meckel's★ Cave.

P. of Anatomy, Vienna (1757–1765). Gasser left no writings or anatomical preparations, and the ganglion was named after him by Anton Hirsch, one of his students, in his thesis (1765).

GAUCHER, Philippe Charles Ernest (1854–1918)
Gaucher's Disease: Familial disorder of cerebroside metabolism. D. 1882.

Physician and Dermatologist to the Hôpital St Louis, Paris.

GAUSS, Karl Friederich (1777–1855)
1. *Gaussian Distribution*: The normal distribution in statistics.
2. *Gauss*: Unit of magnetic flux density.

Born in Brunswick, he was the extraordinarily gifted child of poor illiterate parents. He learned arithmetic before he could talk, and at the age of 3 corrected his father's pay-slip. He taught himself to read, and at the age of 8 he could instantly solve the sum of the first hundred integers. He studied at Brunswick and Göttingen, and became Director of the Observatory there aged 30. A prodigiously brilliant mathematician and astronomer, he worked almost entirely alone; among many discoveries he invented the heliotrope. He lost his first wife young; his second suffered from TB and a hysterical neurosis. He himself would never agree to see a doctor until just before he died, of heart failure, at 78.

GAY, John (1812–1885)
Gay's Glands: Perianal glands.

Surgeon to the Royal Northern Hospital, London.

GEIGER, Hans (1882–1945)
Geiger Counter: Instrument for measuring radioactivity. D. 1908.

German physicist who came to work with Rutherford at Manchester U.

GENGOU, Octave (1875–1957)
1. *Bordet–Gengou Medium*: See *Bordet*.
2. *Bordet–Gengou Phenomenon*: See *Bordet*.

Bacteriologist to the Institute of Hygiene, U. of Brussels. With Bordet* he discovered *Bordetella pertussis* to be the causative organism of whooping-cough (1906). He was also a pioneer of complement-fixation, and helped to develop the Wassermann* reaction.

GENNARI, Francesco (1750–1796)
Stria of Gennari: Lamination line of the occipital (visual) cortex. D. 1782.

Physician and anatomist, Parma, Italy.

GERHARDT, Carl Adolph Christian Jacob (1833–1902)
Gerhardt's Test: Test for acetone in urine by addition of ferric chloride. He also described tests for acetoacetic acid (1865) and bile pigments in urine and blood (1881).

Physician in Berlin.

GEROTA, Dumitru (1867–1939)
Fascia of Gerota: Membrane surrounding kidney. D. 1895.

P. of Surgery and Experimental Surgery, U. of Bucharest, Rumania, who made great contributions to the anatomy of the lymphatics by injection studies, while working as an anatomist in Berlin.

GHON, Anton (1866–1936)
Ghon Focus (or Complex): Primary pulmonary tuberculous lesion. D. 1912.

Born in Villach, Carinthia (Austria), he studied in Vienna, worked in Berlin, and became P. of Pathological Anatomy in Prague.

GIANNUZZI, Giuseppe (1839–1876)
Crescents of Giannuzzi: Distinctive cells in the mucous alveoli of the salivary glands. D. 1865. (Also known as Demilunes of Heidenhain*.)

Anatomist and physiologist in Siena, Italy, who also worked at one time with Claude Bernard in Paris.

GIARD, Alfred (1846–1908)
Giardiasis: Intestinal infection with species of *Giardia*, a genus of flagellate protozoa. D. 1882.

Paris biologist. He was a staunch follower of the doctrine of Lamarck★.

GIBBON, Norman Otway Knight (C)
Gibbon Catheter: Self-retaining urinary catheter.

Consultant in Administrative Charge, Department of Urology, Royal Liverpool Hospital, and Director of Urological Studies in the U. of Liverpool.

GIEMSA, Gustav (1867–1948)
Giemsa's Stain: For protozoan parasites and viral inclusion bodies. D. 1902.

Hamburg chemist and bacteriologist.

Von GIERKE, Edgar Otto Conrad (1877–1945)
Von Gierke's Disease: Type I glycogen storage disease. D. 1929.

German pathologist.

Van GIESON, Ira (1866–1913)
Van Gieson's Stain: Trinitrophenol and acid fuchsin, for nerve and connective tissue. D. 1889.

Neuropathologist in New York (where he was born), who processed the brain sections of the first cases of Tay★–Sachs★ disease, and drew the illustrations for Sachs' paper.

GIGLI, Leonardo (1863–1908)
Gigli Saw: Flexible wire saw. D. 1894.

Obstetrician and Gynaecologist in Florence. He invented the saw for pubiotomy in obstructed labour; today it is more commonly used by orthopaedic surgeons for osteotomies.

GILBERT, Nicolas Augustin (1858–1927)
Gilbert's Disease: Benign familial non-haemolytic hyperbilirubinaemia. D. 1900.

Paris physician, the author of a standard medical textbook.

GILLES de la TOURETTE, Georges Edouard Albert Brutus (1855–1909)
Gilles de la Tourette's Syndrome: Childhood psychosis

including chorea, coprolalia, echolalia and various tics. D. 1885.

Neurologist at the Salpêtrière Hospital, Paris, who wrote famous treatises on hypnotism and hysteria.

GILLIES, Sir Harold Delf (1882–1960)
Gillies Forceps, Needle-holders, etc.: Various surgical instruments.

Originally an ENT surgeon, he later specialised in plastic and reconstructive surgery after service in the First World War. He became the first plastic surgeon at Barts, and originated the tubed pedicle flap (1932) in England, independently of Filatov in Russia. Sir Archibald McIndoe★ was his cousin.

GIMBERNAT y ARBOS, Manuel Louise Antonio don (1734–1816)
Gimbernat's Ligament: Lacunar ligament. D. 1768.

Catalan surgeon who became P. of Anatomy in Barcelona (1762–1774), Surgeon to the Santa Cruz Hospital, Director of the Royal College of Surgeons of Spain, and Surgeon to King Carlos III. On a visit to London in 1777 he attended William Hunter's★ lectures, and demonstrated operations to him.

GIRALDÈS, Joachim Albin Cardozo Cazado (1808–1875)
Organ of Giraldès: Paradidymis. D. 1859.

Born in Oporto, Portugal; he was educated in France and became Surgeon to the Hôpital Beaujou, Paris, and then P. of Surgery. He died of a wound sustained while performing a post-mortem.

GIRDLESTONE, Gathorne Robert (1881–1950)
Girdlestone Procedure: Pseudarthrosis of the hip.

Born in Oxford, the son of an honorary canon of Christ Church, he trained at St Thomas's and worked at Oswestry under Robert Jones★, having initially gone to Shropshire as a general practitioner/surgeon, and came to the Orthopaedic Hospital to assist at operations. A lung injury sustained in a motor-cycle accident prevented active service during the First World War, when instead he set up a military orthopaedic hospital in Oxford, and in 1937 became Nuffield P. of Orthopaedic Surgery there, the first orthopaedic Chair in Britain. In 1942 he was President of the British Orthopaedic Association. A much loved and deeply religious man, he was responsible for building up the regional organisation of orthopaedics in Britain, and was also an outstanding golfer.

von GLANZMANN, Edward (1887–1959)
Glanzmann's Disease: Autosomal recessive alymphocytic agammaglobulinaemia with vestigial thymus. D. 1950. (Also called Glanzmann and Riniker's Disease, or Swiss-type agammaglobulinaemia.)

Swiss paediatrician.

GLAUBER, Johann Rudolph (1604–1670)
Glauber's Salt: Sodium sulphate, first made artificially, as 'sal mirabile' in 1656.

Born in Karlstadt, Germany, the son of a barber, he never attended university, but visited laboratories in Paris, Basle, Salzburg and Vienna. He earned his living by casting metallic mirrors, and in 1635 became Court Apothecary in Giessen. He left Germany in 1639 for Amsterdam because of the Thirty Years' War, after which he returned to work in the wine industry, but his main interest was always alchemy. In 1655 he returned to Amsterdam, built 'the most magnificent laboratory in Europe', and before he died believed he had discovered the material of the Philosophers' Stone.

GLISSON, Francis (1597–1677)
Glisson's Capsule: Fibrous capsule of the liver. D. 1659.

Born in Rampisham, Dorset, he studied at Cambridge, where he became a Lecturer in Greek, and later Regius P. of Physic, from 1636 to 1677. He rarely spent any time in Cambridge, however, treating the Chair as a sinecure. During the Civil War he practised at Colchester, and during the Plague he remained working in London with his friend Thomas Wharton★. In 1650 he wrote a classic treatise on The Rickets, described abroad at that time as 'The English Disease'. In 1654 he described the Sphincter of Oddi★ (described by Oddi 233 years later). Glisson was one of the founders of the Royal Society, and was President of the Royal College of Physicians from

1667 to 1669. He died in London and is buried in St Bride's, Fleet Street.

GOLDTHWAIT, Joel Ernest (1866–1961)
Goldthwait's Operation: Patellar tendon realignment procedure for recurrent dislocation. D. 1899.

Orthopaedic Surgeon, Boston, USA, who had tried studying agricultural science before medicine. He founded the Orthopaedic Department at Massachusetts General Hospital.

GOLGI, Camillo (1843–1926)
Golgi Apparatus: Intracellular network of membranous tubules and vesicles related to cell metabolism. D. 1898.

Born in Corteno (now called Corteno Golgi) in Lombardy, Italy, the son of a doctor, he studied in Pavia and worked there for 7 years after qualifying, writing papers on pellagra, smallpox, and psammomas. In 1875 he became P. of Histology at Pavia, and was later Rector of the University there, and a member of the Royal Senate. He pioneered chrome-silver nitrate staining for neural tissue (working by candle-light in the kitchen of his home), and shared the 1906 Nobel Prize with Santiago Ramon y Cajal (despite their life-long rivalry) for work on the structure of the nervous system.

GOLL, Friedrich (1829–1903)
Column of Goll: Fasciculus gracilis. D. 1860.

Born in Zürich, he studied there under Ludwig★, and under Claude Bernard in Paris and Virchow★ in Berlin. He became P. of Anatomy in Zürich, and was also known as a neurologist and physiologist.

GOMORI, George (1904–1957)
Gomori Stain: For demonstration of phosphatases, lipases, and other enzymes.

Hungarian-born histochemist who emigrated to the USA and worked in Chicago.

GOODPASTURE, Ernest William (1886–1960)
Goodpasture's Syndrome: Glomerulonephritis with intra-pulmonary haemorrhage. D. 1919.

American pathologist at Johns Hopkins Hospital, who first recognised the syndrome in association with the 1919 influenza pandemic. He also introduced the fertile egg as a culture medium for viruses, in 1931.

GOODSALL, David H. (1843–1906)
Goodsall's Rule: Anal fistulae opening anteriorly are usually direct; those opening posteriorly usually have a curving track.

Surgeon to the Metropolitan Hospital, London.

GOSSELIN, Léon Athenase (1815–1887)
Gosselin Fracture: Unstable V-shaped intra-articular distal tibial fracture. D. 1855.

Paris surgeon. He described the Tillaux★ fracture 18 years before Tillaux.

GOWERS, Sir William Richard (1845–1915)
Gowers' Tract: The superficial antero-lateral fasciculus of the spinal cord. D. 1879.

Born in London, he studied at UCH, later becoming P. of Clinical Medicine there, and Neurologist to the National Hospital, Queen Square. He was elected FRS in 1887, and knighted in 1897. He wrote *Gowers' Plain Words*, and textbooks of neurology and ophthalmology which he illustrated himself. He referred to Sir Victor Horsley★ the patient who became the first to undergo operative removal of a spinal cord tumour. The haemoglobinometer he invented in 1877 remained in use for half a century. His paintings were frequently hung at the Royal Academy, and he was also an obsessional proponent of the use of shorthand.

De GRAAF, Regnier (1641–1673)
Graafian Follicle: Maturing ovarian follicle. D. 1672. (Named after him by Haller in 1730.)

Born in Schoonhaven, Holland, where his father was an architect and hydraulic engineer, he studied (together with Niels Stensen★) under Sylvius de la Böe★ in Utrecht and Leyden, but failed to succeed Sylvius as P. of Anatomy at Leyden as he was a Catholic. He worked instead at Delft as anatomist and physician, after travelling and studying in France in 1665–1666. In 1664 he had demonstrated the function of the pancreas, in 1668 wrote a classic account of the testis, and in 1672 published a great work on the female reproductive cycle, based on dissections of 100 rabbits, 40 goats, cows, dogs, cats,

and other animals. In 1673 he communicated the
letters of Antoni van Leeuwenhoek to the Royal
Society in London, which founded the science of
microscopy. De Graaf died of plague in Delft.

Von GRAEFE, Friedrich Wilhelm Ernst Albrecht
(1828–1870)
   Von Graefe's Sign: Lid-lag on downward gaze in
   Graves'★ Disease (primary thyrotoxicosis). D. 1864.

The son of a surgeon, he rapidly became the greatest
ophthalmologist of the nineteenth century,
pioneering iridectomy for glaucoma, cataract
extraction, and many other eye operations. As P. of
Ophthalmology in Berlin, Horner★ was one of his
pupils. He died at 42 of TB.

GRÄFENBERG, Ernest (1881–1957)
   Gräfenberg Ring: The first widely-used intra-uterine
   contraceptive device.

German-born gynaecologist who emigrated to the
USA.

GRAM, Hans Christian Joachim (1853–1938)
   Gram Stain: Selective bacterial staining technique. D.
   1884.

Born in Copenhagen, the son of the P. of Law, he
was a botanist before taking up medicine. He
discovered the stain by accident while a postgraduate
student in Berlin with Friedländer★: he spilt some
Lugol's★ Iodine over a bacterial preparation and tried
to wash it off with alcohol. In 1891 he became P. of
Pharmacology in Copenhagen; in 1892,
Physician-in-Chief to the Royal Frederik's Hospital,
Copenhagen, and in 1900, P. of Medicine in
Copenhagen. Gram was a widely respected clinician
with a large private practice.

GRATIOLET, Louis Pierre (1815–1865)
   Radiation of Gratiolet: Optic radiation.

Like Broca★, born in Ste Foy-la-Grande near
Bordeaux (where today Boulevard Gratiolet leads
into Place Broca), he studied in Paris, became P. of
Anatomy there, and with Broca founded the Société
d'Anthropologie. He had a relatively hard, poor, life,
and attempted to demonstrate anatomical differences
in the skulls and brains of 'superior' and 'inferior'
races.

GRAVES, Robert James (1796–1853)
Graves' Disease: Primary thyrotoxicosis. D. 1835.
(The condition had in fact previously been described
by Caleb Hillier Parry (1825), a Physician of Bath,
who also described Hirschsprung's★ Disease before
Hirschsprung.)

The third son of the Dean of Armagh, he studied at
Trinity College, Dublin, and travelled widely,
becoming so perfectly fluent in German that he was
imprisoned for 10 days as a spy in Austria. He
returned to become Physician to the Meath Hospital,
Dublin, where he was the first to introduce clinical
ward work for medical students. He gave the first
description (1833) of rib fracture from coughing. At
his request his epitaph read: 'He Fed Fevers'.

GRAWITZ, Paul Albert (1850–1932)
Grawitz Tumour: Adenocarcinoma of kidney
(sometimes referred to as 'hypernephroma' as it was
formerly thought to arise from adrenal tissue). D.
1883.

Born in Pomerania, he studied medicine in Berlin and
Halle, becoming Assistant to Virchow★ at the Berlin
Pathological Institute. He was for 37 years P. of
Pathology at Griefswald.

GRAY, Henry (1827–1861)
Gray's Anatomy: Famous standard textbook.

The son of the private messenger to George IV and
William IV, he entered St George's Hospital Medical
School as a 'perpetual student' in 1845, winning the
triennial prize of the Royal College of Surgeons in
1848 for an essay on the nerve supply of the eye.
Elected FRS aged 25, in 1853 he won the Astley
Cooper★ Prize of the Royal College of Surgeons for a
thesis on the spleen. He became successively
Anatomy Demonstrator, Curator of the Museum,
and Anatomy Lecturer at St George's, dedicating the
first edition of *Gray's Anatomy* (1858) to Sir Benjamin
Brodie★, 'in remembrance of many acts of kindness'.
Gray died at 34 of confluent smallpox, contracted
while looking after his nephew who was suffering
from the disease.

GRITTI, Rocco (1820–1920)
Stokes–Gritti (or Gritti–Stokes) Operation: Amputation
of lower limb through femoral condyles bringing the

patella over the femoral stump. D. 1857. (D. 1858 by Stokes.)

Surgeon in Milan.

GROVES, Ernest William Hey (1872–1944)
Hey Groves Clamps: Self-retaining bone-holding forceps.

Born in India, the son of a civil engineer, he came to Bristol at the age of 3 when his father retired. He studied at Barts and Tübingen, and was a biology demonstrator while still a student. He married a nurse at Barts, and after a short period in general practice in Bristol, turned his home into a private hospital, operating in the sitting-room, with his wife assisting. He introduced intramedullary nailing for fractures, and used ivory and walrus tooth as well as bone for grafting, and described external fixation of fractures in 1913. He founded (with Moynihan★), and edited (for 27 years), the *British Journal of Surgery*. His chief interest was in orthopaedics, on which he gave the Hunterian Lectures in 1914. He became P. of Surgery at Bristol in 1922, and President of the British Orthopaedic Association in 1929. He translated Böhler's★ writings into English in 1935.

GUARNIERI, Giuseppi (1856–1918)
Guarnieri Corpuscles: Inclusion bodies in smallpox. D. 1894.

Italian physician in Genoa.

GUEDEL, Arthur Ernest (b. 1883)
Guedel Airway: Black rubber oro-pharyngeal airway. D. 1911.

Anaesthetist, Indianapolis, USA. He described the stages of anaesthesia in 1920.

GUÉRIN, Camille (b. 1872)
Bacille Calmette-Guérin: See *Calmette*.

Veterinary surgeon in charge of the serum and vaccine laboratory of Calmette's★ Institute at Lille. A painstaking and meticulous worker, he developed BCG by repeated sub-culturing of the tubercle bacillus for 12 years. It was first used (orally) in 1921.

GUIDO GUIDI (VIDUS VIDIUS) (1500–1567)
Guido's (or Vidian) Canal, Artery, and Nerve: Structures in the pterygoid bone.

Born in Florence, he became P. of Medicine at the Collège de France, Paris, and personal physician to Francis I. Cosimo I de Medici recalled him to be P. of Philosophy and Medicine at Pisa (1548–1567), where he also practised as anatomist and surgeon (recommending the use of the rack to reduce shoulder dislocations), and was a teacher of Vesalius★.

GUILLAIN, Georges (1876–1961)
Guillain–Barré Syndrome: Acute infective polyneuritis. D. 1916.

P. of Neurology, Paris. He was Director of the Neurological Unit of the Sixth Army during the First World War, in which Barré★ was working.

GUYON, Felix Jean Casimir (1831–1920)
Guyon's Canal: Tunnel through which the ulnar nerve passes at the wrist, where it may be subject to compression. D. 1861.

Born on Isle Réunion, a French possession in the Indian Ocean, he studied medicine in Paris, and later became P. of Surgical Pathology there (at the same time as Tillaux★ was P. of Surgery), retiring in 1906. He was the greatest teacher of genito-urinary surgery of the day, with a clinic at the Hôpital Necker.

H

HAGEDORN, Werner (1831–1894)
Hagedorn Needle: Flat-sided curved cutting needle with large eye. D. 1885.

Surgeon in Magdeburg, Germany, who also designed an operating table which bears his name.

HALDANE, John Scott (1860–1936)
Haldane Apparatus: For measurement of respiratory gases. D. 1892.

Born in Edinburgh, the younger brother of Viscount Haldane of Cloan, he studied there and at Jena, qualifying in medicine in Edinburgh in 1884. He was Physiology Demonstrator in Dundee and Berlin, and in 1897 came to Oxford as Physiology Demonstrator (where C. G. Douglas★ was among his pupils), under

his uncle, Professor J. S. Burdon-Sanderson
(1828–1905), (who in 1871 (58 years before Fleming)
had described the antimicrobial effect of penicillium
mould.) He became a Fellow of New College (1901)
and Reader in Physiology (1907), and after directing a
mining research laboratory near Doncaster (1912)
was made Honorary P. of Mining at Birmingham U.
(1921) and President of the Institute of Mining
Engineers (1924–1928). He was elected FRS in 1897,
and Companion of Honour in 1928.

HALSTED, William Stewart (1852–1922)
   1. *Halsted's Operation*: Radical mastectomy. D. 1890,
though first performed by him in 1882.
   2. *Halsted's Needle-holding Forceps*.
   3. *Halsted Suture*: Mattress suture of gut wall. D.
1887.

He studied at Yale and in New York, where he was
Attending Surgeon to the Presbyterian and Bellevue
Hospitals, and became in 1893 the first P. of Surgery
at Johns Hopkins Medical School, Baltimore, where
Harvey Cushing★ was his assistant. Halsted was a
great surgical pioneer of wide repute: he introduced
rubber gloves to surgery (made for him by Goodyear
in 1889 to protect a theatre nurse whose skin was
sensitive to mercuric chloride), and was one of the
first to use regional 'block' anaesthesia, with cocaine
(1885).

HAMMAN, Louis (1877–1946)
Hamman-Rich Syndrome: Diffuse interstitial
pulmonary fibrosis. D. 1937.

Physician to Johns Hopkins Hospital, Baltimore.

HAND, Alfred (Jr) (1868–1949)
Hand–Schüller–Christian Disease: Disseminated
histiocytosis with a disorder of lipid metabolism. D.
1893. (D. 1915 by Schüller and 1920 by Christian.)

Paediatrician in Philadelphia.

HANOT, Victor Charles (1844–1896)
Hanot's Cirrhosis: Primary biliary cirrhosis.

Physician in Paris who described the condition in his
thesis in 1875.

HANSEN, Gerhard Henrik Armauer (1841–1912)
Hansen's Disease: Leprosy.

Born in Bergen, Norway, Hansen was the 8th of 15 children. The local leprosarium had been opened to non-lepers and the disease was fairly common. His discovery of the bacillus, *Mycobacterium leprae* (1873) disproved previous theories about the heritability of the disease. His (unsuccessful) experimental attempt to transmit the disease by injection into a patient's eye resulted in a court action which removed his licence to practise in hospital, but he remained a consultant to the Norwegian Government, highly respected by his colleagues, until his death from a heart attack.

HARRIS, Henry Albert (1886–1968)
Harris's Lines: Transverse lines seen on radiographs near the ends of long bones, representing periods of retarded growth. D. 1924.

Born in Rhymney, Wales, he became P. of Anatomy in Khartoum, then returned to be P. of Anatomy at Cambridge and a Fellow of St John's College.

HARRIS, S. Harry (1881–1937)
Harris's Boomerang Needle: Instrument for inserting haemostatic lateral sutures during open (e.g. Millin's★) prostatectomy.

Urologist to Lewisham Hospital, Sydney, Australia.

HARRISON, Edward (1766–1838)
Harrison's Sulcus: Indentation below ribs in rickets and undernutrition, due to abdominal distension 'spreading' lower ribs.

General practitioner, Horncastle, Lincolnshire. The sign is also ascribed to Edwin Harrison (1779–1847), a Physician at St Marylebone Infirmary, London.

HARTMANN, Alexis Frank (1898–1964)
Hartmann's Solution: Ringer★-lactate solution for intravenous infusion. D. 1932.

Paediatrician, St Louis, Missouri, USA.

HARTMANN, Henri Albert Charles Antoine (1860–1952)
Hartmann's Pouch: Dilatation at the neck of the gall-bladder.

Born in Paris, in 1909 he became P. of Surgery in the Faculty of Medicine there, and wrote the encyclopaedic four-volume *Traité de Chirurgie*

Anatomo-Clinique. (The Pouch is sometimes attributed to Robert Hartmann★.)

HARTMANN, Robert (1831–1893)
Hartmann's Operation: Excision of the rectum and colostomy with preservation of the anal canal.

P. of Anatomy, Berlin. 'Hartmann's Pouch' is also sometimes ascribed to him rather than to Henri Hartmann★.

HARVEY, William (1578–1657)
1. *Harveian Oration*: Prestigious medical lecture.
2. *Harvey's Sign*: Assessment of the speed of venous refilling by exerting digital pressure on a superficial vein.

Born in Folkestone, he studied at Caius College, Cambridge, and at Padua under Fabricius★, becoming MD there in 1602. He became a Physician at Barts, and Surgeon–Anatomist to, and later President of the Royal College of Physicians. *De Motu Cordis*, the book in which Harvey gave the first coherent account of the circulation of the blood, was first published in Frankfurt in 1628 (and dedicated to his patient and patron King Charles I), though the first public statement of his discovery of the circulation was in 1616, in his first Lumleian Lecture as Professor at the Royal College of Physicians. He studied the animals in the Royal Parks, and was Physician to James I as well as Charles I. As a Royalist during the Civil War, the King appointed him Warden of Merton College, Oxford, from 1640 to 1642. He died of gout and a cerebral haemorrhage.

HASHIMOTO, Hakaru (1881–1934)
Hashimoto's Thyroiditis: Struma lymphomatosa; auto–immune thyroiditis. D. 1912, found to be auto–immune in 1956.

Japanese surgeon who studied in Europe for 2 years, worked at the U. of Kyushu from 1908 to 1912, and became Director of the Hashimoto Hospital, Miyo Prefecture, Japan. He died of typhoid.

HASSALL, Arthur Hill (1817–1894)
Hassall's Corpuscles: Characteristic lymphoid structures in the thymus. D. 1846.

Born in Teddington, Middlesex, he became Physician to the Royal Free Hospital, London, and later practised in the Isle of Wight, where he died. At the age of 29 he wrote the first English textbook on microscopic anatomy, and was also a noted botanist.

HASSELBALCH, Karl A. (b. 1874)
Henderson–Hasselbalch Equation: See *Henderson*. D. 1912.

Copenhagen scientist.

HAVERS, Clopton (1657–1702)
Haversian System: Vascular canal surrounded by concentric layers of cortical bone. D. 1689 (though they had first been demonstrated in 1674 by Antoni van Leeuwenhoek (1632–1723), the pioneer Dutch microscopist).

Born in Essex, the son of the chaplain to the Earl of Warwick, he studied first at Cambridge, but left without a degree, becoming MD in Utrecht in 1685, and FRS in London the following year (the President at the time was the diarist Samuel Pepys). In 1698 he was appointed the first Gale Lecturer at Surgeon's Hall.

HAWLEY, George Waller (1875–1940)
Hawley Table: Orthopaedic operating table with adjustable leg traction extensions. D. 1913.

Surgeon in Bridgeport, Connecticut, USA.

HEBERDEN, William (1710–1801)
Heberden's Nodes: Swellings over the terminal interphalangeal joints in osteoarthrosis. D. 1802.

Born in London, he studied classics then medicine at Cambridge from the age of 14, became a Fellow of St John's College at 20, and practised there and lectured on materia medica for 10 years before returning to London. He was elected FRCP in 1746, and FRS in 1748. He had a large private practice, was Physician to George III, and was summoned by Dr Johnson in his last illness. In 1778 he was made an Associate of the Royal Society of Medicine in Paris. He was the first to recognise angina pectoris, gave the first description of night-blindness, and was the first to distinguish chicken-pox from smallpox (all in 1768). He wrote up all his case-notes in Latin, and many of his observations were published posthumously.

HEGAR, Alfred (1830–1914)
Hegar's Dilators: Graded metal sounds for dilatation of uterine cervix.

The son of a doctor, he studied at Heidelberg,
Vienna, Berlin and Giessen, qualifying MD in 1852.
In 1864 he became P. of Obstetrics and Gynaecology
in Freiburg, where he introduced antisepsis, being a
strong follower of Semmelweis. His operating lists
began at 5 a.m.

HEIDENHAIN, Rudolf Peter Heinrich (1834–1897)
Demilunes of Heidenhain: Distinctive cells in the
mucous alveoli of the salivary glands. (Also known as
Crescents of Gianuzzi★.)

He studied in Königsberg, Halle and Berlin, and from
the age of 25 until his death was P. of Histology and
Physiology at Breslau.

HEINEKE, Walter Hermann (1834–1901)
Heineke–Mikulicz Pyloroplasty: Longitudinal incision
in pylorus resutured transversely. D. 1886, by F.
Fronmüller.

German surgeon.

HEINZ, Robert (1865–1924)
Heinz Bodies: Fragments of denatured haemoglobin
found in red cells in drug-induced haemolytic
anaemias.

Born in Silesia, he studied in Breslau and in 1888 was
appointed Assistant at the Pharmacological Institute
there. From 1893 he worked in Jena and Munich; in
1904 became P. of Pharmacology and Toxicology,
Erlangen; and in 1910 Director of the
Pharmacological Institute there, where he died.

HEISTER, Lorenz (Laurentius) (1683–1758)
Spiral Valve of Heister: Mucosal fold in cystic duct. D.
1720.

Born in Frankfurt, he studied art, music and painting
before medicine, and in 1710 toured the British Isles,
before taking up the Chair of Surgery at Altorf, in
Nuremberg. In 1719 he became P. of Anatomy and
Surgery at Helmstädt; he was a great proponent of
therapeutic baths. He dedicated his *Compendium
Anatomicum* (translated as *General System of Surgery*) to
Morgagni★.

HELLER, Ernst (b. 1877)
Heller's Operation: Oesophago-cardiomyotomy. D.
1913.

P. of Surgery, Leipzig.

Von HELMHOLTZ, Hermann Ludwig Ferdinand.
(1821–1894)
Young–Helmholtz Theory of Colour Vision: See *Young*.
D. 1852. (D. 1801 by Young.)

Born in Potsdam, in 1848 he became Assistant to
Johannes Müller in Berlin, and between 1850 and
1871 was P. of Physiology, Pathology and Physics
successively at Königsberg, Bonn, Heidelberg and
Berlin (where Hertz★ was his pupil and later
Assistant). He gave dreadful lectures which were
eventually attended by only three students. In 1851 he
invented the ophthalmoscope, and designed a
galvanometer to measure the speed of conduction of
nerve impulses. He eventually became President of
the Research Institute at Charlottenburg, and died in
Berlin.

HENDERSON, Lawrence Joseph (1878–1942)
Henderson–Hasselbalch Equation: Formula for
calculating the pH of a buffer solution:

$$pH = pK + \log \frac{[base]}{[acid]} \quad D. 1910.$$

Biochemist at Harvard U. He was a pioneer in the
study of acid–base balance and water metabolism.

HENLE, Friedrich Gustav Jakob (1809–1885)
Loop of Henle: Portion of renal tubule. D. 1862.

Born at Furth, near Nuremberg in Bavaria, he
studied in Bonn and Heidelberg under Müller,
whom he followed to Berlin. After qualifying, he
became Anatomy Demonstrator in Berlin, and at 31,
P. of Anatomy in Zürich, then Heidelberg (in 1844),
and from 1852 to 1885 was P. of Anatomy in
Göttingen, where he taught Robert Koch★. A
well-known microscopical anatomist, he described
the smooth muscle of blood vessels (1841), and
promoted Virchow's★ Cell Theory. He also
maintained, before Pasteur★, that small living
organisms were responsible for infectious disease
(1840).

HENOCH, Eduard Heinrich (1820–1910)
Henoch–Schönlein Purpura: 'Allergic'
non-thrombocytopenic purpura in children
associated with capillary hyperpermeability and
diffuse vasculitis. D. 1865. (D. 1832 by Schönlein.)

P. of Paediatrics, Berlin; a nephew of Moritz Romberg★. He also described spasmodic tic (1868).

HENRY, William (1774–1836)
Henry's Law: The solubility of a gas in a liquid is proportional to its partial pressure. D. 1803.

Born in Manchester, the son of a chemist, a wooden beam fell on him at the age of 10, after which he could never play games, so he concentrated on study. He studied medicine for a year (1795) in Edinburgh, then helped his father as a chemist, but qualified MD in 1807, specialised in urinary diseases, was elected FRS in 1808, and won the Copley Medal. He was a great friend of Dalton★. Chronic pain plagued him from his childhood injury, and he committed suicide at 52.

HENSEN, Viktor (1835–1924)
Hensen's Node: Thickening of primitive streak in embryo.

Born in Schleswig, in 1868 he became P. of Physiology at Kiel, where he remained until his death.

HENSING, Friedrich Wilhelm (1719–1745)
Hensing's Ligament: Tissue attaching the upper end of the left colon to the abdominal wall. D. 1742.

German anatomist at Giessen who died at 26. He was the son of the P. of Medicine at Giessen who reported the first chemical examination of the brain, and was the grandson of a surgeon.

d'HERELLE, Felix Hubert (1873–1949)
Twort–d'Herelle Phenomenon: See *Twort*. D. 1917. (D. 1915 by Twort.)

Born in Montreal, he studied in Lille and Leyden. From 1902 to 1908 he was Director of Bacteriological Laboratories in Guatemala and Mexico, and then went to the Pasteur★ Institute in Paris where he was head of the bacteriology department from 1914 to 1921. In 1922–1923 he was P. of Bacteriology in Leyden, and in 1923–1927 Director of the International Sanitary Commission in Egypt. In 1928 he became P. of Protobiology at Yale.

HERTZ, Heinrich Rudolf (1857–1894)
Hertz (Hz): Unit of vibration frequency, 1 cycle per second.

Born in Hamburg, the son of a wealthy barrister and Hanseatic Senator of Jewish descent (though Hertz was Lutheran, and his first and only assistant was a devoted Nazi), he studied engineering in Frankfurt, Dresden and Munich. He was a student of, then Assistant to, Helmholtz★ in Berlin, then physics lecturer at Kiel (where Max Planck was his successor), and P. of Physics in Karlsruhe, then Bonn. He died of septicaemia secondary to a bone tumour of the jaw, aged 36.

HERXHEIMER, Karl (1861–1944)
Herxheimer Reaction: (Or Jarisch–Herxheimer Reaction.) Adverse pyrexial reaction in antibiotic treatment of syphilis, possibly due to release of toxins from dead spirochaetes. D. 1902. (Hypoglycaemia associated with pancreatic secretory duct obstruction is sometimes called Herxheimer–Mansfeld Phenomenon.)

German dermatologist.

HESS, Alfred Fabian (1875–1933)
Hess's Test: Tourniquet test for capillary fragility. D. 1914.

Clinical P. of Paediatrics, New York U.

HESSELBACH, Franz Kaspar (1759–1816)
Hesselbach's Triangle: Bounded by the inguinal ligament, inferior epigastric artery, and rectus abdominis; through it protrudes a direct inguinal hernia. D. 1806.

P. of Surgery, Würzburg.

HEY, William (1736–1819)
Hey's Ligament: Falciform ligament of the saphenous opening.

Born in Pudsey, Yorkshire, he studied with John Hunter★ at St George's Hospital, London, returning to Leeds as a Surgeon in 1759. He founded Leeds Medical School and was one of the founders of Leeds General Infirmary. Elected FRS in 1775, he coined the term 'internal derangement of the knee' (1784).

HIGGINSON, Alfred (1808–1884)
Higginson's Syringe: Enema syringe.

Born in Stockport, the son of a clergyman, he

qualified MRCS in 1832 and practised in Liverpool. In 1857 he was elected Surgeon to Liverpool Southern Hospital and Liverpool Children's Hospital, and was a pioneer of blood transfusion (before the blood groups were identified).

HIGHMORE, Nathaniel (1613–1685)
Antrum of Highmore: Maxillary sinus. D. 1651. (It had previously been described by Leonardo da Vinci and other earlier anatomists.)

Born at Fordingbridge, Hampshire, he gained his degree at Oxford in 1641 with a treatise on anatomy, and practised as a physician at Sherborne, Dorset, where he died.

HILTON, John (1804–1878)
1. *Hilton's Law*: A joint is innervated by nerves serving the muscles which control it. D. 1863.
2. *Hilton's Method*: Drainage of abscess by inserting closed forceps and opening the blades. D. 1879.
3. *White Line of Hilton*: Peritoneal reflection on abdominal wall, 1.5 cm above the anal verge. D. 1879.

Born at Sible Hedingham, Essex, he was educated at Chelmsford and Boulogne, becoming a medical student at Guy's in 1824. He was Anatomy Demonstrator to Bransby Cooper at Guy's, was elected FRS in 1839, and in 1854 became Lecturer in Anatomy at Guy's and from 1849 to 1871 was Full Surgeon, and was also Hunterian★ P. of Anatomy. In 1843 he was one of the original Fellows of the Royal College of Surgeons, and in 1867 its President. He wrote *Lectures on Rest and Pain* (London, 1863), and was the first to diagnose and operate on a patient with internal strangulation of the small bowel. He died in Clapham.

von HIPPEL, Eugen (1867–1939)
von Hippel–Lindau Syndrome: Angiomatosis of skin, retina, brain and spinal cord, with cysts of liver and pancreas. D. 1895. (D. 1926 by Lindau.)

Ophthalmologist in Berlin.

HIPPOCRATES of Cos (460–367 B.C.)
1. *Hippocratic Oath*: Physicians' ethical code.

2. *Hippocratic Facies*: Appearance in advanced peritonitis, or any condition in which death is imminent.
3. *Hippocratic Method*: For reduction of shoulder dislocation.

'The Father of Medicine' was the son of Heraclides, a physician, and was born on the Greek Island of Cos, where he was taught by his father. He founded a School of Medicine, teaching his own sons and many others beneath a plane tree: his main contribution was the written recording of many accurate clinical descriptions. His main work, 'Aphorisms' contains many proverbial generalisations (e.g. 'Ars longa, vita brevis'). Some sources suggest he lived to be 109.

HIRSCHSPRUNG, Harald (1830–1916)
Hirschsprung's Disease: Congenital dilatation of colon due to aganglionic segment. D. 1888. (Caleb Hillier Parry, a Physician, in Bath, had described the condition in 1825; he also described Graves* Disease before Graves.)

He studied at Copenhagen, qualifying MD in 1855, and in 1877 became P. of Paediatrics in Copenhagen, and in 1879 Head Physician to the Queen Louise Children's Hospital there.

HIS, Wilhelm (Jr) (1863–1934)
Bundle of His: Cardiac atrioventricular conducting tissue, also known as Bundle of Kent. D. 1893 (same year as Kent).

Born in Basle, His was successively P. of Anatomy in Leipzig, Basle, Göttingen and Berlin. The Bundle was in fact originally described by his father, Wilhelm His Sr. (1831–1904), who had also been P. of Anatomy and Physiology at Basle and Leipzig.

HODGE, Hugh Lenox (1796–1873)
Hodge Pessary: Ring pessary. D. 1866.

Gynaecologist and Obstetrician, Philadelphia, who promoted his pessary for backache and pelvic pain.

HODGKIN, Thomas (1798–1866)
Hodgkin's Disease: Lymphadenoma. D. 1832.

Born in Pentonville, London, the son of a tutor, Hodgkin was a Quaker who studied at Guy's, qualified MD Edinburgh in 1823, and was one of the first to use a stethoscope in England, having been taught in Paris by Laennec★, who invented it. He became Curator of the Museum at Guy's and his original paper described seven cases of the disease (the first was a patient of Richard Bright's★). A humble and unworldly man and a strong opponent of slavery, when he failed to be appointed Physician to Guy's he gave up medicine, became a missionary, and died of dysentery at Jaffa.

HOFFA, Albert (1859–1908)
Hoffa's Syndrome: Synovitis of the knee with fat pad hyperplasia. D. 1904.

P. of Orthopaedic Surgery, Berlin (succeeding Julius Wolff★ in 1902); he was well known for his work on tendon transplantation and congenital dislocation of the hip.

von HOFMEISTER, Max Friedrich (1867–1926)
Hofmeister Valve: Modification of Billroth★ II gastro–enterostomy. D. 1908.

Berlin surgeon.

HOHMANN, Georg (b. 1880)
Hohmann Osteotomy: First metatarsal osteotomy for hallux valgus. D. 1923.

German surgeon.

HOLLANDER, Frederick G. (b. 1899)
Hollander Test Meal: Insulin meal to test completeness of vagotomy.

Surgeon to Sharp Memorial Hospital, San Diego, California, USA.

HOLMES, Sir Gordon Morgan (1876–1965)
Holmes–Adie Syndrome (Pupil): Myotonic pupil with absent deep tendon reflexes. D. 1931 (independently of Adie).

Born in Dublin, where he qualified in medicine, he then studied in Frankfurt with Edinger★ and Weigert★. Predominantly a neurologist, he was on the staffs of the National Hospital, Queen Square, Moorfields, the Seamen's, and Charing Cross Hospitals. He was rejected for Army Service on the grounds of myopia, so went to France in the First World War with a Red Cross Hospital: the RAMC changed its mind and made him consultant to the British Expeditionary Force. He wrote a classic paper with Henry Head on sensory disturbances from cerebral lesions, and recorded the regression of virilisation with extirpation of an adrenal cortical tumour. He was elected FRS in 1933 and knighted in 1951.

HOLMGREN, Alarik Frithiof (1831–1897)
Holmgren's Skeins: Coloured woollen yarn for testing colour vision. D. 1874.

Physiologist in Uppsala, then Stockholm.

HOLT, Mary (C)
Holt–Oram Syndrome: Ostium secundum atrial septal defect with hypoplastic thumb containing accessory phalanx. D. 1960.

She studied at King's College Hospital (MB 1947), and is now Consultant Cardiologist in Croydon, Surrey, and to the Brompton Hospital, London; and Physician to the South London Hospital for Women and Children.

HOMANS, John (1877–1954)
Homan's Sign: Calf pain on dorsiflexion of the ankle in the presence of a deep vein thrombosis. D. 1941.

P. of Clinical Surgery, Harvard University Medical School, Boston. The sign was originally described in thrombophlebitis.

HORNER, Johann Friedrich (1831–1886)
Horner's Syndrome: Ptosis, miosis, hypohidrosis and apparent enophthalmos, with damage to the cervical sympathetic. D. 1869.

Born in Zürich, the son of a doctor, he wrote a thesis on spinal curvature and in 1862 became P. of Ophthalmology in Zürich.

HORSLEY, Sir Victor Alexander Horden (1857–1916)
Horsley's Wax: Seven parts beeswax to one part almond oil, for control of skull bone bleeding. D. 1887.

The son of a Royal Academician who opposed the pre-Raphaelites, he was born in Kensington and educated at Cranbrook and University College, London, winning the Gold Medal in Surgery in 1881.

A founder of modern neurosurgery, he was the first to remove a tumour of the spinal cord (in a patient referred to him by Gowers★), and also attempted to transplant the thyroid gland. He was a supporter of the suffragettes, but a strong opponent of alcohol and tobacco. At 29, he was appointed Surgeon to the National Hospital, Queen Square, and was also on the staff of UCH. He was knighted in 1902, and in the First World War, despite his age (57) requested active duty, developed paratyphoid fever serving with the RAMC in Mesopotamia, and died of heatstroke when he went walking at midday without his sun-helmet.

HOUSTON, John (1802–1845)
Valve of Houston: Folds of rectal mucous membrane. D. 1830.

An Ulsterman by birth, he became Physician at the City of Dublin Hospital, and Lecturer in Surgery, and died in Dublin. He discovered a muscle for compressing the dorsal vein of the penis in man, and compared it with a similar muscle in the chameleon's tongue.

HOWELL, William Henry (1860–1945)
Howell–Jolly Bodies: Nuclear remnants seen in mature red cells in leukaemia, some anaemias, and after splenectomy. D. 1890. (D. 1905 by Jolly.)

Born in Baltimore, Maryland, he studied at Michigan, Harvard, and John's Hopkins, becoming P. of Physiology at Johns Hopkins Medical School in 1893, Assistant Director (1916) and then Director (1926) of the School of Hygiene, and in 1931 Emeritus P. of Physiology. He did pioneer work on blood coagulation, and discovered heparin in 1916.

HOWSHIP, John (1781–1841)
1. *Howship's Lacunae*: Absorption spaces in bone, possibly eroded by osteoclasts. D. 1812.
2. *Howship–Romberg Sign*: Pain referred to the knee in a strangulated obturator hernia, via the genicular branch of the obturator nerve.

He was Surgeon to St George's and Charing Cross Hospitals, London, Hunterian★ Lecturer in 1833, and Member of Council of the Royal College of Surgeons. He developed osteomyelitis of the tibia and studied the lacunae in the sequestrum from his own bone. He died at his house in Savile Row, London.

HUET, G. J. (b. 1879)
Pelger–Huet Anomaly: See *Pelger*. D. 1931. (D. 1928 by Pelger.)

Dutch physician.

HUMPHRY, Sir George Murray (1820–1896)
Ligament of Humphry: Anterior menisco-femoral ligament, running from the posterior horn of the lateral meniscus to the inner aspect of the medial femoral condyle, in front of the posterior cruciate. D. 1858.

Born in Suffolk, he studied medicine at Barts (1839), becoming MRCS in 1841, FRCS in 1854, and was elected FRS in 1859. From 1866 to 1883 he was P. of Anatomy at Cambridge, and founded the *Journal of Anatomy*. In 1883 he became the first P. of Surgery at Cambridge, was knighted in 1891, and died in Cambridge.

HUNNER, Guy Le Roy (1868–1957)
Hunner's Ulcer: Ulcer developing in bladder in chronic cystitis. D. 1932.

Emeritus P. of Gynaecology, Johns Hopkins University, Baltimore.

HUNTER, Charles H.
Hunter's Syndrome: A mucopolysaccharidosis, with less severe mental retardation than in Hurler's★ Syndrome. D. 1917.

Winnipeg physician and a Major in the Canadian Army Medical Corps, who described two affected brothers at a meeting of the Royal Society of Medicine in London; his paper was discussed by F. P. Weber★ and Bankart★.

HUNTER, John (1728–1793)
1. *Hunter's Canal*: Subsartorial canal in thigh. D. 1786.
2. *Hunterian Chancre*: Hard chancre in primary syphilis. D. 1786.

He was born in Lanarkshire, Scotland, the son of a laird, and the youngest of ten, seven of whom died before adulthood. He joined his older brother

William (1718–1783) as Assistant in his Covent Garden Street School of Anatomy in London, and studied at Barts and St George's. He was a Staff Surgeon in the Belle Isle and Portugal campaigns of the Seven Years' War, leaving England principally for his health, as he had developed pneumonia at 33. He was elected FRS in 1767 and the following year was appointed Surgeon to St George's. The greatest exponent of surgery of his day, Hunter was the first to demonstrate the formation of a collateral circulation, by ligating the external carotid artery of a stag from Richmond Park, and observing the regrowth of the antler. He inoculated himself with syphilis in 1767 to test the hypothesis that syphilis and gonorrhoea were due to the same infective agent, and in old age probably suffered from cerebral syphilis. In 1790 he introduced artificial feeding, using an oro–gastric tube. He built up a great menagerie of exotic animals in the grounds of his large house in Earls Court. Over 30 years, he assembled a great surgical museum (including the skeleton of the Irish giant O'Bryan), which was purchased by Parliament in 1799. It was partially destroyed by German bombing in 1940, and is now in the Royal College of Surgeons. Hunter died of a ruptured aortic aneurysm, and is buried in Westminster Abbey.

HUNTINGTON, George (1850–1916)
Huntington's Chorea: Dominant familial form of progressive dementia commencing in middle age. D. 1872.

A 3rd-generation doctor, born in Long Island, New York, he studied at Columbia, and practised at first with his father, then, apart from 2 years each in Ohio and N. Carolina, independently in Duchess County, NY until the age of 65. He played the flute well, fished, shot, and drew from nature, and wrote a single medical paper – at the age of 22 – in which he described the condition which bears his name, which he had first observed while making rounds with his father and grandfather in Long Island.

HURLER, Gertrud (C)
Hurler's Syndrome: A severe systemic mucopolysaccharidosis with early death from mental and physical degeneration. D. 1920.

Paediatrician in Munich.

HUTCHINSON, Sir Jonathan (1828–1913)
1. *Hutchinson's Incisors*: Peg-shaped, notched, permanent incisors in congenital syphilis. D. 1858.
2. *Hutchinson's Pupil*: Dilated pupil on the side of an extradural haemorrhage.
3. *Hutchinson's Potato Tumour*: Carotid body tumour.

A Quaker, he was apprenticed in York, then studied at Barts under Paget★, qualifying MRCS in 1850. In 1853 he became Surgeon to Blackfriars Hospital for Diseases of the Skin and to the Metropolitan Hospital, and in 1858 wrote a classic paper on interstitial keratitis in congenital syphilis. He became Assistant Surgeon to the London Hospital in 1860, FRCS in 1862 (President in 1889), and Surgeon to Moorfields Eye Hospital in 1863. He was elected FRS in 1882 and knighted in 1908. He was the first to operate successfully on intussusception in an infant.

HYNES, Wilfred (C)
Anderson–Hynes Pyeloplasty: See *Anderson*.

He studied at Leeds (MB 1927), became Surgeon-in-Charge of the Plastic and Jaw Department, United Sheffield Hospitals; and is now retired in Sheffield.

I

ISHIHARA, Shinobu (b. 1879)
Ishihara Charts: Colour-confusion diagrams for testing colour vision.

P. of Ophthalmology, Tokyo.

ISRAEL, James Adolf (1848–1926)
Actinomyces israelii: Causative organism of Actinomycosis. D. 1878.

Urologist in Berlin; Director of Surgery at the Jewish Hospital.

J

JABOULAY, Mathieu (1860–1913)
Jaboulay Procedure: Partial excision and eversion of the sac of a hydrocoele.

P. of Surgery, Lyon, France. He described an abdominal incision usually given Battle's★ name, and was one of the first to report arterial suture, in 1896.

JACKSON, John Hughlings (1835–1911)
Jacksonian Epilepsy: 'Focal' fits starting in one muscle group. D. 1863.

The son of a Yorkshire farmer, he studied medicine in York and at Barts, qualifying MRCS and Licenciate of the Society of Apothecaries in 1856. He practised in York, and returned to London in 1859, when Sir Jonathan Hutchinson★ dissuaded him from giving up medicine in favour of philosophy. Indeed in 1860 he became Lecturer in Pathology, then Assistant Physician at The London Hospital and also held a post at Moorfields Eye Hospital. He became MRCP and gained an MD from St Andrews. 'The Father of English Neurology', Jackson took up the specialty after himself developing Bell's★ palsy, on the persuasion of Brown-Séquard★. In 1862 he became Assistant Physician to the National Hospital for the Paralysed and Epileptic (now the National Hospital for Nervous Diseases), Queen Square, and married his cousin, who died of a stroke associated with Jacksonian epilepsy.

Hughlings Jackson wrote extensively in a most confusing and repetitious style (described as 'resembling the love of God, which passeth all understanding'). He did not enjoy music, sport, eating, or people, and developed various odd habits such as tearing up any part of a book which did not interest him; he died of pneumonia aged 76.

JACOBSON, Ludwig Leven (1783–1843).
1. *Jacobson's Nerve*: Tympanic branch of the glosso-pharyngeal. D. 1818
2. *Jacobson's Canal*: Canaliculus tympanicus. D. 1818.

Anatomist and physician in Copenhagen, where he was born and died. He was also for a period Physician in the French Army.

JAKOB, Alfons Maria (1884–1931)
Jakob–Creutzfeld Syndrome: Cerebral cortical atrophy arising in middle age, possibly due to a 'slow virus'. D. 1921. (D. 1920 by Creutzfeld.)

Born in Bavaria, the son of a shopkeeper, he trained in Munich, Berlin, and Strasbourg (MD 1909), then returning to Munich where he worked with Nissl*, Alzheimer* and Kraepelin. In 1911 he went as clinical assistant to the State Hospital at Hamburg, and in 1930 he became Prosektor. He served at the Front in the First World War, and became Privatdozent in Hamburg in 1918, and P. of Neurology in 1924. He had over 200 patients with neurosyphilis on the wards at any one time. In 1928 he went to South America as visiting Professor, and wrote a paper on the neuropathology of yellow fever. He died of a streptococcal osteomyelitis of the femur, which after 7 years eventually caused a retroperitoneal abscess.

JAQUES, James Archibald (1815–1878)
Jaques Catheter: Rubber urethral catheter.

Works manager of William Warne and Co. Ltd, India Rubber Mills, Barking, Essex. He developed and patented the first soft rubber catheter.

JEGHERS, Harald Jos (C)
Peutz–Jeghers Syndrome: See *Peutz*.

P. of Internal Medicine, New Jersey College of Medicine and Dentistry, Jersey City, USA. Formerly P. of Medicine, Tufts U. School of Medicine, Boston.

JENDRASSIK, Ernst (1858–1921)
Jendrassik Manoeuvre: Reinforcement of lower–limb reflexes by resisted abduction (or other isometric contraction) in the upper limbs.

Physician in Budapest, Hungary.

JENNER, Louis Leopold (1866–1904)
Jenner's Stain: Methylene blue and eosin dissolved in methyl alcohol, for blood corpuscles. D. 1899.

Director of the Clinical Pathology Laboratory, St Thomas's Hospital, London, to which post he was appointed only 5 years after qualifying. (Not the same man as Edward Jenner (1749–1823), the pioneer of vaccination.)

JEWETT, Eugene Lyon (b. 1900)
Jewett Nail-plate: Implant for fixation of hip fractures. D. 1941.

Orthopaedic Surgeon in Orlando, Florida.

JOHNE, Heinrich Albert (1839–1910)
Johne's Disease: 'Pseudotuberculosis': infiltration of the gut in cattle due to *Mycobacterium johnei*.

Born in Dresden, he was a pupil of Cohnheim in Leipzig, and became P. of Pathological Anatomy in Dresden. He died near Pirna (Sachsen).

JOHNSON, Frank Bacchus (b. 1919)
Dubin–Johnson Syndrome: See *Dubin*.

Born in Washington, he studied at the U. of Michigan, and is now Chief of Histochemistry at the Armed Forces Institute of Pathology, Washington, DC.

JOHNSON, Frank Chambliss (1894–1934)
Stevens–Johnson Syndrome. See *Stevens*. D. 1922.

Paediatrician in New York.

JOLLY, Justin Marie Jules (1870–1953)
Howell–Jolly Bodies: See *Howell*. D. 1905. (D. 1890 by Howell.)

Born in Melun, he became Director of the Histological Laboratory and P. of Histophysiology at the Collège de France, Paris, and was a pioneer of modern haematology.

JONES, Sir Robert (1858–1933)
1. *Robert Jones Bandage*: Three successive layers of wool and Domette bandage on the lower limb.
2. *Robert Jones Operation*: Tendon transfer of extensor hallucis longus to neck of first metatarsal.

Several other operative procedures, and various orthopaedic splints, frames and braces also bear his name.
    Jones' father gave up his architectural studies to be a writer, and sent his son to stay with his uncle Hugh Owen Thomas★, a well-established bone-setter in Liverpool, who sent Robert Jones to Medical School there; after qualifying in 1878 he worked part-time with Thomas, in 1888 organised the Casualty Service of the Manchester Ship Canal, and in 1889 was appointed General Surgeon to the Royal Southern Hospital, Liverpool. From 1905 he restricted his practice to orthopaedics, and was consulted by Agnes Hunt, Matron of a small home for crippled children, about her own stiff hip; from this consultation grew

the renowned Robert Jones and Agnes Hunt
Orthopaedic Hospital at Oswestry.

Robert Jones, a much-loved man, was Director of
Military Orthopaedics in the First World War, helped
found the British Orthopaedic Association in 1918,
and, with Girdlestone★ after the War, built up the
whole organisation of orthopaedic care in Britain.
From 1921 he was also Director of Orthopaedic
Studies at Liverpool U.

K

KAHN, Reuben Leon (b. 1887)
Kahn Test: Serum flocculation test for detection of
syphilitic antibody. D. 1922.

Bacteriologist, U. of Michigan Medical School and
Hospital, Ann Arbor, Michigan.

KANAVEL, Allen Buchner (1874–1938)
Spaces of Kanavel: Fascial spaces in the forearm.

P. of Surgery, Northwestern U., Chicago, and
Surgeon to Cook County Hospital, Chicago, one of
the largest in the world. He wrote extensively on the
spread and treatment of infections in the hand and
forearm.

KANTOR, John Leonard (1890–1947)
Kantor's 'String Sign': Constriction of the terminal
ileum seen on barium follow-through in
long-standing Crohn's★ Disease. D. 1934.

Gastroenterologist to Presbyterian Hospital, New
York.

KAPOSI, Moricz Kohn (1837–1902)
Kaposi's Sarcoma: Multiple pigmented skin neoplasms
occurring in East European and Italian Jews (also
known as Kaposi's Varicelliform Eruption). D. 1872.
The highest incidence in the world has been found in
Zaire, where this accounts for 12% of all
malignancies.

P. of Dermatology, Vienna.

KAY, Sir Andrew Watt (C)
Kay's Test: Augmented histamine test indicating size
of oxyntic cell mass in peptic ulcer.

He studied in Glasgow (MD 1944), winning the Bellahouston Gold Medal and Brunton Medal, became P. of Surgery, Sheffield, President of the Royal College of Physicians and Surgeons, Glasgow, and Regius P. of Surgery, U. of Glasgow, Chief Scientist of the Scottish Home and Health Department, and Fellow of the Royal Society of Edinburgh.

KAYSER, Bernhard (1869–1954)
Kayser–Fleischer Rings: Pigmented rings seen in Descemet's★ membrane of the cornea in patients with Wilson's★ Disease (hepatolenticular degeneration). D. 1902 (D. 1903 by Fleischer.)

German Ophthalmologist.

KEETLEY, Charles Robert Bell (1848–1909)
Keetley–Torek Operation: Orchiopexy involving temporary anchoring of testis and scrotum to deep fascia of thigh. D. 1905.

Surgeon to the West London Hospital.

KEHR, Hans (1862–1916)
Kehr's Sign: Left shoulder-tip pain when the foot of the bed is elevated, in a patient with a ruptured spleen, due to diaphragmatic irritation by free blood in the peritoneum.

P. of Surgery, Halberstädt, Saxony, then in Berlin. He described an incision for cholecystectomy, and died of septicaemia contracted while performing an operation.

KEITH, Sir Arthur (1866–1955)
Sino-atrial node of Keith and Flack: Site of initiation of cardiac contraction. D. 1906.

Born in Aberdeen, he studied at Marischal College, and went into practice before becoming medical officer to a mining company in Siam. He returned in 1895, as Lecturer in Anatomy to the London Hospital Medical School. From 1908 to 1934 he was Conservator of the Royal College of Surgeons' Museum, and then became Master of Buckston Browne Farm Research Station. He was elected FRS in 1913, and from 1930 to 1933 was Rector of Aberdeen U. In 1919 he published a book of lectures on principles of orthopaedic management: *Menders of the Maimed*.

KELLER, Colonel William Lordan (1874–1959)
Keller's Procedure: Proximal hemiphalangectomy for hallux rigidus, or hallux valgus with bunions. D. 1904. (The same operation had been performed in 1885 by N. Davies–Colley of Guy's Hospital, London.)

Born in Connecticut, he studied in Virginia, gained his MD in 1899, and devised this operation while working in Manila during the Philippine War. A pioneer chest surgeon, he was Director of Professional Services of the American Expeditionary Forces in the First World War. In 1919 he succeeded Freiberg★ as Director of Surgery at Walter Reed Military Hospital, retiring in 1935. He never slept more than 4 hours a night.

KELLY, Adam Brown (1865–1941)
Paterson–Brown Kelly–Plummer–Vinson Syndrome: See *Paterson*. D. 1919. (D. 1912 by Plummer; 1919 by Paterson and Vinson.)

ENT Surgeon to the Victoria Infirmary, Glasgow.

KENT, Albert Frank Stanley (1863–1958)
Bundle of Kent: Cardiac atrioventicular conducting tissue, also known as Bundle of His★. D. 1893 (same year as His).

Born in Wiltshire, he became Demonstrator in Physiology at the U. of Manchester in 1887, in 1889 P. of Physiology, U. of Manchester, and in 1909 P. of Physiology, Bristol U. He was subsequently Director of Industrial Administration, Manchester College of Technology, and was also a pioneer radiologist, setting up the X-ray Department at St Thomas's Hospital, London. He died at Bath.

KERNIG, Vladimir Mikhailovich (1840–1917)
Kernig's Sign: In meningitis, pain on extension of the knee with the hip flexed. D. 1882.

Neurologist, and Director of the Obuchovsky Hospital, St Petersburg from 1865 to 1911.

KIENBÖCK, Robert (1871–1953)
Kienböck's Disease: Avascular necrosis of the lunate. D. 1910.

P. of Radiology, Vienna. He described a method of hair removal by low-dose radiation.

KILLIAN, Gustav (1860–1921)
Dehiscence of Killian: Lowermost fibres of the inferior
constrictor of the pharynx. D. 1908.

Born in Mainz, he became successively Director of
the ENT Clinic at Freiburg; P. of
Otorhinolaryngology at Freiburg (1900); and at
Berlin (1911), where he died.

KIMMELSTIEL, Paul (1900–1970)
Kimmelstiel–Wilson disease of kidneys: Diabetic
glomerulosclerosis with hypertension, proteinuria,
oedema and renal failure. D. 1936.

German-born pathologist who emigrated to the USA
and worked in Boston.

KING, Earl Judson (1901–1962)
King–Armstrong Unit: Measure of phosphatase level.
D. 1934.

Toronto biochemist who became P. of Chemical
Pathology at the Royal Postgraduate Medical School,
Hammersmith, London.

KIRSCHNER, Martin (1879–1942)
Kirschner Wire: Thin rigid stainless steel wire used for
skeletal traction and for fixation of bone fragments.
D. 1909.

Born in Greifswald and a pupil of Trendelenburg★,
he became P. of Surgery at Heidelberg, and
performed one of the first successful Trendelenburg
operations (pulmonary embolectomy). He
demonstrated such a case to his old teacher in 1924,
when the latter was 80, just before he died.

KJELLAND, Christian (1871–1941)
Kjelland's Forceps: Obstetric forceps for rotation in
deep transverse arrest. D. 1915.

Norwegian obstetrician and gynaecologist.

KLEBS, Theodor Albrecht Edwin (1834–1913)
Klebsiella: A genus of Gram★-negative bacteria.
Klebsiella pneumoniae is also known as Friedländer's★
bacillus. D. 1883.

This peripatetic bacteriologist was born in
Königsberg, studied there under Rathke★ and von
Helmholtz★ and in Würzburg under Virchow★. He
later worked with Virchow in Berlin, then became P.
of Pathological Anatomy in Bern and took up Swiss

citizenship. He then held Chairs in Würzburg (1872) and Prague (1873) and was P. in Zürich from 1882 to 1893. He then lived in Karlsruhe and Strasbourg, before emigrating to America, settling initially in Asheville, North Carolina. He was then P. of Pathological Anatomy at Rush Medical College, Chicago, but from 1900 to 1905 was back in Europe working in a private laboratory in Hanover, then at 71 went to Orth's Institute in Berlin. He next lived in Lausanne, and finally Bern again, where he died. He was 'one of the first in every advance in bacteriology, but had the misfortune to miss almost every discovery that has turned out to be correct' (Bulloch, 1938), though he did discover the diphtheria bacillus with Loeffler★ in 1883.

KLINEFELTER, Harry Fitch, Jr (b. 1912)
Klinefelter's Syndrome: Male hypogonadism with XXY chromosome complement. D. 1942.

Born in Baltimore, he studied at the U. of Virginia and Johns Hopkins, and is now Associate P. of Medicine, Johns Hopkins Medical School, Baltimore, Maryland.

KLIPPEL, Maurice (1858–1942)
1. *Klippel–Feil Syndrome*: Congenital fusion of cervical vertebrae. D. 1912.
2. *Klippel–Trénaunay Syndrome*: Unilateral hypertrophy of skeleton and soft tissues with angiomatosis. D. 1900. (Also called Klippel–Trénaunay–Weber★ Syndrome.)

Neurologist at the Salpêtrière, Paris.

KLUMPKE, Augusta (Madame Dejerine-Klumpke) 1859–1927)
Klumpke's Paralysis: Due to birth injury to lower roots of brachial plexus. D. 1885.

Born in San Francisco, she was educated in Lausanne and Paris, where she qualified as one of the first women doctors, in 1888. While still a student, she described this paralysis, and in 1890 married Jules Dejerine★, then Clinical Chief of the Salpêtrière.
She became President of the Société de Neurologie, an officer of the Légion d'Honneur, and founded a laboratory to commemorate her husband and continue his work on the nervous system.

KNOWLES, Frederick (1888–1973)
Knowles Pins: Implants for fixation of femoral neck fractures.

Orthopaedic Surgeon, Fort Dodge, Iowa. He studied at Oberlin and Iowa City College of Medicine, worked with Steindler★ at the Children's Hospital, and then in Chicago. (He had spent 1 year at the Chicago Art Institute before changing to medicine.) He was a noted painter and orchid-grower, and designed his own house with special tennis courts and bowling greens.

KOCH, Robert (1843–1910)
1. *Koch's Bacillus*: *Mycobacterium tuberculosis*. D. 1882.
2. *Koch-Weeks Bacillus*: *Haemophilus aegyptius*, causing acute conjunctival catarrh, or 'pinkeye'.

Born in Clausthal, Hanover, the son of a mining engineer, he qualified at Göttingen in 1866, Henle★ and Meissner★ having been among his teachers. He was initially in general practice in Niemegk and Rakwitz, becoming an army surgeon in the Franco-Prussian War (1870), and later a Medical Officer of Health. In 1876 he proved for the first time that a specific disease – anthrax – was caused by a specific micro-organism. By 1881 he had solved the problem of pure bacterial cultures, though Lister★ had been the first to obtain a pure culture of a bacterium three years earlier. In 1885 he became P. of Hygiene in Berlin, then from 1891 to 1904 Director of the Institute for Infectious Diseases, receiving the Nobel★ Prize in 1905. He discovered the tubercle bacillus in 1882, the cholera vibrio in 1883, and tuberculin in 1890, and travelled the world investigating the causes of epidemics of cholera, plague, malaria and sleeping sickness. He was ennobled by the State with the title of Excellenz, became a foreign FRS in 1897, and died of cardiac failure in Berlin. His ashes are in his Institute.

KOCHER, Emil Theodor (1841–1917)
1. *Kocher's Fracture*: Osteochondral fracture of the capitellum.
2. *Kocher's Manoeuvre*: Combination of adduction and rotation to reduce a shoulder dislocation, a method first used by him in public when Billroth★ was failing to reduce a shoulder in a lecture-demonstration. D. 1870.
3. *Kocher's Incision*: Right subcostal incision for exposure of the gall-bladder.

4. *Kocherisation*: Mobilisation of the second part of the duodenum. D. 1893.
5. *Kocher's Forceps*: Self-retaining tissue-holding forceps.

Born in Berne, he studied there (MD 1865), and in Berlin, London, Paris and Vienna and was P. of Clinical Surgery at Berne University for almost 50 years, succeeding de Quervain★ at the age of 31. A brilliant operator, and one of the founders of modern scientific surgery, he was the first to perform thyroidectomy for thyrotoxicosis, and won the 1909 Nobel★ Prize for his work on the physiology, pathology and surgery of the thyroid gland (the first award of the Prize to a surgeon).

KÖHLER, Alban (1874–1947)
1. *Köhler's First Disease*: Osteochondritis of the tarsal navicular. D. 1908.
2. *Köhler's Second Disease*: Oesteochondritis of the head of the 2nd metatarsal. D. 1920. Also called Freiberg's★ Disease (D. 1926).

Radiologist, Wiesbaden, Germany. He never held a hospital appointment. He described Pellegrini★– Stieda★ disease in the same year as Pellegrini.

KOPLIK, Henry (1858–1927)
Koplik's Spots: Red spots on buccal mucosa in early measles. D. 1896. Many previous writers had recognised them, but Koplik was the first to point out their diagnostic significance.

Born in New York, he studied at City College and Columbia University (MD 1881), and did postgraduate work in Berlin, Vienna and Prague, before returning to become Attending Paediatrician to Mount Sinai Hospital, New York. He was also Consulting Physician to the Jewish Maternity Hospital and the Hebrew Orphan Asylum, pioneering the provision of free milk for babies. He was a founder of the American Paediatric Society, and was well-loved for the many anecdotes he told. He died of a coronary.

KOROTKOFF, Nicolai Sergeyevitch (b. 1874)
Korotkoff Sounds: Heard during auscultation of an artery when recording blood pressure. D. 1905.

Physician in St Petersburg, Russia.

KORSAKOV, Sergei Sergeivitch (1853–1900)
Korsakov's Psychosis: Syndrome of confabulation and peripheral neuritis in alcoholics. D. 1887.

This great humanitarian, who was the foremost
psychiatrist and neurologist during the Tsarist
regime, was born on the Gus Estate in Vladimir
Province, the son of a glass-factory manager. He
studied in Moscow, writing his MD thesis on
alcoholic paralysis. After study with Meynert★ in
Vienna, he became P. of Neurology and Psychiatry at
the Preobrazhensky Mental Hospital, and was one of
the first to urge the abandonment of restraints in
psychotic patients.

KRAUSE, Wilhelm Johann Friedrich (1833–1910)
End-bulbs of Krause: Sensory cutaneous end-organs.
D. 1860.

P. of Anatomy at Göttingen and then Berlin.

KREBS, Sir Hans Adolf (b. 1900)
Krebs Cycle: Citric acid (tricarboxylic acid) cycle.

Born in Hildesheim, Germany, he studied medicine
(MD Hamburg 1925) then chemistry, and worked in
Berlin as a chemist, then as lecturer in internal
medicine at Freiburg. He fled the Nazi regime to
England in 1933, working first at the Biochemical
Laboratory at Cambridge, then became P. of
Biochemistry, U. of Sheffield, and in 1954 became
Whitley P. of Biochemistry at Oxford. He was
elected FRS in 1947 and was knighted in 1958. He
shared the 1953 Nobel Prize with F. A. Lipmann for
the discovery of Coenzyme A and its place in
intermediary metabolism.

KRETSCHMER, Ernst (1888–1964)
Kretschmer Types: Variants of personality linked to
physical type. (Pyknic, leptosome and athletic.)

German psychiatrist.

KRUKENBERG, Friedrich Ernst (1871–1946)
Krukenberg Tumours: Intra-abdominal secondaries
from ovary. D. 1896.

P. of Ophthalmology, Halle, who wrote a classic
thesis on malignant tumours of the ovary at the age of
24.

KUNTSCHNER, Gerhard (1900–1972)
Kuntschner Nail: Intramedullary device for fracture
fixation. D. 1940.

Born in Saxony, the son of a factory director, he studied at Würzburg and Hamburg, and qualified summa cum laude at Jena in 1926. He worked briefly as a radiologist, then as a surgeon at Kiel, becoming Professor in 1942. He served on the Eastern Front in the Second World War, where the introduction of the nail greatly shortened the period spent away from active duty of a soldier with a fractured femur, but early unrestrained enthusiasm for its application led to many disastrous infections. In 1946 he became Surgeon-in-Charge of Kries Hospital, Schleswig-Hesterberg, and in 1956 Medical Director of Hafen Hospital in Hamburg. After retiring he set up a centre for intramedullary nailing in Spain in 1966 and was visiting physician to St Franziskus Hospital, Flensburg.

KUNTZ, Albert (1879–1957)
Nerve of Kuntz: Grey ramus communicans running from the second thoracic ganglion to the first thoracic nerve, which is divided in cervical sympathectomy. D. 1927.

P. of Histology, St Louis University, Kentucky, USA.

von KUPFFER, Karl Wilhelm (1829–1902)
Kupffer Cells: Cells lining the blood sinusoids in the liver. D. 1876.

Successively P. of Anatomy in Kiel (1867), Königsberg (1875) and Munich (1880), he made several contributions to embryology. He was born and died in Munich.

KUSSMAUL, Adolf (1822–1909)
Kussmaul Breathing: Hyperventilation ('air hunger') in diabetic ketoacidosis. D. 1874.

A pupil of Friedreich★ at Heidelberg, he became P. of Internal Medicine at Strasbourg. A superb diagnostician who wrote a classic book on aphasia, he was an influential teacher of Edinger★, and Sachs★. He coined the terms 'hemiballismus', and 'word-blindness', and was the first to diagnose mesenteric embolism ante-mortem.

KÜSTNER, Heinz (b. 1897)
Prausnitz–Küstner Reaction: See *Prausnitz*.

German Gynaecologist.

KVEIM, Morten Ansgar (b. 1892)
Kveim test: Intradermal test for sarcoidosis.

Norwegian-born pathologist in Copenhagen.

L

LABBÉ, Léon (1832–1916)
Vein of Labbé: Vena anastomotica superior in cerebral circulation.

French surgeon.

LADD, William Edwards (1880–1967)
Transduodenal Band of Ladd: Persistent peritoneal band due to arrested midgut rotation, causing neonatal intestinal obstruction. D. 1932.

P. of Child Surgery, Harvard U. Medical School, Boston, USA.

LAENNEC, René–Théophile–Hyacinthe (1781–1826)
Laennec's Cirrhosis: Fatty degeneration of the liver in malnutrition and alcoholism. D. 1819.

Born in Quimper, capital of Brittany, he studied with Dupuytren★ in Paris, becoming Physician at the Hôpital Necker, and P. of Medicine at the Collège de France. He invented the stethoscope in 1819, and died in Brittany of TB at the age of 45.

LAHEY, Frank Howard (1880–1953)
Lahey Forceps: Long self-retaining forceps with curved ends.

Head of Surgery, The Lahey Clinic, Boston, USA.

de LAMARCK, Jean Baptiste Pierre Antoine de Monette (1744–1829)
Doctrine of Lamarck; Lamarckism: Theory of the inheritance of acquired characteristics. D. 1801 in lectures.

P. of Natural History at the Jardin des Plantes, Paris. His ideas opposed those of Darwin★.

LAMBL, Vitem Dusan (1824–1895)
Giardia★ lamblia: Protozoan parasite of the small intestine. D. 1860.

Born in Kharkov, he became physician to the
Franz-Josef Children's Hospital in Prague.

LAMBRINUDI, Constantine (1890–1943)
Lambrinudi operation: Triple fusion with anterior
wedge tarsectomy, for drop-foot. D. 1927.

Orthopaedic Surgeon to Guy's, where he succeeded
Trethowan★. He is remembered for his mechanistic
view of orthopaedic complaints and their functional
analysis, and great enthusiasm despite a chronic
cardiac complaint from which he died.

LANCEFIELD, Rebecca Craighill (b. 1895)
Lancefield Groups: Serological classification of
haemolytic streptococci. D. 1933.

Born in Fort Wadsworth, New York, she was
educated at Wellesley and Columbia U., and is now
Emeritus P. of Microbiology, Rockefeller U., New
York.

LANDOUZY, Louis Théophile Joseph (1845–1917)
Landouzy–Dejerine Dystrophy: Facio-scapulo-humeral
progressive muscular dystrophy. D. 1884.

Physician and neurologist in Paris.

LANDSTEINER, Karl (1868–1943)
Donath–Landsteiner Syndrome: See *Donath*.

Austrian-born physician who settled in New York.
He also discovered the ABO blood groups in 1900,
for which he received the Nobel Prize in 1930. In
1940 he discovered the rhesus (Rh) factor, with A. S.
Wiener.

LANE, Sir William Arbuthnot (1856–1943)
Lane's Forceps, Retractors, and other instruments.

Born in Inverness, the son of an Army surgeon, he
studied at Guy's from the age of 16. He was
particularly interested in relating skeletal form to
occupation. He became a ship's surgeon, then
Surgeon to Guy's Hospital, and pioneered internal
fixation of fractures using wood screws (1894): he
introduced the meticulous 'no-touch technique', in
1892. Lane was the first to open the mastoid antrum
and to ligate the internal jugular vein for infection,
and to resect a rib for empyema, but he was above all
an enthusiastic abdominal surgeon, who, however,

unfortunately believed rheumatoid arthritis and many
other conditions were due to constipation, for which
he regularly performed colectomy. He gradually
became obsessed with softening the nation's faeces,
founded the New Health Society, and occupied the
first Chair of Dietetics.

LANGE, Karl Friedrich August (b. 1883)
Lange Reaction: Curve expressing the degree of
precipitation of colloidal gold on a scale of 0–5, in 10
tubes containing increasing dilutions of CSF; certain
patterns are characteristic in neurosyphilis. D. 1912.

German physician in Berlin who later emigrated to
the USA.

von LANGENBECK, Bernhard Rudolf Konrad
(1810–1887)
Langenbeck retractor.

Probably the greatest clinical teacher and surgeon in
Germany, he was P. of Surgery in Kiel, then from
1847 to 1882 in Berlin. Esmarch★ was his Assistant,
and he also trained many notable surgeons of the later
nineteenth century. He was possibly the first to
internally fix a femoral neck fracture (in 1850) but the
nail corroded.

von LANGER, Carl Ritter von Edenburg (1819–1887)
Langer's Lines: Tension lines in the skin, due to the
orientation of collagen bundles in the dermis.
Incisions are best made parallel to these lines. D.
1861. (Dupuytren★ had described them in 1832.)

Born in Vienna, he became P. of Zoology in
Budapest at the age of 32, and returned to Vienna in
1870 as P. of Anatomy, and died there.

LANGERHANS, Paul (1847–1888)
Islets of Langerhans: Groups of (mainly) pancreatic
β-cells, secreting insulin. D. 1869.

Born in Berlin, he became P. of Pathological
Anatomy at Freiburg, and retired early to Madeira
and died in Funchal.

LANGHANS, Theodor (1839–1915)
1. *Langhans Layer*: The cytotrophoblast in the
embryo.
2. *Langhans Cells*: Giant cells in tubercle. D. 1867.

German pathologist.

LANTERMANN, A. J.
Schmidt–Lantermann Clefts: See *Schmidt*. D. 1877. (D.
1874 by Schmidt.)

Born in Cleveland, Ohio, he became an anatomist,
and worked at the Strasbourg Anatomical Institute.

LANZ, Otto (1865–1935)
1. *Lanz Incision*: Low oblique incision in right iliac
fossa.
2. *Lanz's Point*: Junction of the right and middle
thirds of a line joining the two anterior superior iliac
spines. D. 1908.

Lecturer in Surgery at Berne, then P. of Surgery,
Amsterdam (1902).

LARSEN, Christian Magnus Falsen Sinding (b. 1874)
Sinding Larsen Disease: Osteochondritis of lower pole
of patella. D. 1921. D. 1922 by Sven Johansson
(Swedish surgeon, b. 1880) thus sometimes called
Sinding Larsen–Johannson Disease.

Norwegian surgeon.

LASÈGUE, Charles Ernest (1816–1883)
Lasègue's Sign: Pain on dorsiflexion of foot with hip
flexed and knee extended, in sciatica.

Born in Paris, he shared rooms with Claude Bernard
as a student: they were always short of money for
their rent as they had spent it on rabbits and
guinea-pigs for experiments. He changed course
from philosophy to medicine on hearing Trousseau★
lecture, and became his favourite pupil, and from
1852 to 1854 his 'Chef de clinique'. In 1847 the French
government sent him to study a cholera epidemic in
Southern Russia, and he returned to become P. of
Medicine in Paris, and physician to the Salpêtrière,
Necker and Pitié Hospitals. He wrote widely on
hysteria, malingering, exhibitionism, and the
psychoses. He is said to have devised his sign on
seeing the taut strings of the violin his son-in-law was
tuning, resembling the sciatic nerve, but never wrote
of it himself; it was described by his pupil J. J. Forst in
his doctoral thesis in 1881. Remembered as a
'universal specialist' in clinical medicine, he died of
diabetes at 67.

LASSAR, Oskar (1849–1907)
Lassar's Paste: Preparation originally used for eczema,

consisting of a mixture of equal parts of Vaseline, zinc oxide and starch.

German dermatologist.

LATARGET, André (1876–1947)
Nerve of Latarget: Presacral sympathetic. D. 1913. He also described the anterior gastric nerves which are sectioned in the operation of highly selective vagotomy.

Born in Dijon, he was a pupil of the celebrated French anatomist and anthropologist Testut. In 1925 he became P. of Anatomy at Lyon: his investigations ranged widely, including angiography of the fetal gut, bone growth, and vascularisation of the thymus.

LAURENCE, John Zachariah (1830–1874)
Laurence–Mood–Biedl Syndrome: Autosomal recessive trait comprising obesity, retinitis pigmentosa, mental retardation, polydactyly and hypogonadism. D. 1886.

London Ophthalmologist.

Le FORT, René (1829–1893)
Le Fort Classification: of fractures of the middle third of the facial skeleton.

Born in Lille, he became P. of Surgery in Paris and Surgeon to the Hôtel–Dieu. He described the fractures after experiments in which he dropped rocks and other heavy objects onto the faces of cadavers.

LEGG, Arthur Thornton (1874–1939)
Calvé–Legg–Perthes–Waldenström Disease: See *Perthes*. D. 1910 (February), (D. 1910 (July) by Calvé; D. 1910 (October) by Perthes).

He graduated from Harvard Medical School in 1900 and was Goldthwait's★ Assistant in the early years of the Orthopaedic Department at Massachusetts General Hospital. He was Assistant P. of Orthopaedic Surgery at Harvard Medical School, and Surgeon to the Boston Children's Hospital for 39 years, and at 62 married the Sister of the Private Ward. He died suddenly at the Harvard Club.

LEISHMAN, General Sir William Boog (1865–1926)
1. *Leishmaniasis*: Tropical disease spread by sandflies

caused by the protozoon *Leishmania donovani*★. D. 1903.

2. *Leishman–Donovan Bodies*: Small round structures seen in the spleen and liver of patients with kala-azar (visceral leishmaniasis). D. 1903. (Possibly described previously (1884) by David Douglas Cunningham (1834–1914), a Calcutta physician.)

3. *Leishman's stain*: A type of Romanowsky★ dye containing eosin and methylene blue. D. 1901.

Born in Glasgow, where he studied medicine, he joined the Army in 1887 and was posted to India. On his return he became Assistant P. of Pathology at the Army Medical School at Netley, then P. of Pathology at the Royal Army Medical College, and finally Director-General of Army Medical Services. He was knighted in 1909 and elected FRS in 1910.

LEMBERT, Antoine (1802–1851)
Lembert Suture: Inverting suture for gut anastomoses. D. 1826.

Paris surgeon.

LERICHE, René (1879–1956)
Leriche's Syndrome: Intermittent claudication of the buttocks, pale cold legs, and impotence; due to atherosclerotic obstruction of the aortic bifurcation. D. 1940.

P. of Clinical Surgery, Strasbourg; a proponent of sympathectomy. He later became P. of Medicine at the Collège de France, Paris, the most prestigious medical post in France.

LESCH, Michael (b. 1939)
Lesch–Nyhan Syndrome: X-linked recessive disorder of cerebral palsy, mental retardation and hyperuricaemia, due to deficiency of hypoxanthine–guanine phosphoribosyl-transferase. D. 1964.

American Cardiologist. He described the syndrome while a medical student at Johns Hopkins, Baltimore.

LETTERER, Erich (b. 1895)
Letterer–Siwe Disease: Acute disseminated histiocytosis X. D. 1924. (D. 1933 by Siwe.)

Pathologist in Frankfurt, Germany.

LEVENTHAL, Michael Leo (1901–1971)
   Stein–Leventhal Syndrome: See *Stein*. D. 1935.

American Obstetrician and Gynaecologist.

von LEYDEN, Ernst Victor (1832–1910)
   Charcot–Leyden Crystals: See *Charcot*.

Neurologist at Heidelberg; he taught Edinger★, who
took his book on comparative histology for holiday
reading.

von LEYDIG, Franz (1821–1908)
   Leydig Cells: Interstitial cells of testis. D. 1850.

Born in Rothenburg, in 1855 he became P. of
Histology in Würzburg, and later held the same post
in Tübingen and Bonn. He was one of the first
comparative histologists.

LIBMAN, Emanuel (1872–1946)
   Libman–Sacks Disease: Verrucous endocarditis in
   systemic lupus erythematosus. D. 1924. A syndrome
   of anaemia, fever, and purpuric and erythematous
   rash also bears their names.

Physician, New York.

LIEBERKÜHN, Johann Nathaniel (1711–1756)
   Crypts of Lieberkühn: Glands in the wall of the small
   bowel. D. 1745. (They had previously been described
   by Malpighi★ in 1688, Brunner★ in 1715, and Galeati
   in 1731.)

Physician and anatomist who was born and worked
in Berlin. He developed a noted technique of injecting
anatomical preparations and was elected FRS for his
demonstrations of these in London.

LIGHTWOOD, Reginald (C)
   Lightwood's Disease: Hypercalciuria in infants with
   inability to acidify urine. D. 1935.

He studied at King's College Hospital, London (MB
1922), became P. of Paediatrics at the American U. of
Beirut, then P. of Paediatrics and Child Health at the
U. of Rhodesia; and is now Consulting Paediatrician
to St Mary's and Great Ormond Street Hospitals,
London.

LINDAU, Arvid (b. 1892)
   Von Hippel–Lindau Syndrome: See *von Hippel*. D.
   1926. (D. 1895 by von Hippel.)

Swedish pathologist.

von LINNÉ, Carolus (1707–1778)
Linnaean System: Binomial nomenclature in natural science (generic and specific names). D. 1735.

Swedish biologist and physician.

LISFRANC de ST MARTIN, Jacques (1790–1847)
1. *Lisfranc Amputation*: Through the tarso-metatarsal joint ('Lisfranc's Joint'). D. 1815. The fracture-dislocation occurring through this joint bears his name, though Lisfranc never described this injury. The amputation took him just 1 minute to perform. (A through-shoulder amputation also bears his name.)
2. *Lisfranc's Tubercle*: The scalene tubercle on the first rib.

Born in St Paul (Loire), he studied under Dupuytren★ in Paris, qualified in 1813, and was a military surgeon with Napoleon's armies before becoming P. of Surgery and Operative Medicine in Paris. He lectured in a booming voice, frequently attacking Dupuytren, his former teacher. In the pre-anaesthetic era, he resected nine rectal tumours perineally with only three deaths. He died in Paris, of 'angina and pernicious fever'.

LISSAUER, Heinrich (1861–1891)
Tract of Lissauer: Ascending dorso–lateral tract in spinal cord. D. 1885.

The son of Abraham Lissauer, a well-known anthropologist, he studied in Heidelberg, Berlin and Leipzig, and worked in Breslau as a neurologist.

LISTER, Lord Joseph (1827–1912)
1. *Lister's Tubercle*: Bony prominence on dorsum of distal radius.
2. *Listerian Method*: Antisepsis in surgery.
3. *Listeria monocytogenes*: Gram★-positive organism which may rarely cause respiratory infection or encephalitis.

'The apostle of antisepsis' was born in Stoke Newington, London, and studied Arts and Medicine at University College, London, gaining the BA in 1847, and MB and FRCS in 1852. In 1853 he worked with Syme★ in Edinburgh, married Syme's daughter, and succeeded him as P. of Surgery in 1869, coming from Glasgow, where he had become P. of Surgery

in 1860. In 1877 he returned to London as P. of
Clinical Surgery at King's College Hospital and the
following year was the first to obtain a pure culture
of a bacterium. In 1883 he was knighted and in 1897
was raised to the peerage. In 1895 he was awarded
the Albert Medal of the Royal Society of Arts for
the application of antisepsis to surgery, and in 1902
received the Order of Merit. He was President
of the Royal Society from 1895 to 1900. In
1902, with Treves★ assisting, he drained King
Edward VII's appendix abscess at Buckingham
Palace, 2 days before the Coronation had been
due to take place. Lister died of pneumonia in
Walmer, Kent, and is buried in Westminster
Abbey.

LITTLE, James Laurence (1836–1885)
Little's Area: Region of confluence of arteries on nasal
septum. D. 1876.

Born in Brooklyn, New York, he became lecturer in
operative surgery and P. of Surgery, U. of Vermont,
and then surgeon to St Luke's Hospital, New York.

LITTLE, William John (1810–1894)
Little's Disease: Cerebral palsy (specifically spastic
diplegia). D. 1843.

Little was educated in France, and first worked for an
apothecary; he was appointed Physician to the
London Hospital in 1845. He founded the Royal (later
Royal National) Orthopaedic Hospital, pioneered the
use of intravenous saline for dehydration, and had a
large private practice. Called 'the apostle of
tenotomy', he himself had had polio in childhood,
and had a club-foot: he was one of the first to undergo
subcutaneous Achilles tenotomy, performed by G. F.
L. Stromeyer (1804–1876) in Hanover.

LITTRÉ, Alexis (1658–1726)
1. *Glands of Littré*: Penile urethral glands. D. 1700.
2. *Littré's Hernia*: Hernia containing a Meckel's★
diverticulum, which Littré described in 1700 before
Meckel was born.

Born in Cordes, he practised as a surgeon and
Lecturer of Anatomy in Paris, where he died.

LOCKWOOD, Charles Barrett (1856–1914)
1. *Lockwood's Operation*: 'Low' operation for femoral
hernia, approached below the inguinal ligament. D.
1893.

2. *Ligament of Lockwood*: Suspensory ligament of the globe of the eye. D. 1886.

Surgeon to Barts.

LOEFFLER, Wilhelm (b. 1887)
Loeffler's Syndrome: Pulmonary eosinophilia, sometimes related to ascariasis. D. 1932. A form of fibroplastic myocardial disease is also associated with his name.

Swiss physician who worked in Basle and Zürich.

LÖFFLER, Friedrich August Johannes (1852–1915)
Löffler's Serum: Nutrient broth medium containing dextrose for diphtheria cultures. D. 1884.

Born in Frankfurt, the son of a military surgeon, he studied in Berlin, served in the Franco-Prussian War and was Koch's★ assistant in Berlin from 1879 to 1884. After a period as P. of Hygiene in Griefswald he became Director of the Institute for Infectious Disease in Berlin. He founded the Centralblatt für Bakteriologie, and with Klebs★ discovered the diphtheria bacillus (Klebs–Löffler bacillus). He discovered the virus of foot-and-mouth disease, and introduced methylene blue as a staining agent. A bacterial genus in the family Pseudomonadaceae is named *Lofflerella*. The name is sometimes spelled Loeffler. He won the Iron Cross in the First World War and died after an operation.

LOOSER, Emil (1877–1936)
Looser's Zones: Transverse lucent lines in long bones in osteomalacia due to local calcium loss. D. 1920.

Surgeon in Zürich.

LORAIN, Paul Joseph (1827–1875)
Lorain Types: Classification of dwarfism and sexual infantilism. D. 1871.

Paris physician, who gave the description in his thesis.

LOTHEISSEN, Georg (1868–1941)
Lotheissen Operation: Femoral herniorrhaphy by suturing conjoint tendon to ilio-pectineal line. D. 1898.

Surgeon to the Kaiser Franz Josef Hospital, Vienna. He also described an operation for Dupuytren's★ contracture (1900).

LOUIS, Pierre Charles Alexandre (1787–1872)
Angle of Louis: Junction of manubrium with body of sternum.

Born in Ai (Champagne), he became physician to the Hôpital de la Pitié, Paris, and was a leading authority on pulmonary tuberculosis. (The Angle is sometimes attributed to Antoine Louis (1723–1792), Surgeon to the Hôpital de la Charité, Paris, better remembered for perfecting the guillotine, which was first used in 1792 to execute a highwayman.)

LØVSET, Jørgen (20th. C.)
Løvset's Manoeuvre: Rotation of fetus and extraction of arms in breech delivery.

Obstetrician, Bergen, Norway.

LOWER, Richard (1631–1691)
Tubercle of Lower: Intervenous tubercle on posterior wall of atrium, above fossa ovalis. D. 1669.

Born in Cornwall, he studied at Westminster School, and Christ Church College, Oxford, where he studied medicine under Willis★, whom he followed to practise in London in 1666. In 1667 he was elected FRS, and in 1675 FRCP. Lower acquired much of Willis's practice on his death in 1675. He performed the first animal blood transfusion (on dogs) in 1666 at Oxford, following preliminary experiments by Sir Christopher Wren, and in 1667 from animal to man. He disproved Galen's★ theory that nasal secretions came from the pituitary (1672).

LOWMAN, Charles LeRoy (1879–1977)
Lowman's Clamp: Bone-holding instrument.

Born in Illinois, he worked his way through college in Los Angeles collecting ice-bills from saloons on a bicycle. He qualified from the U. of Southern California Medical School in 1907, studied orthopaedics at the Massachusetts General Hospital in Boston, and in 1922 he founded the Orthopaedic Hospital in Los Angeles. He received the Presidential Medal of Freedom, the highest US civilian honour, and died of a stroke at 97.

LUC, Henri (1855–1925)
Caldwell–Luc Operation: See *Caldwell*. D. 1889.

Internationally famous Paris ENT Surgeon.

von LUDWIG, Wilhelm Friedrich (1790–1865)
Ludwig's Angina: Submandibular cellulitis. D. 1836.

He studied at Tübingen, becoming an Army Surgeon during the Napoleonic Wars, and was a Russian prisoner-of-war for 2 years. He returned to be P. of Surgery and Midwifery at Tübingen, and Court Physician to King Frederick II. He first observed the inflammation which bears his name in Queen Catherine of Württemburg, and described it in his very first paper, which he published 20 years after becoming Professor, a great encouragement to us all.

LUER (d. 1883)
Luer Syringe: With locking device for needle.

German-born instrument-maker who worked in Paris.

LUGOL, Jean Guillaume Auguste (1786–1851)
Lugol's Iodine: 5% iodine in 10% potassium iodide. D. 1829.

Born in Montauban, he studied in Paris (MD 1812) and became Physician to the Hôpital St Louis. He made a special study of scrofula, for which he developed his iodine mixture; H. S. Plummer★ was the first to use it in the pre-operative treatment of thyrotoxicosis. Paul Broca★ married his daughter. Lugol died in Geneva.

von LUSCHKA, Hubert (1820–1875)
Foramen of Luschka: Opening in the lateral recess of the 4th ventricle. D. 1855.

Born in Constance, he was P. of Anatomy in Tübingen from 1849 until his death.

LYON, Mary Frances (b. 1925)
Lyon Hypothesis: All X-chromosomes in a cell except one are inactivated.

Mammalian geneticist who studied at Cambridge; she was appointed to the Scientific Staff of the Medical Research Council in 1950, and is now at the Radiobiological Research Unit, Harwell.

M

McBURNEY, Charles (1845–1913)
1. *McBurney's Point*: Site of maximum tenderness in the right iliac fossa in acute appendicitis. D. 1889.

2. *McBurney's Incision*: Oblique muscle-splitting incision for appendicectomy. D. 1894.

Born in Roxbury, Massachusetts, he obtained an arts degree at Harvard in 1866, then an MD at the New York College of Physicians and Surgeons, and followed this with 2 years' postgraduate study in Europe. In 1880 he became Assistant Surgeon to the Bellevue Hospital, New York, and in 1888 Surgeon-in-Chief to the Roosevelt Hospital. He was subsequently P. of Surgery at the College of Physicians and Surgeons of New York, and died of a heart attack while out hunting.

McCARTHY, Joseph Francis (1874–1965)
McCarthy Resectoscope: Endoscopic prostatic resector.

P. of Urology, New York Polyclinic Medical School.

MacCONKEY, Alfred Theodore (1861–1931)
MacConkey's Medium: Culture medium for coliform organisms, containing 0.5% sodium taurocholate, 1% lactose, and 0.07% neutral red as indicator. D. 1900.

Born in Liverpool, he studied at Cambridge and Guy's, and became Assistant Bacteriologist to the Royal Commission on Sewage Disposal, London. He later worked in Leeds, and in 1901 became a member of staff of the Lister★ Institute, and later Head of the antitoxin department there. He retired in 1926.

McEVEDY, Peter George (1890–1951)
McEvedy's Approach: 'High' operation for femoral herniorrhaphy, approached above the inguinal ligament.

Surgeon to Ancoats Hospital, Manchester.

MacEWEN, Sir William (1848–1924)
MacEwen's Triangle: Suprameatal triangle.

Born on the Isle of Bute, Scotland, the 12th child of a master mariner, he trained under Lister★ and Syme★ in Edinburgh. In his first post, as Medical Superintendent of the Glasgow Fever Hospital, he introduced laryngeal intubation for diphtheria, and went on to become, at 28, Surgeon to the Royal Infirmary, Glasgow, and then P. of Surgery in Glasgow and Honorary Surgeon to the King in

Scotland. A proud and intolerant surgeon, he cooperated poorly with colleagues, but was a pioneer of chest surgery and neurosurgery, introduced bone grafting and invented (and named) the osteotome. He made studies of bone growth and antler formation in deer, and died of pneumonia in Glasgow.

McINDOE, Sir Archibald Hector (1900–1960)
McIndoe Scissors: Long curved scissors.

Several plastic operations bear his name, including one for hypospadias, and a vaginoplasty. Born in New Zealand, he trained at the U. of Otago and did postgraduate work at the Mayo Clinic, before he came to work with his cousin Sir Harold Gillies★ in London as a plastic surgeon. He was on the staff of Barts and became the most successful specialist in London. He was Consultant Plastic Surgeon to the RAF during the Second World War, when he built up the internationally famous unit at Queen Victoria Hospital, East Grinstead, and supervised the total rehabilitation of badly disfigured airmen, who later formed the Guinea Pig Club, with McIndoe as their president. He was Senior Vice President of the Royal College of Surgeons when he died, of a heart attack in his sleep.

MACINTOSH, Charles (1766–1843)
Macintosh: Material waterproofed by treatment with india–rubber dissolved in naphtha. Formerly used for surgical dressings, the process had been originally discovered by James Syme★, though Macintosh patented it in 1823.

The son of a dyer, he was born in Glasgow and at 19 gave up working as a clerk, to manufacture sal ammoniac, and develop new processes in dyeing. He started the first Scottish alum works in 1796, and helped invent bleaching powder. By 1836 the waterproof coat had become generally known as a Mackintosh (*sic*).

McINTOSH, James
McIntosh–Fildes Jar: Receptacle for anaerobic bacterial culture. D. 1916.

London pathologist and bacteriologist.

McKEE, George Kenneth (C)
McKee Prosthesis: Metal-on-metal total hip replacement.

Orthopaedic Surgeon, Norfolk and Norwich Hospital.

MACKENRODT, Alwin Karl (1859–1925)
Mackenrodt's Ligaments: Transverse bands on either side of the uterine cervix. D. 1895.

P. of Gynaecology, Berlin; also a noted pathologist.

McMURRAY, Thomas Porter (1888–1949)
1. *McMurray Osteotomy*: Upper femoral displacement osteotomy for osteoarthrosis of the hip.
2. *McMurray's Test*: Clinical test for meniscal tears by rotation of the knee in varying degrees of flexion.

After studying medicine at Belfast, he became houseman to Robert Jones★ in Liverpool, and later shared with him the Consulting Rooms at 11, Nelson St, which had been built by Hugh Owen Thomas★. He was the first P. of Orthopaedic Surgery in England, at Liverpool.

M'NAUGHTEN, Daniel
M'Naughten Rule(s): Judgement given to the house of Lords, following the acquittal (the first in a British Court) on grounds of insanity, of Daniel M'Naughten, who shot dead Sir Robert Peel's private secretary in 1843.

MADELUNG, Otto Wilhelm (1846–1926)
Madelung's Deformity: Developmental abnormality of the wrist and carpus, with a short radius, dorsally and laterally bowed distally, and dorsal subluxation of the distal ulna. D. 1878. (Previously D. by Robert Smith★.)

In 1881 he became Assistant P. of Surgery in Bonn, then in Rostock, and in 1894 P. of Surgery, Strasbourg, at the time when von Recklinghausen★ was P. of Pathology there. A serious and strong-willed man, his main interest was abdominal surgery.

MAFFUCCI, Angelo (1847–1903)
Maffucci's Syndrome: Chondrodystrophy with vascular malformations. D. 1881.

Italian physician who used living organisms for prophylaxis against TB.

MAGENDIE, François (1783–1855)
1. *Foramen of Magendie*: Median opening in the 4th ventricle. D. 1828.
2. *Bell–Magendie Law*: See *Bell*. D. 1822. (The priority for this discovery was strongly disputed.)

Born in Bordeaux, the son of a surgeon, Magendie was the pioneer of experimental physiology in France. He studied in Paris, and worked at the Charité Hospital, and Hôtel-Dieu under Dupuytren*, later becoming Physician to the Hôtel-Dieu, and P. of Medicine, Pathology and Physiology at the Collège de France, where he was succeeded by Claude Bernard. He died in Paris of a coronary and is buried in Père Lachaise.

MAGILL, Sir Ivan Whiteside, KCVO (C)
Magill tube: Endotracheal tube.

He studied at Belfast (MB 1913) and became Senior Consultant Anaesthetist to the Westminster and Brompton Hospitals, London. He also described the 'Magill Circuit', part of a Boyle's* Apparatus on an anaesthetic machine.

MAISONNEUVE, Jules Germain François (1809–1897)
Maisonneuve Fracture: Fracture of proximal third of fibula with rupture of distal tibio–fibular syndesmosis. D. 1840.

Paris surgeon. His name is also given to a bandage, a urethrotome, and a method of amputation (breaking the bone before dividing the soft tissues); and he gave the first formal description of gas gangrene (1853), though it had previously been recorded by Fabricius Hildanus in 1607.

MALASSEZ, Louis Charles (1842–1909)
Rests of Malassez: Epithelial remnants in periodontal membrane from which dental cysts may develop.

Paris physiologist.

MALÉCOT, Achille-Étienne (b. 1852)
Malécot Catheter: Large-bore suprapubic urinary catheter.

Paris surgeon who invented the catheter while a houseman.

MALGAIGNE, Joseph François (1806–1865)
1. *Malgaigne Fracture*: Double fracture of the pelvic ring, in front of and behind the acetabulum. D. 1847, and differentiated from a femoral neck fracture.
2. *Malgaigne's Triangle*: Superior carotid triangle.
3. *Malgaigne's Bulgings*: Bilateral groin swellings in patients with weak abdominal wall musculature.

Anatomist and P. of Surgery, Paris.

MALLORY, Franklin Burr (1863–1941)
Mallory's Stain: Phosphotungstic acid haematoxylin after alcohol fixation, for elastic fibres. D. 1900.

Pathologist in Boston. A number of other staining methods bear his name.

MALLORY, G. Kenneth (b. 1900)
Mallory–Weiss Syndrome: Haematemesis due to a gastro–oesophageal mucosal tear after persistent vomiting. D. 1929.

P. of Pathology Boston U., USA. He made extensive investigations of streptococcal infections.

MALPIGHI, Marcello (1628–1694)
1. *Malpighian Body*: Glomerular apparatus in kidney. D. 1666.
2. *Malpighian Corpuscles*: Aggregates of lymphocytes in the spleen. D. 1669.
3. *Malpighi's Layer*: Germinal layer of epidermis.

'The Father of Histology' was born near Bologna, became P. of Physic there at the age of 25, subsequently holding the same post in Pisa (1656) and Messina (1662). In 1666 he returned to Bologna as P. of Anatomy, where he was succeeded by his pupil Valsalva★. He founded the science of microscopical anatomy, describing the capillaries in 1660 (thus completing the evidence for Harvey's★ exposition of the circulation of the blood) and the Crypts of Lieberkühn★ in 1688, 57 years before Lieberkühn. His writings were published in England in 1687 and he became FRS, but many of his original manuscripts were burned by a relative in a family quarrel. In 1691 he became Physician to Pope Innocent XII, and died in Rome three years later, but was buried, as he had requested, in Bologna. He was a close friend of Niels Stensen★.

MALTHUS, Rev. Thomas Robert (1766–1834)
Malthusian Law or Doctrine: Population size tends to exceed the means to supply it, implying the operation of a constant check.

Born near Guildford, the son of a dissenter and admirer of Rousseau, he studied mathematics at Cambridge and led a full social life despite a cleft palate and hare-lip. He was then ordained, becoming a curate in Surrey, then held a sinecure as rector of Walesbury, Lincolnshire. On travels through Europe he developed his theory of population growth, and became a Fellow of Jesus College Cambridge in 1793, but had to resign in 1804 when he married. (His wife was his cousin.) In 1805 he was appointed P. of History and Political Economy at Haileybury, and in 1819 was elected FRS. His *Essay on the Principle of Population* strongly influenced Darwin and Alfred Russell Wallace, and nineteenth-century social theory generally.

MANCHESTER
Manchester Repair: Operation for uterine prolapse.

Operation described in 1908 by Sir Archibald Donald, P. of Gynaecology, Manchester.

MANSON, Sir Patrick (1844–1922)
Schistosoma mansoni: Causative organism of intestinal schistosomiasis.

Born in Aberdeen, the son of a bank manager, his first jobs after qualifying were as medical officer to Durham Lunatic Asylum, then medical officer to the Chinese Imperial Maritime Customs in Formosa. Political unrest there drove him to Amoy on the Chinese mainland, then Hong Kong as lecturer and physician. On his return to England he became Physician to the Dreadnaught Hospital, Greenwich, founded the London School of Tropical Medicine, became medical adviser to the Colonial Office, and taught tropical medicine at St George's, Charing Cross, and the Royal Free Hospitals. He did his reading in the British Museum: across the table sat Karl Marx writing *Das Kapital*. Latterly, crippled by gout, he did his ward rounds in a wheelchair, and finally retired to Galway in Ireland, where he died.

MANTOUX, Charles (1877–1947)
Mantoux Test: Intradermal hypersensitivity test to old tuberculin. D. 1908.

Paris physician who retired to Le Cannet in the South of France.

MARCILLE, Maurice (1871–1941)
Triangle of Marcille: Bounded by psoas, the vertebral column and the ilio-lumbar ligament, and containing the obturator nerve.

The son of a doctor, he worked as a surgeon with Poirier and Faraboeuf. He designed an ambulance in the First World War and protective apparatus for gas warfare in the Second.

MARFAN, Bernard Jean Antonin (1858–1942)
Marfan's Syndrome: An autosomal dominant condition of variable penetrance comprising arachnodactyly, ectopia lentis, high-arched palate, cardiovascular defects, and joint hypermobility. Abraham Lincoln was probably affected. D. 1896.

He qualified in Paris in 1887, became Assistant P. of Paediatrics to the Paris Faculty in 1892, P. of Therapeutics in 1910, and in 1914 was the first P. of Hygiene. He made numerous contributions to infant feeding, and pointed out that rickets in rural France was sometimes due to direct suckling of infants by goats.

MARIE, Pierre (1853–1940)
1. *Marie–Strümpell Arthritis*: Ankylosing spondylitis. D. 1898. (D. 1884 by Strümpell.)
2. *Charcot–Marie–Tooth Disease*: See *Charcot*. D. 1886.

'Charcot's★ greatest pupil' first became a lawyer, to please his father, before studying medicine. He was Charcot's houseman (and eventually his Chef de Clinique), and described peroneal muscular atrophy three years after qualifying. He became P. of Pathological Anatomy and P. of Clinical Neurology at the Salpêtrière following Charcot and Dejerine★, and gave the first descriptions of acromegaly (1886), hypertrophic pulmonary osteoarthropathy (1890), congenital cerebellar ataxia (1893) and cranio-cleidal dysostosis (1898), yet still had time to make an important collection of painting and sculpture. From 1897 to 1907 he was P. of Neurology at the Hospice de Bicêtre, then P. of Pathological Anatomy, and finally in 1918, P. of Neurology (the Chair founded for Charcot). In 1925, at 72, he retired to the Côte d'Azur, dying at 87 having outlived all his immediate family.

MARION, Jean Baptiste Camille Georges (1869–1960)
Marion's Disease: 'Prostatisme sans prostate'; muscular hypertrophy of internal sphincter at bladder neck in young men, producing bladder diverticulum or hydronephrosis.

P. of Urology, Faculty of Medicine, Paris.

MARJOLIN, René (1812–1895)
Marjolin's Ulcer: Development of carcinoma in chronic ulcer.

Surgeon to Hôpital Sainte-Eugénie, Paris. The ulcer is sometimes ascribed to Jean Nicholas Marjolin (1780–1850), another Paris surgeon.

MARSHALL, John (1818–1891)
Oblique Vein of Marshall: Vein on the posterior wall of the left atrium.

Born in Ely, the son of a solicitor, he became Fullerian P. of Physiology at the Royal Institution, P. of Anatomy at the Royal Academy (he published a large *Anatomy for Artists*), and P. of Surgery at University College London, where he had been a student. He was elected President of the Royal College of Surgeons in 1883, and of the GMC in 1887.

MARTIN, Peter Guy Cutlack (C)
Martin's Pump: Rotary pump for accelerated blood transfusion.

He studied at Cambridge and Manchester, becoming Surgeon to the Hammersmith and Chelmsford Hospitals, and Vice-President of the International College of Angiology.

MASTER, Arthur Morris (b. 1895)
Master Step Test; Standardised exercise tolerance test for assessment of cardiorespiratory function. D. 1929.

New York physician.

MAYDL, Carl (1853–1903)
Maydl's Hernia: Rare form of groin hernia-in-W with

the strangulated loop of bowel within the abdomen.
D. 1898.

P. of Surgery, Prague, and later Vienna.

MAYO, Charles Horace (1865–1939) and William
James (1861–1939)
1. *Mayo's Vein*: The pre-pyloric vein. D. 1900
(Previously D. by Latarget*.)
2. *Mayo Operation*: Repair of umbilical hernia by
double-breasting layers of rectus sheath. D. 1901. A
number of other operations (for bunions, varicose
veins, and abdominal cancer) also bear their name.
3. *Mayo Table, Mayo Scissors, etc.*: Numerous
instruments and items of operating-theatre
equipment.

The Mayo Brothers' father, William Worrall Mayo,
emigrated from England to America in 1845, settled
in Rochester, Minnesota, as a pharmaceutical
chemist, and qualified MD in 1854. He captured a
Sioux chief and taught his sons anatomy from his
bones – the skeleton is in the Mayo Clinic today. As
children, they assisted their father at operations:
Charles had to stand on a biscuit-tin to reach the
table. In 1883 the father (then 70) and his two sons
opened the 13-bed St Mary's Hospital in Rochester,
to deal with victims of a cyclone: this developed into
the Mayo Clinic, the largest private hospital in the
world. The two brothers were Chief Surgical
Consultants for all services in the US Army in
the First World War. Between them they published
over 1000 papers, and died within 2 months of each
other.

MECKEL, Johann Friedrich I (The Elder) (1714–1774)
1. *Meckel's Ganglion*: Sphenopalatine ganglion. D.
1748.
2. *Meckel's Cave*: Dural space containing the
Gasserian* ganglion. D. 1748.

Born in Wetzlar, he became P. of Anatomy, Botany
and Gynaecology in Berlin, where he died, 7 years
before the birth of his grandson, Johann Friedrich
Meckel II (The Younger)*. His own son also became
a P. of Anatomy.

MECKEL, Johann Friedrich II (The Younger)
(1781–1833)
1. *Meckel's Diverticulum*: Persistent remnant of the

vitello-intestinal duct arising from the terminal ileum, typically 2 ft (60 cm) from the ileo-caecal valve. D. 1809.

2. *Meckel's Cartilage*: Cartilage of the 1st branchial arch. D. 1805.

Born in Halle, he studied there, and in Göttingen, Würzburg, and Vienna, succeeding his father as P. of Anatomy and Surgery at Halle in 1808. As well as his father, his grandfather (Johann Friedrich Meckel I★) and several younger brothers were all Professors of Anatomy. He was one of the greatest comparative anatomists in Germany and developed (with his father and grandfather) a famous pathology and anatomy museum at Halle. This lively and witty man became paranoid in early middle age; he retired at 50, became a recluse, and died 2 years later.

MEDUSA
Caput Medusae: Enlarged superficial veins radiating from the umbilicus in cirrhosis.

One of the three Gorgons in Greek mythology whose hair turned into snakes.

MEIBOM (MEIBOMIUS) Heinrich (1638–1700)
Meibomian Glands: Sebaceous follicles in the eyelids. D. 1666. (Previously D. by Casserio in 1609.) A chronic granuloma of these glands is called a chalazion (= hailstone, in Greek).

Born in Lubeck, he became P. of Medicine, then of History and Poetry, at Helmstadt, where he died. His father, J. Henricus Meibom (1590–1655) wrote extensively on the anatomy of veins.

MEIGS, Joseph Vincent (1892–1963)
Meig's Syndrome: Ovarian fibroma with pleural effusions. D. 1937.

P. of Gynaecology at Harvard, and Director of the Gynaecology Department at the Massachusetts General Hospital, he was a much-loved man who died of a coronary during an airline flight on his 71st birthday.

MEISSNER, Georg (1829–1905)
1. *Meissner's Corpuscles*: Touch nerve endings in skin. D. 1852.
2. *Meissner's Plexus*: Submucous nerve plexus in gut wall. D. 1853.

Born in Hanover, he studied in Göttingen, Trieste and Berlin (under Müller★) and was successively P. of Anatomy and Physiology at Basle, of Zoology and Physiology at Freiburg, and of Physiology at Göttingen. He developed techniques for preservation of organs without disinfectants.

MENDEL, Gregor Johann (1822–1884)
Mendel's Law: Independent assortment and segregation of inherited factors. D. 1865.

Austrian Augustinian monk and naturalist of Brno, whose experiments on breeding sweet peas and other plants laid the foundations of modern genetics. In 1868 he was appointed Abbot of the monastery and abandoned his studies which were 're-discovered' by de Vries in 1900, 16 years after Mendel's death.

MENDELSON, Curtis L. (C)
Mendelson's Syndrome: Pneumonitis due to aspiration of acid gastric contents during obstetric anaesthesia. D. 1945.

Obstetrician and Gynaecologist, Cornell U. Medical College and New York Hospital.

MÉNIÈRE, Prosper (1799–1862)
Ménière's Disease: Progressive deafness with episodic vertigo, tinnitus and vomiting. D. 1861.

The son of a wealthy tradesman, he studied medicine in Paris, winning the Gold Medal in 1826, and qualifying MD in 1828. He was clinical assistant to Dupuytren★ at the Hôtel-Dieu, and was the Casualty Officer on duty on the day in 1830 when 2000 injured rioters were admitted to the Paris hospitals: an experience about which he wrote a book. In 1832 he became Assistant P. of Medicine, but his thesis on the subject of clothes and cosmetics did not gain him the post he sought, of P. of Medicine and Hygiene, and in 1838 he became Physician-in-Chief to the Imperial Institute for Deaf-Mutes. He was an expert on orchids, a close friend of Victor Hugo and Honoré de Balzac, and was made Chevalier de la Lègion d'Honneur for dealing with a cholera outbreak. He died of influenzal pneumonia. (He added an accent to the second 'E' in his name: that on the first 'E' was added by his son: the name had no accents when he was born.)

MESMER, Friedrich Anton (1734–1815)
Mesmerism: Hypnosis induced by the will-power of another person.

Swiss physician born in Geneva who in 1776 described a theory of 'animal magnetism' (a term used 100 years before by Valentine Greatarick): that the heavenly bodies diffused a fluid through the universe, which acted on the nervous system. He demonstrated a form of hypnotism in Vienna, stroking patients with magnets, or with his own hands, and then continued his work in Paris, founding a 'Magnetic Institute' supported by Louis XVI and Marie Antoinette.

METCHNIKOFF, Ilia Illyich (Elie) (1845–1916)
Metchnikoff's Theory: Phagocytosis. D. 1884.

Born in Kharkov, Russia, he studied there, and at Giessen and Naples. He worked in Messina, then became P. of Zoology in Odessa from 1886 to 1887. He went to work with Pasteur★ in Paris in 1888, and on Pasteur's death in 1895 succeeded him as Director of the Pasteur Institute. He shared the 1908 Nobel Prize for Medicine with Paul Ehrlich★, for work on immunity, and was awarded the Copley Medal of the Royal Society in 1906.

MEYNERT, Theodor Herman (1833–1892)
Meynert Cells: Pyramidal cells in cerebral cortex. D. 1867.

Born in Dresden, the son of an opera-singer and a writer, his student days in Vienna were Bohemian and he only qualified at 28. In 1865 he became Dozent, in 1870 Director of the Psychiatric Clinic, and in 1873 P. of Nervous Diseases in Vienna, founding a School which rivalled the Salpêtrière in Paris and Queen Square in London, and influenced Forel★, Sachs★, Wernicke★ and Freud★. Sachs translated his classic book on psychiatry into English; Edinger★ said to him: 'You have translated Meynert into English; we can hardly understand him in German'. His Department in Vienna was dirty and untidy: his wife had died young and his two children wandered amongst the brain sections in the histology laboratory. A poor teacher and difficult to work with, he was brilliant in his writings and an accomplished poet and draughtsman.

MICHEL, Gaston (1874–1937)
Michel Clips: Skin closure clips.

P. of Clinical Surgery, Nancy, France.

von MIKULICZ-RADECKI, Johann (1850–1905)
1. *Paul–Mikulicz Operation*: See *Paul*. D. 1902. (D. 1903 by Paul.)
2. *Mikulicz Disease*: Enlargement of salivary and lachrymal glands with dryness of the mouth. D. 1892.
3. *Heineke–Mikulicz Pyloroplasty*: See *Heineke*.

Polish-born surgeon who was for several years Billroth's★ Assistant in Vienna, then P. of Surgery in Königsberg and Breslau. A number of abdominal operations bear his name.

MILKMAN, Louis Arthur (1895–1951)
Milkman Fractures: Multiple spontaneous stress fractures in osteomalacia. D. 1930.

Radiologist in Scranton, New Jersey, USA.

MILLER, Thomas Grier (b. 1886)
Miller–Abbott Tube: Double-lumen tube with balloon-end propelled by peristalsis, for suction drainage of the small bowel. D. 1934.

Emeritus P. of Medicine, U. of Pennsylvannia, Philadelphia.

MILLIN, Terence John (d. 1980)
Millin's Prostatectomy: Retropubic ('open') prostatectomy.

He studied at Dublin, The Middlesex and Guy's (MB 1927), became Honorary Consultant Surgeon to the Westminster Hospital, London (All Saints' Hospital Urological Centre), and was Ex-President of the British Association of Urological Surgeons, and the Royal College of Surgeons of Ireland. He retired to Ireland.

MILROY, William Forsyth (1855–1942)
Milroy's Disease: Familial lymphoedema of the leg. D. 1892. (Nonne in Berlin had described the condition in 1891.) It was named for Milroy by Sir William Osler★.

P. of Clinical Medicine, U. of Nebraska, Omaha.

MINERVA
Minerva Jacket: Plaster cast for vertebral stabilisation.

Roman goddess of memory and warfare, and patroness of arts and trades, identified with the Greek Athena.

MONCKEBERG, Johann George (1877–1925)
Monckeberg's Sclerosis: Calcification of the media of
arterial walls. D. 1903.

Physician and pathologist in Bonn.

MONDOR, Henri (1885–1962)
Mondor's Disease: Superficial thrombo-phlebitis of
breast and chest wall. D. 1951.

P. of Clinical Surgery and Chief Surgeon to the
Hôpital Salpêtrière, Paris.

MONRO, Alexander (Secundus) (1733–1817)
Foramen of Monro: Interventricular foramen in
forebrain. D. 1783.

At the age of 25 he succeeded his father, Monro
Primus (1697–1767) as P. of Anatomy in Edinburgh.
In 1774 he was the first to pass an endotracheal tube to
ventilate the lungs, using a bellows. His son, Monro
Tertius (1773–1859) was a neuroanatomist.

MONTEGGIA, Giovanni Battista (1762–1815)
Monteggia Fracture–Dislocation: Fracture of proximal
third of the ulna with anterior dislocation of the radial
head. D. 1814 (the same year Colles★ described his
fracture).

Born on Lake Maggiore, he studied in Milan, and in
his first job as a pathologist, contracted syphilis from
a cut sustained while performing a post-mortem on a
patient who had died of the disease. He later became
P. of Anatomy and Surgery at the Ospedale
Maggiore, Milan.

MONTGOMERY, William Fetherstone (1797–1859)
Glands (or Tubercles) of Montgomery: Sebaceous glands
in the areola of the breast.

P. of Midwifery, Dublin.

MOON, Richard C. (b. 1926)
Laurence–Moon–Biedl Syndrome: See *Laurence*.

Born in Beech Grove, Indiana, he studied at Butler
U. and the U. of Cincinatti, and is now Head of
Pathophysiology at the Research Institute of the
Illinois Institute of Technology, Chicago.

MOORE, Austin Talley (1899–1963)
Austin–Moore Prosthesis: Femoral head replacement
arthroplasty.

Surgeon and Director, Moore Clinic, Columbia,
South Carolina.

MORAX, Victor (1866–1935)
1. *Morax–Axenfeld bacillus*: *Haemophilus duplex* (the
causative agent of a type of conjunctivitis). D. 1896.
2. *Moraxella*: Genus of Gram*-negative rods.

Born in Switzerland, he studied in Freiburg and Paris,
and became Ophthalmic Surgeon to the Hôpital
Lariboisière. He also worked at the Pasteur*
Institute.

MORGAGNI, Giovanni Battista (1682–1771)
1. *Foramen of Morgagni*: Congenital anterior defect in
the diaphragm, between the sternal and costal
attachments, commoner on the right, through which
herniation may occur. D. 1761.
2. *Hydatids of Morgagni*: Sessile and pedunculated
appendages of the epididymis; the latter may undergo
torsion. D. 1761.

A pupil of Valsalva* in Bologna, he was P. of
Anatomy at Padua for 59 years, and is regarded as the
founder of morbid anatomy. He was the first to
describe the association of hydrocephalus and spina
bifida with lower limb deformities, in 1761. (Spina
bifida had first been described in 1652 by Nicolai
Tulp, the teacher in Rembrandt's 'The Anatomy
Lesson'.) He also gave the first description of heart
block (1761), and described Turner's* Syndrome in
1768, 170 years before Turner.

de MORGAN, Campbell (1811–1876)
Campbell de Morgan Spots: Small red cutaneous lesions
found in middle-aged and elderly persons. They are
of no nosological significance, but were believed by
de Morgan to be a sign of cancer. D. 1872.

Born in Clovelly, the son of an Indian Army Colonel,
he studied at University College, London, and the
Middlesex Hospital (MRCS 1835). In 1842 he became
Assistant Surgeon to the Middlesex, and in 1847 Full
Surgeon, having been made one of the 300 original
Fellows of the Royal College of Surgeons, in 1843.
An inflexibly religious man, he lectured on anatomy,
surgery, physiology and forensic medicine, and was
in charge of the ophthalmic department. He was
elected FRS in 1861.

MORGAN, Thomas Hunt (1866–1945)
Morgan: Unit of distance on chromosome map in which the mean number of recombinations is 1.

Born in Virginia, he studied biology at Kentucky and Johns Hopkins, becoming Associate P. of Zoology, Bryn Mawr (1891–1904); and P. of Biology, California Institute of Technology, Pasadena (1928–1945). A renowned geneticist and embryologist, he formulated the gene theory, and was awarded the 1933 Nobel Prize. He also won the Darwin★ and Copley Medals of the Royal Society and was elected FRS in 1919.

MORISON, James Rutherford (1853–1939)
1. *Pouch of Rutherford Morison*: Right subhepatic space. D. 1894.
2. *Rutherford Morison's Incision*: Oblique muscle-cutting incision for appendicectomy.

After studies in Birmingham, Edinburgh (where he was Lord Lister's★ dresser) and Vienna (under Billroth★), he went into practice in Hartlepool in 1879, where he became Medical Officer of Health and Physician to the local hospital. In 1888 he moved to Newcastle, becoming Surgeon to Newcastle Infirmary in 1897, and in 1910 Emeritus P. of Surgery at the U. of Durham. He popularised 'Bipp' for the treatment of infected war wounds (1918).

MORO, Ernst (1874–1951)
Moro Reflex: 'Startle' reflex of infants.

Paediatrician in Graz and Vienna.

MORQUIO, Luis (1867–1935)
Morquio–Brailsford Disease: Systemic mucopolysaccharidosis with chondro-osteodystrophy. D. 1929.

Paediatrician in Montevideo, Uruguay.

MORRIS, Sir Henry (1844–1926)
Morris Retractor: Broad curved abdominal retractor.

Surgeon to the Middlesex Hospital, London.

MORTON, Thomas George (1835–1903)
Morton's Neuroma: Neuroma of plantar digital nerve, causing Morton's metatarsalgia. D. 1876.

The son of a doctor, he graduated from the U. of Pennsylvania, writing his thesis on cataract. During

the Civil War he was a military surgeon, and returned
to found the Philadelphia Orthopaedic Hospital. He
was also a general and eye surgeon at the
Pennsylvania Hospital, and renowned as a teacher
and daring operator: he performed one of the first
appendicectomies in 1887, after seeing his son and
brother die of untreated appendicitis. He died of
cholera in Philadelphia.

MOYNIHAN, Lord Berkeley George Andrew
(1865–1936)
Moynihan's Gutter: Right paracolic gutter down
which gut contents may track after a perforation,
simulating acute appendicitis. Several surgical
instruments also bear his name.

Born in Malta, the son of an Army Captain who won
the VC in the Crimea, he was a pupil at Christ's
Hospital and studied medicine at Leeds (MB 1887).
He became FRCS in 1890, and won the Gold Medal
for his MS in London. In 1896 he became Surgeon to
Leeds General Infirmary, where he was famous for
his meticulous surgical technique and was also a
compelling speaker. He coined the term 'hunger pain'
(1910).

MÜLLER, Johannes Peter (1801–1858)
Müllerian Duct: The paramesonephric duct; the
primordial female genital duct. D. 1825.

'The founder of scientific medicine in Germany', was
born in Coblenz, the eldest son of a shoemaker. He
studied in Bonn (MD 1822) and then in Berlin (under
Rudolphi, Purinkje's★ father-in-law), returning to
practise in Bonn in 1824, and became P. of Anatomy
there in 1830. In 1833 he became P. of Anatomy and
Physiology in Berlin. His *Handbuch der Physiologie*
was the standard textbook of the mid-nineteenth
century; he also wrote a monumental work on
tumours (1838), and confirmed the Bell★–Magendie★
Law by experiments on frogs (1831). His pupils and
assistants included Schwann★, Henle★, Virchow★ and
von Helmholtz★. In middle age he became dependent
on opium, suffered from depression, and was found
dead in bed at the age of 57.

MURPHY, John Benjamin (1857–1916)
1. *Murphy's Sign*: Pain in the right upper quadrant on
inspiration in cholecystitis. D. 1912.
2. *Murphy's Drip*: Rectal fluid infusion (proctoclysis).
D. 1908.

The son of Irish immigrants to America, he qualified MD at Chicago in 1879, studied in Vienna under Billroth★ and returned to become a resident, and subsequently Attending Surgeon, at Cook County Hospital, Chicago, at that time the largest general hospital in the world. He was then P. of Surgery at Rush Medical College and Northwestern U. of Chicago, and Chief of Surgery at the Mercy Hospital. A pioneer thoracic surgeon, he also made great advances in vascular, abdominal and orthopaedic surgery, and described the classic symptom sequence of peri-umbilical pain–vomiting–right iliac fossa pain in acute appendicitis. He lived at enormous pressure and died of a coronary at 59.

N

NABOTH, Martin (1675–1721)
Nabothian Follicles: Retention cysts of the glands of the cervical mucous membrane.

Born in Kalau, he become an anatomist and P. of Medicine in Leipzig, where he died.

NAJJAR, Victor Assad (b. 1914)
Crigler–Najjar Syndrome: See *Crigler*.

Born in Lebanon, he studied at the American U. of Beirut, becoming Associate P. of Paediatrics, Johns Hopkins U.; P. of Microbiology, Vanderbilt U.; and is now American Cancer Society P. of Molecular Biology, P. of Paediatrics, and Chairman of the Division of Protein Chemistry, Tufts U. Medical School, Boston.

NASMYTH, Alexander (d. 1847)
Nasmyth's Membrane: Tissue covering the enamel of an unerupted tooth.

Scottish dental surgeon and anatomist who practised in London.

NEELSEN, Friedrich Karl Adolf (1854–1894)
Ziehl–Neelsen Stain: See *Ziehl*. D. 1892.

Born in Holstein, he studied in Leipzig, becoming Assistant in the Pathological Institute in 1876. From 1878 to 1885 he was P. of Pathology in Rostock and then Prosector in the State Hospital at Dresden, where he died.

NEGRI, Adelchi (1876–1912)
Negri Bodies: Intracellular bodies seen in rabies and in other viral infections. D. 1903.

Born in Perugia, he studied in Pavia and was Golgi's★ assistant. He became P. of Bacteriology in Pavia, and died at 36.

NEISSER, Albert Ludwig Siegmund (1855–1916)
Neisseria: Genus of Gram★-negative bacteria including gonococcus and meningococcus. D. 1879.

Born in Scheidnitz, he studied in Breslau, later becoming Director of the Dermatological Institute there. He studied leprosy in Norway and Spain, discovered the gonococcus and experimented on syphilis in monkeys in Java. He helped in the development of the 'Wassermann★ reaction'.

NELATON, Auguste (1807–1873)
Nelaton's Line: From the anterior superior iliac spine to the ischial tuberosity by the shortest path: to aid estimation of the position of the greater trochanter. D. 1847.

Born in Paris, he became Surgeon to the Hôpital St Louis and P. of Clinical Surgery, and in 1867 succeeded Jobert as Surgeon to Napoleon III. In 1862 he operated on Garibaldi for a bullet-wound; the porcelain-tipped probe he used became a standard instrument in military surgery. He also invented the rubber catheter. He died in Paris.

NERNST, Hermann Walther (1864–1941)
Nernst Equation: Governing the ionic equilibrium between two phases in a physical system separated by a semi-permeable membrane.

Born in Prussia, the son of a civil servant, he studied at Zürich, Würzburg and Graz, at 30 became the first P. of Physical Chemistry in Göttingen, and in 1904 held the same Chair in Berlin, where he was Rector of the U. in 1922. In 1924 he was made P. of Physics, but was expelled to the country by the Nazis in 1933. In 1905 he discovered the Third Law of Thermodynamics, won the Nobel Prize in 1920, and in 1932 was elected a foreign FRS.

NETTLESHIP, Edward (1845–1913)
Nettleship Syndrome: A chronic urticarial skin disease (urticaria pigmentosa). D. 1869.

London ophthalmologist and dermatologist.

NEUFELD, Ferdinand (1869–1945)
Neufeld Quellung Reaction: Agglutination and swelling occurring on mixing pneumococci and specific immune serum. D. 1902 (but probably D. previously by Roger in 1896.)

Born in Neuteich, he studied in Tübingen, Königsberg, Berlin and Heidelberg. He worked in Koch's★ Institute in Berlin and in 1917 was made Director of the Infectious Diseases Institute in Berlin, but was deprived of his post shortly after, though he continued to work there.

NEWTON, Sir Isaac (1643–1727)
Newton's Rings: Coloured rings on thin surfaces (e.g. soap bubbles) due to light wave interference. D. 1704.

English physicist, mathematician and astronomer, who discovered the Laws of Gravity.

NIEMANN, Albert (1880–1921)
Niemann–Pick Disease: Lipoid histiocytosis, an autosomal recessive lipid storage disease, commonest in Jewish children, with accumulation of sphingomyelin in reticulo–endothelial cells. D. 1914. (D. 1926 by Pick.)

German paediatrician and surgeon.

NISSL, Franz (1860–1919)
Nissl's Granules: Basophil granules in the cytoplasm of nerve cells. D. 1894.

Born in Frankenthal, Bavaria, he studied in Munich, where he developed important stains for neural tissue. In 1889 he became Assistant Physician in Frankfurt, where he worked with Alzheimer★, and in 1895 moved to Heidelberg, eventually becoming P. of Psychiatry there in 1904, after Kraepelin. In 1918 he again moved, to Munich, but died a year later of renal disease. He was known as an early great enthusiast for lumbar puncture. A small man with a large birthmark, he never married, but was kindly and modest, and a fine pianist, with a great sense of humour.

NOBEL, Alfred Bernard (1833–1896)
1. *Nobel Prizes*: Annual awards for endeavours in the fields of Chemistry, Physics, Medicine and

Physiology, Literature, Economics, and Peace. First awarded in 1901.
2. *Nobelium*: Element of atomic number 102.

Swedish chemist and engineer who invented dynamite and left a fortune.

NOCARD, Edmund Isidore-Étienne (1850–1903)
Nocardiasis: Bovine farcy (suppuration of lymph nodes) due to *Nocardia* organisms (a genus of actinomycetes). D. 1888.

Born at Provins, near Paris, he studied at the Veterinary School at Alfort, where he became P. of Pathology, and in 1887 Director. He also worked at the Pasteur★ Institute in Paris.

NUCK, Anton (1650–1692)
Canal of Nuck: Patent processus vaginalis in female (hydrocoele muliebris). D. 1691.

Born in Harderwyk, Holland, he became P. of Anatomy and Medicine in Leyden, where he died.

NUHN, Anton (1814–1889)
Glands of Blandin and Nuhn: See *Blandin*. D. 1845.

P. of Anatomy, Heidelberg.

NYHAN, William Leo (b. 1926)
Lesch–Nyhan Syndrome: See *Lesch*. D. 1964.

Born in Boston, he studied at Columbia and the U. of Illinois, and is now P. of Paediatrics, U. of California Medical School, San Diego.

O

OCHSNER, Albert John (1858–1925)
Ochsner–Sherren Regime: Non-operative treatment for appendix mass. D. 1901. (D. 1905 by Sherren.)

Of German origin, he also claimed descent from Vesalius★. He studied at Rush Medical College, Chicago (BSc 1884; MD 1886) and then in Berlin, Vienna and London. He became Chief Surgeon at St. Mary's and Augustana Hospitals in Chicago, and in 1900 P. of Clinical Surgery at the U. of Illinois. From 1923 to 1924 he was President of the American College of Surgeons.

ODDI, Ruggero (1845–1906)
Sphincter of Oddi: Muscular fibres at the orifice of the
common bile duct. D. 1887. (Previously D. by
Glisson★ in 1654.)

Physiologist at the U. of Perugia, who later worked
as a surgeon and anatomist in Rome.

OEDIPUS
Oedipus Complex: Sexual attraction to mother.

Character in Greek mythology raised by
foster-parents, who kills his real father, marries his
real mother, blinds himself when he discovers the
truth, and reads the riddle of the Sphinx.

OGILVIE, Sir William Heneage (b. 1887)
Ogilvie's Syndrome: Functional large bowel
obstruction in the elderly. D. 1948.

Surgeon to Guy's Hospital, London.

OLLIER, Louis Xavier Édouard Léopold. (1830–1901)
Ollier's Disease: Multiple enchondromas. D. 1889.

He studied in Lyon and Montpellier, becoming the
Senior Surgeon at Lyon at the age of 30, and then P.
of Surgery there. He also practised in Paris, and was a
well-recognised orthopaedic surgeon. In 1870 he was
military surgeon to both sides in the Franco-Prussian
War, and in 1894 was decorated with the Légion
d'Honneur by the French President – who was shot a
few hours later and died despite Ollier's attentions.

OMBRÉDANNE, Louis (1871–1956)
Ombrédanne Operation: (1) Trans-scrotal orchiopexy.
D. 1910. (2) Plastic repair for hypospadias. D. 1911.

Surgeon to the Hôpital des Enfants Malades, Paris,
and subsequently P. of Orthopaedics. He was well
known for plastic surgery and paediatric
orthopaedics, and described an operation for
pollicisation in 1920.

ORAM, Samuel (C)
Holt–Oram Syndrome: See *Holt*.

He studied at King's College Hospital, London (MB
1939), won the Gold Medal with his London MD
thesis in 1940, and became Senior Physician and
Director of the Cardiac Department, King's College
Hospital, and Censor of the Royal College of
Physicians.

ORTOLANI, Marino
Ortolani Test: Clinical test for congenital hip
dislocation. D. 1937.

Director of the Children's Hospital, Ferrara, Italy,
and P. of Paediatrics and Child Health.

OSGOOD, Robert Bayley (1873–1956)
Osgood–Schlatter's Disease: Osteochondritis of tibial
tubercle. D. 1903 (D. by Schlatter independently in
1903 also.)

Graduating from Harvard in 1899, he became
orthopaedic surgeon to the Massachusetts General
Hospital in Boston, and encouraged contact between
British and American orthopaedic surgeons. During
the First World War he worked with Harvey
Cushing★ in France, and with Robert Jones★ in
England (helping him to found the British
Orthopaedic Association). He ran the first X-Ray
Department at the Massachusetts General, with the
hospital pharmacist; the pharmacist died of
radiation-induced skin cancers, and Osgood
developed several which were removed surgically.

OSLER, Sir William (1849–1919)
1. *Osler's Nodes*: Cutaneous nodules in subacute
bacterial endocarditis. D. 1885.
2. *Osler–Rendu–Weber Syndrome*: Multiple hereditary
telangiectasia. D. 1901. (D. 1896 by Rendu and 1904
by Weber.)
3. *Osler–Vaquez Disease*: Polycythaemia vera. D.
1903.

Born in Canada, the son of an immigrant Cornish
Missionary, he studied at McGill U., Montreal, then
travelled in Europe with Harvey Cushing★, whom he
taught clinical neurology, and in London was the first
to see platelets. At 25 he became P. of Medicine at
McGill; in 1884 at the U. of Pennsylvania, in
Philadelphia; in 1889 at Johns Hopkins Hospital in
Baltimore; and in 1904 in Oxford. He had become
MRCP in 1878 and in 1892 published the first edition
of his famous *Principles and Practice of Medicine*. In
1898 he was elected FRS, and in 1911 made a baronet.
He attended medical meetings tirelessly, even on
honeymoon, and is remembered as a great clinician
and a charming, kindly man. His only son was killed
at Ypres; Osler never fully recovered from the
tragedy, and died in Oxford 2 years later.

OTTO, Adolph Wilhelm (1786–1845)
Otto Pelvis: Pelvis narrowed by bilateral protrusio acetabuli.

German surgeon.

P

PACINI, Filippo (1812–1883)
Pacinian Corpuscles: End-organs of sensory nerves. D. 1835. (Previously D. in 1717 by Vater★.)

Born in Pistoia, Emilia, Italy, he studied in Florence and became P. of Anatomy and Physiology in Pisa, and in 1849 P. of Histology in Florence, where he died.

PAGET, Sir James (1814–1899)
1. *Paget's Disease of Bone*: Osteitis deformans; a condition of rapid bone turnover. D. 1877.
2. *Paget's Disease of the Nipple*: Slowly growing duct carcinoma presenting as an eczematous lesion. D. 1874.
3. *Paget's Disease of the Penis*: Carcinoma developing after long-standing balanitis. D. 1853. Also known as Erythroplasia of Queyrat★.

One of 17 children of a brewer and ship-owner of Yarmouth, he wrote a book on the local natural history while a schoolboy, then went to London and studied medicine at Barts: one of his brothers paid the fees. He qualified MRCS in 1836, added to his salary by contributing to the *Penny Encyclopaedia*, and the following year became Curator of the Museum at Barts, then Anatomy Demonstrator, and in 1843 Lecturer in Anatomy and Physiology, and Sub-Editor of the *London Medical Gazette*. In 1847 he became Assistant Surgeon to Barts, in 1851 FRS, and in 1858 Surgeon Extraordinary to Queen Victoria. In 1871 he retired from Barts (having nearly died from an infected cut sustained at a post-mortem), and was made a baronet. In 1875 he became President of the Royal College of Surgeons (having been one of the 300 original Fellows in 1843), and in 1876 became Serjeant Surgeon to the Queen, and a Member of the GMC, then Vice-Chancellor of London U. By 1878 he had the largest private practice in London and was earning £10,000 a year, with William Morrant Baker★

as his private assistant. An untiring worker, who never took a holiday until he was 47, he was operating until the age of 64, and though not technically brilliant he was hugely influential, partly through his superb and popular lectures. His funeral was in Westminster Abbey: one son became a surgeon, the other, Bishop of Oxford. He is buried in Finchley, North London.

PANCOAST, Henry Khunrath (1875–1939)
Pancoast Tumour: Apical bronchial carcinoma associated with lesion of T1 sympathetic fibres. D. 1932.

P. of Roentgenology, U. of Pennsylvania, Philadelphia, USA.

PANETH, Joseph (1857–1890)
Paneth Cells: Secretory cells in the base of crypts of Lieberkühn★ in the small intestinal mucosa. D. 1888.

P. of Physiology, Vienna, and Breslau. Born and died in Vienna.

PAPANICOLAOU, George Nicolas (1884–1962)
Papanicolaou Smear (Stain): Exfoliative cytology test for uterine cervical disease. D. 1933.

New York physician, later P. of Anatomy, Cornell U.

PARDEE, Harold Ensign Bennett (b. 1886)
Pardee Sign: S–T segment elevation on ECG following acute myocardial infarction. D. 1920.

New York physician.

PARHAM, Frederick William (1856–1927)
Parham's Bands: Encircling wires formerly used in internal fixation of long bone fractures. D. 1913.

Surgeon in New Orleans, USA.

PARKINSON, James (1755–1824)
Parkinson's Disease: Paralysis agitans; an affection of the basal ganglia. D. 1817. (Charcot gave Parkinson's name to the disease 40 years later.)

Born at No. 1 Hoxton Square, in the East End of London, the son of a doctor, he inherited his father's practice in Shoreditch, after studying at the London Hospital. He attended John Hunter's★ lectures, and was also a noted palaeontologist – a number of fossils

are named after him – and founder member of the
Geological Society of London, and was involved in
politics as a pamphleteer under the pseudonym of
'Old Hubert'. With his son, he reported the first case
of appendicitis in English (1812), and also wrote
several studies on gout, from which he suffered
himself. He was the first recipient of the Honorary
Gold Medal of the Royal College of Surgeons. No
portrait of him has ever come to light.

PARKINSON, Sir John (b. 1885)
Wolff–Parkinson–White Syndrome: See *Wolff*.

London cardiologist.

PARONA, Francesco (1861–1910)
Space of Parona: Deep intermuscular space in forearm.
D. 1876.

Surgeon to the Ospedale Maggiore, Milan; then
Chief Surgeon to Novara Hospital; he was chiefly an
orthopaedic surgeon.

PASCAL, Blaise (1623–1662)
Pascal's Law: Pressure applied to a liquid is
transmitted equally in all directions. D. 1653.

This French physicist, born in Clermont-Ferrand,
where his father was President of the Court of Aids,
was educated by his sisters (his mother died when he
was 4), wrote a study on geometry at 12, and
invented an adding machine at 19. He was a fervent
Jansenist (a sect opposed to the Jesuits).

PASSAVANT, Philipp Gustav (1815–1893)
Passavant's Ridge: Elevation on posterior wall of
pharynx caused by contraction of the superior
constrictor on swallowing. D. 1869.

Surgeon in Frankfurt.

PASTEUR, Louis (1822–1895)
1. *Pasteurisation*: Process of bacterial destruction by
heating.
2. *Pasteurella*: Bacterial genus which includes the
causative organism of plague.

Born in Dôle in the Jura Mountains of France, the son
of a tanner, he trained as a chemist and bacteriologist
in Besançon and Paris, and though he never qualified
in medicine, was the founder of modern

microbiology. He was P. of Physics at the Lycée in Dijon in 1848, and P. of Chemistry in Strasbourg in 1852. He was Dean of the Faculty of Science in Lille in 1854, then Director of Studies at the École Normale in Paris, where he had been a student. His early work in Paris was on anthrax and rabies; he discovered tartaric and racemic acids in 1848, and the use of polarisation to detect laevo- and dextro-crystalline forms, for which he received the Rumford Medal of the Royal Society in the same year. His germ theory disproved spontaneous generation and the Pasteur Institute was founded in his honour in Paris in 1888. He was elected a foreign FRS in 1869 and received the Copley Medal in 1874. He died at Villeneuve L'Étang, near Garches and is buried in a crypt in the Institut Pasteur in Paris.

PATERSON, Donald Ross (1863–1939)
Paterson–Brown Kelly–Plummer–Vinson Syndrome: Achlorhydria, anaemia, koilonychia and oesophageal web formation with dysphagia. D. 1919. (D. 1919 by Brown Kelly in another paper in the same journal; D. 1919 by Vinson and 1912 by Plummer.)

ENT Surgeon to the Royal Infirmary, Cardiff.

PAUL, Frank Thomas (1851–1941)
1. *Paul's Tubing*: Penile tubing for incontinence.
2. *Paul's Tube*: Curved glass tube for draining colostomy. D. 1891.
3. *Paul–Mikulicz Operation*: Intestinal resection by two-stage exteriorisation with temporary double-barrelled colostomy. D. 1903. (D. 1902 by Mikulicz.)

Born in Norfolk, he qualified at Guy's in 1871, and at the age of 24 was the first Resident Medical Officer at the Liverpool Royal Infirmary, where he was subsequently on the surgical staff. He later became P. of Medical Jurisprudence at Liverpool, but continued operating until he was 80. A modest man and gentle operator, he was also an orchid expert, and a pioneer of colour photography.

PAUL, John Rodman (b. 1893)
Paul–Bunnell Test: Test for heterophile antibody against sheep red cells, positive in infectious mononucleosis (glandular fever). D. 1932.

Emeritus P. of Preventive Medicine, Yale U. School of Medicine, New Haven, Connecticut.

PAVLOV, Ivan Petrovitch (1849–1936)
1. *Pavlovian Theory*: Behavioural theory of
'conditioned reflex'.
2. *Pavlov Pouch*: Exteriorised gastric pouch in
experimental animal, retaining nerve and blood
supply, by which Pavlov established the psychic
secretion of gastric juice in 1879.

The son of a poor priest in Riazan in Central Russia,
Pavlov was destined for the Church, but instead
studied medicine at St Petersburg, and later worked
with Ludwig★ in Leipzig and with Heidenhain★ in
Breslau, on the circulation, and digestive physiology,
respectively. A brilliant physiologist, and a man of
exceptionally rigid habits, he became physiologist at
the Military Academy of St Petersburg, and was
awarded the 1904 Nobel Prize for studies on the
physiology of digestion.

PAYR, Erwin (1871–1946)
Payr's Clamp: Occlusive clamp used in gastric
surgery.

Surgeon in Leipzig. His name is associated with an
operation for hydrocephalus and a plastic procedure
on the ear; in 1900 he devised a resorbable tube to
connect the ends of severed blood vessels.

PEL, Pieter Klaases (1859–1919)
Pel–Ebstein Fever: Cyclical bouts of pyrexia said to be
associated with Hodgkin's★ Disease. D. 1885.

P. of Medicine, Amsterdam.

PELGER, Karel (1885–1931)
Pelger–Hüet Anomaly: Dominant condition of
hypersegmented leucocyte nuclei. D. 1928. (D. 1931
by Hüet.)

Dutch physician.

PELLEGRINI, Augusto
Pellegrini–Stieda Disease: Calcification at femoral
attachment of medial collateral ligament of knee
following avulsion fracture. D. 1905. (D. 1905 by
Köhler★ and 1908 by Stieda.)

Chief Surgeon to Ospedale Mellini, Chiari, Italy, and
later to Ospedale San Francesco, Florence.

PENDRED, Vaughan (b. 1869)
Pendred's Syndrome: Recessive condition of defective

iodine-binding with deaf-mutism and goitre. D. 1896.

London physician.

PENROSE, Charles Bingham (1862–1925)
Penrose Drain: 'Cigarette drain': rubber tube containing gauze wick. D. 1890.

P. of Gynaecology, U. of Pennsylvania, Philadelphia.

PERKINS, George (1892–1979)
1. *Perkin's Traction*: Skeletal traction over a pillow with split bed for functional treatment of femoral shaft fractures: a method of fracture treatment which does not require immobilisation.
2. *Perkin's Formula*: Guide to time taken for union and consolidation of fractures.

He trained at Oxford and St Thomas's, qualified in 1916, and served two years in the RAMC in the East African campaign. He was captured by the Germans, won the MC, and returned as house-surgeon to Max Page at St Thomas's, then worked with Naughton Dunn★ and Robert Jones★ at Shepherd's Bush. He was later First Assistant to Rowley Bristow at the Orthopaedic Department at St Thomas's, succeeding him as Head of the Department in 1946, when he also became President of the British Orthopaedic Association. In 1948 he became the first P. of Orthopaedic Surgery at St Thomas's.

PERTHES, Georg Clemens (1869–1927)
Perthes Disease: Osteochondritis of femoral capital epiphysis. D. 1910 (October). The same condition was described in February 1910 by Legg★ and July 1910 by Calvé;★ hence often is given the name of all three.

Surgeon in Leipzig, later P. of Surgery, Tübingen. He also described a tourniquet test for patency of the femoral vein, performed a 'Bankart'★ repair for anterior shoulder dislocation in 1906, 17 years before Bankart, and devised a pollicisation operation in 1921. He originated the use of deep X-ray therapy for the treatment of cancer in 1903.

PETIT, Jean Louis (1674–1750)
1. *Triangle of Petit*: Inferior lumbar triangle, bounded by external oblique, latissimus dorsi and iliac crest.
2. *Petit's Hernia*: Hernia through Triangle of Petit.

A child prodigy, he began to study anatomy at 7, was Littré's★ Demonstrator at 12, and Surgeon to La

Charité Hospital in Paris at 16. He performed the first mastoidectomy, became a foreign FRS in 1729, and was Director of the Academie de Chirurgie in Paris.

PETRI, Richard Julius (1852–1921)
Petri Dish: Shallow receptacle for bacterial culture. D. 1887.

Born in Barmen, he was curator of the Hygiene Museum in Berlin, then assistant to Robert Koch★, in whose Institute in Berlin he invented his dish.

PEUTZ, John Law Augustine (1886–1957)
Peutz–Jeghers Syndrome: Familial intestinal polyposis with circumoral pigmentation. D. 1921. (D. 1949 by Jeghers in USA.)

Chief of Internal Medicine, St John's Hospital, The Hague, Holland.

PEYER, Johann Conrad (1653–1712)
Peyer's Patches: Aggregates of lymph follicles in the ileum. D. 1677.

Born of a noble family in Schaffhausen, Switzerland, he studied in Basle, and under Duverney in Paris, and became P. of Logic, Rhetoric and Medicine in Schaffhausen. He died in Basle. His patches had previously been described by Stensen★, and had been seen by Marco Aurelio Severino (1580–1656) in 1645.

PEYRONIE, François de la (1678–1747)
Peyronie's Disease: Fibrosis of the shaft of the penis. D. 1743.

Surgeon to Louis XV in Paris, and founder of the Royal Academy of Surgery; in 1743 he was responsible for separating the surgeons from the barbers. One of the most renowned surgeons in Paris in the eighteenth century, he was known as a skilful operator for hernia and on the gut.

PFANNENSTIEL, Hermann Johannes (1862–1909)
Pfannenstiel Incision: Curved suprapubic incision. D. 1900.

Breslau gynaecologist.

PFEIFFER, Richard Freidrich Johannes (1858–1945)
1. *Pfeifferella*: Bacterial genus now included under Brucellaceae (see Bruce★). D. 1892.
2. *Pfeiffer's Phenomenon*: Bacteriolysis, which he first observed in animal injection studies of vibrios during the Hamburg cholera epidemic of 1892 (D. 1894); this was the foundation of clinical serology.

Born in Posen, he was educated at Schweidnitz and studied in Berlin. He entered the Army, worked as a bacteriologist in Wiesbaden, and in 1884 was Koch's★ Assistant in Berlin. In 1894 he became P. in Berlin, from 1899 to 1909 was P. of Hygiene in Königsberg, and from 1909 to 1926 in Breslau. He was probably the first to isolate typhoid organisms from faeces, and successfully immunised humans against typhoid in 1896. He discovered the influenza bacillus in 1892. He was a hygienist with the rank of General in the First World War, and was on the German Plague Commission in India in 1896 and on the Malaria Commission in Italy.

PHALEN, George S. (C)
Phalen's Test: Forced palmar-flexion of wrist which induces paraesthesiae in the median-innervated fingers in carpal tunnel syndrome.

Orthopaedic surgeon from Dallas, Texas, who worked at the Cleveland Clinic Foundation, Cleveland, Ohio.

PHEMISTER, Dallas Burton (1882–1951)
Phemister Graft: Cortico-cancellous bone graft.

Born on a farm in Illinois, he trained at Rush Medical College, Chicago, and was an intern at Cook County Hospital (then the largest in the world). He did postgraduate work in Vienna and England, returning as P. of Surgery, first to Rush Medical College, then to the U. of Chicago Medical School. Though mainly an orthopaedic surgeon, he was the first successfully to remove the oesophagus for carcinoma, and studied gallstone formation, and the treatment of shock. He was President of the American College of Surgeons in 1940, was awarded the French Légion d'Honneur, and died following appendicectomy.

PICK, Friedel (1867–1926)
Pick's Disease: Chronic constrictive pericarditis with multiple serositis. D. 1896.

P. of Laryngology and Director of the Laryngological Institute, Prague.

PICK, Ludwig (1868–1935)
Niemann–Pick Disease: See *Niemann*. D. 1926. (D. 1914 by Niemann.)

Berlin physician, who described arrhenoblastoma in 1905.

von PIRQUET, Clemens Peter Freiherr (1874–1929)
von Pirquet's Reaction: Skin reaction to old tuberculin applied by scarification. D. 1907.

Born in Vienna, he studied there and was registrar to Escherich★ in the Children's Hospital. He was later P. of Paediatrics at Johns Hopkins Hospital, Baltimore then in Breslau in 1910 and in Vienna in 1911. He suggested the term 'allergy', and introduced the concept of allergy to TB.

PLATT, Sir Harry. Bt. (C)
Putti–Platt Procedure: See *Putti*.

Emeritus P. of Orthopaedic Surgery, U. of Manchester, and a past President of the Royal College of Surgeons. He trained in Manchester and London, winning the Gold Medal in both places, and qualified in 1909. He worked in New York and Boston, returning as Orthopaedic Surgeon to Ancoats Hospital, Manchester, where he set up the first hospital fracture clinic. He became P. of Orthopaedic Surgery in Manchester in 1939, and from 1940 to 1963 was Consultant Adviser on Orthopaedics to the Ministry of Health.

PLUMMER, Henry Stanley (1874–1937)
Paterson–Brown Kelly–Plummer–Vinson Syndrome: See *Paterson*. D. 1912. (D. 1919 by the other three.)

Physician to the Mayo Clinic, who introduced the use of Lugol's★ Iodine in the preparation of thyrotoxic patients for surgery, in 1923.

POISEUILLE, Jean Léonard Marie (1797–1869)
Poiseuille's Law: Equation governing flow in relation to density, pressure difference, and dimensions of the tube. This is the fundamental principle used to determine blood viscosity.

Born in Paris, the son of a carpenter, he studied at the École Polytechnique, becoming Doctor és Science in 1828. In 1842 he was elected to the Academie de Medicine in Paris, and in 1860 became Inspector of Primary Schools. He experimented on blood-flow with a haemodynamometer of his own construction. He died in Paris.

POLITZER, Adam (1835–1920)
Politzerisation: Inflation of the middle ear using a Politzer's Bag. D. 1863.

P. of Otology, Vienna, and the world's leading otologist of his day. He described otosclerosis in 1893.

POLYA, Eugen Alexander (1876–1944)
Polya Gastrectomy: Partial ('Billroth★ II')
Gastrectomy. D. 1911. (Kronlein described this
operation in 1888.)

Surgeon to St Stephen's Hospital, Budapest,
Hungary. An operation for femoral hernia repair (D.
1905) also bears his name.

PORGES et Compagnie
Porges Catheter: Red rubber catheter.

Surgical instrument-making firm in Paris.

PORTEUS, Stanley David (b. 1883)
Porteus Maze Test: Non-language psychological test
requiring subject to trace through mazes of increasing
complexity. D. 1920.

Hawaii psychologist and psychiatrist.

POTT, Sir Percivall (1714–1788)
1. *Pott's Fracture*: Ankle fracture–dislocation with
lower fibular fracture 2–3 in. above lateral malleolus
and rupture of the medial ligament. D. 1765. (He
described this injury as 'a case which gives infinite
pain and trouble both to patient and surgeon,
frequently ending in the lameness and
disappointment of the former and the disgrace and
concern of the latter').
2. *Pott's Puffy Tumour*: Oedema overlying
osteomyelitis of the skull secondary to frontal
sinusitis or extradural abscess. D. 1760.
3. *Pott's Disease*: Vertebral tuberculosis (spinal
caries). D. 1779.
4. *Pott's Paraplegia*: Resulting from Pott's Disease. D.
1779.

Pott was born in Threadneedle Street in the City of
London, on the present site of the Bank of England.
At 15 he was apprenticed to the surgeon Edward
Nourse at Barts for 200 guineas (the fee was paid by
his relative the Bishop of Rochester). In 1736 he
obtained the Grand Diploma of the Barber–Surgeons'
Company, in 1744 became Assistant Surgeon to
Barts, and in 1749 Full Surgeon. The most celebrated
lecturer in London, he pioneered lecture-
demonstrations and virtually founded Barts Medical
School. He was the first to describe an occupational
cancer – of the scrotum in chimney-sweeps. In 1755
he fell off his horse in the Old Kent Road sustaining a
compound tibial fracture. His old teacher Nourse

attended him, and saved the leg from amputation. He had nine children, and the largest private practice in London. At 73 he retired from Barts, and the next year died of pneumonia, contracted while travelling 20 miles to visit a patient in winter.

POUPART, Francois (1661–1709)
Poupart's Ligament: Inguinal ligament. D. 1705. (D. by Fallopio★ in 1584.)

Born in Le Mans, he was mainly a naturalist, writing extensively on invertebrates while working in Reims. He became Surgeon to the Hôtel-Dieu in Paris but returned to Reims, where he died.

PRAUSNITZ, Carl Willy (b. 1876)
Prausnitz–Küstner Reaction: Intradermal test now recognised as being for reaginic immunoglobulin (IgE). D. 1921.

Bacteriologist in Breslau.

PROSKAUER, Bernhard (1851–1915)
Voges–Proskauer Reaction: See *Voges*.

Bacteriologist and physician in Berlin, who worked with Koch★.

von PURKINJE, Johannes (Jan) Evangelista (1787–1869)
1. *Purkinje fibres*: Subendocardial muscle fibres. D. 1839.
2. *Purkinje cells*: Cells of cerebellar cortex with many dendrites. D. 1837.

Born in Bohemia of Czech peasant stock, he was educated by monks and at first taught as a novice, but at 21 left the Order and walked 200 miles to Prague to study philosophy. Two years later he became tutor to a Baron's family, and began to study medicine. His early experiments involved self-administration of ipecac, belladonna and camphor; he later wrote on colour vision, and visual perception, discovered the skin sweat glands (1833), noted the uniqueness of finger-prints, helped develop the animated cartoon, and was eventually co-editor of the leading Czech daily paper. He translated Shakespeare into Czech, married the daughter of the P. of Anatomy in Berlin, K. A. Rudolphi, in 1825 (having been introduced by Goethe), and became P. of Physiology in Breslau (the first such Chair in the world) from 1832 to 1850. He coined the term 'protoplasm', and did experiments on vertigo on the roundabouts in a Prague amusement park. In 1850 he became P. of Physiology in Prague, where he died at 82, a patriot and popular hero.

PUTTI, Vittorio (1880–1940)
Putti–Platt Procedure: Operation for recurrent dislocation of the shoulder.

Born in Bologna, the son of the P. of Surgery, after qualifying he became Assistant to Alessandro Codivilla, a renowned orthopaedic surgeon, and Director of the Instituto Ortopedico Rizzoli, Bologna, in 1903, and 9 years later succeeded him as Surgeon-in-Chief, becoming also P. of Orthopaedic Surgery in Bologna. His library was covered with frescoes and he made important contributions to medical history as well as orthopaedics, and lectured world-wide. The King of Italy bestowed upon him the Order of Grand Officiali of the Crown of Italy.

Q

QUECKENSTEDT, Hans Heinrich Georg (1876–1918)
Queckenstedt's Test: Compression and release of the internal jugular vein to test for spinal block to circulation of the CSF. D. 1916.

Physician in Rostock, who became Chief of Medical Services, Hamburg, and was killed by an army truck on the last day of the First World War.

de QUERVAIN, Fritz (1868–1940)
1. *de Quervain's Tenosynovitis*: Stenosing tenovaginitis of the sheaths of abductor pollicis longus and extensor pollicis brevis at the wrist. D. 1895.
2. *de Quervain's Disease*: Painful subacute thyroiditis (now believed to be viral). D. 1902.
3. *de Quervain's Fracture*: Scaphoid fracture with volar dislocation of the proximal fragment together with the lunate. D. 1907.

The son of a pastor in Sion in the Valais canton of Switzerland, he became Reader to Kocher★ in Berne, and succeeded him as P. of Surgery.

QUETELET, Lambert Adolphe Jacques (1796–1874)
1. *Quetelet's Rule*: Body Weight (kg) = Height in cm minus 100. D. 1871.

2. *Quetelet's Index of Constitution*: Weight/Height. D.
1871.

Belgian mathematician and anthropologist; a pioneer
of anthropometry.

QUEYRAT, Louis Auguste (1856–1933)
Erythroplasia of Queyrat: Red, shiny, exudative,
pre-cancerous lesion of the penis. D. 1911. Also
known as Paget's★ Disease of the Penis.

Physician to the Hôpital Cochin, Paris.

QUICK, Armand James (b. 1894)
Quick Test: One-stage prothrombin time, for
coumarin-type anticoagulants. D. 1935.

Emeritus P. of Biochemistry, Marquette School of
Medicine, Milwaukee, Wisconsin.

R

RAMPLEY
Rampley's Sponge-Holding Forceps: Surgical
instrument.

Surgery beadle at the London Hospital in the 1880s.
He would relate: 'The Surgeon watched me to see if I
made any mistakes, and I watched the Surgeon . . .'.

RAMSTEDT, Wilhelm Conrad (1867–1963)
Ramstedt's Operation: Pyloromyotomy for infantile
hypertrophic pyloric stenosis. D. 1912. (Previously
D. 1888 by Hirschsprung★.)

Born in Prussia, he studied at Heidelberg, Berlin and
Halle, where he qualified MD in 1894. From 1895 to
1901 he was Assistant Surgeon in Halle, then became
a military surgeon, and in 1919 Chief Surgeon to the
Rafaelklinik at Münster (which was completely
destroyed in an Allied bombing raid in the Second
World War). Most of his early patients with pyloric
stenosis were the infant sons of other doctors. He was
a connoisseur of Dutch painting. Ramstedt's family
name originally had two 'm's', said to be a
mis-spelling by his grandfather due to an attack of
nerves when signing his marriage register, so in 1928
Ramstedt dropped the second 'm'.

RANDALL, Alexander (1883–1951)
Randall's Plaques: Microliths of urinary salts deposited on erosions of renal papillae. D. 1937.

P. of Urology, U. of Pennsylvania, Philadelphia.

RANVIER, Louis Antoine (1835–1922)
Nodes of Ranvier: Interruptions in the myelin sheath of nerves (previously thought to be artefacts). D. 1875.

Physician, pathologist and histologist; P. of Histology at the Collège de France, Paris. In 1868 he introduced picro-carmine, the first 'double-stain' which distinguished cytoplasm and nuclei.

RATHKE, Martin Heinrich (1793–1860)
Rathke's Pouch: Depression in roof of embryonic mouth in front of the bucco-pharyngeal membrane. D. 1838.

P. of Physiology and Pathology at Dorpat, then of Zoology and Anatomy at Königsberg, where the bacteriologist Klebs★ was among his pupils.

RAYNAUD, A. G. Maurice (1834–1881)
1. *Raynaud's Disease*: Condition of abnormal sensitivity of the direct response of arterioles to cold, causing intermittent acute and prolonged vasospasm, especially in the upper limbs. D. 1862 in his Paris MD thesis.
2. *Raynaud's Phenomenon*: Peripheral vasospasm secondary to organic disease of the main artery to a limb, vibration, connective tissue disease, or phaeochromocytoma. D. 1862.

Physician to the Hôpital Lariboisière, Paris.

de RÉAUMUR, René-Antoine Ferschault (1683–1757)
Réaumur Temperature Scale: 0°–80°. A Paris Métro station is also named after him.

'A modern Leonardo', this French natural philosopher and scientist, born in La Rochelle, was elected to the Paris Académie des Sciences at 25, where he was Director 12 times, and an active member for 50 years. His studies on iron and steel technology (1722) established steel-making in France: he was rewarded with a pension of 12,000 livres a year by the Duc d'Orleans, Regent of France. Apart from many studies of the application of science to industry, he isolated gastric juice and demonstrated its solvent effect on foods, in 1752. He died in Paris.

von RECKLINGHAUSEN, Friedrich Daniel (1833–1910)
1. *von Recklinghausen's Disease of Nerves*: Neurofibromatosis. D. 1882.
2. *von Recklinghausen's Disease of Bone*: Osteitis fibrosa cystica (occurring in about 30% of cases of parathyroid adenoma). D. 1890. (It had been described by Robert Smith* of Dublin in 1849.)

After qualifying MD in Berlin in 1855, he was Virchow's* Assistant for 6 years; in 1865 he became P. of Pathological Anatomy at Königsberg, and in the following year in Würzburg. In 1872 he became P. of Pathology in Strasbourg (when Madelung* was P. of Surgery). He described haemochromatosis in 1889 and invented the silver stain for nerve tissue in 1900.

REED, Dorothy M. (Mrs Mendenhall) (1874–1964)
Reed–Sternberg Cells: Giant cells in the spleen in Hodgkin's* Disease. D. 1906. (D. 1898 by Sternberg.)

Pathologist to Johns Hopkins Hospital, Baltimore.

REICHERT, Karl Bogislaus (1811–1883)
Reichert's Cartilage: Cartilage of 2nd branchial arch in embryo. D. 1836.

Born in Rastenburg, Germany, he was from 1853 to 1885 P. of Human and Comparative Anatomy at Dorpat, and later in Breslau and Berlin, where he died.

REISSNER, Ernst (1824–1878)
Reissner's Membrane: Basement membrane of the cochlea. D. 1851, in his inaugural dissertation at Dorpat.

Born in Riga, Lithuania, in 1851 he became P. of Anatomy in Dorpat, and later in Breslau. He died at Schloss Ruhenthal.

REITER, Hans Conrad (1881–1969)
1. *Reiter's Disease*: Non-gonococcal syndrome of urethritis, arthritis and conjunctivitis. D. 1916. (It had been described by Brodie* in 1818.)

2. *Reiter Protein Complement Fixation Test*: For syphilis.

Born in Leipzig, the son of a factory owner, he studied there (MD 1906) and in Breslau and Tübingen. After postgraduate training in bacteriology in Paris, Berlin and under Sir Almroth Wright at St Mary's Hospital, London, he became Lecturer at the Institute of Hygiene, Königsberg. He discovered the causative organism of Weil's★ Disease in 1914, as an Army doctor on the Western Front, and from 1919 to 1923 he was P. of Hygiene at Rostock U. He then worked under von Wassermann★ at the Kaiser Wilhelm Institute of Experimental Therapy, Berlin, and became P. of Hygiene at the Friederich Wilhelm Universität. An enthusiastic Nazi, he was President of the Health Service in Berlin, and Honorary P. of Hygiene during the Second World War; after retiring he devoted himself to a study of the problems of illegitimacy. He died at his country house in Hesse at 88.

RENDU, Henry Jules Louis Marie (1844–1902)
Osler–Rendu–Weber Syndrome: See *Osler*.

Paris physician.

RETZIUS, Andreas Adolf (1796–1860)
Cave of Retzius: Prevesical space. D. 1849.

Born in Lund, Sweden, he was from 1840 until his death P. of Anatomy and Physiology at the Carolinska Institute, Stockholm. His son Magnus Gustav (1842–1919) (after whom a cerebral gyrus and a foramen are named) succeeded him in the same chair, and after his death published many of his father's anthropological writings, including the description of a 'Cranial Index'.

RICH, Arnold Rice (1893–1968)
Hamman–Rich Syndrome: See *Hamman*.

Pathologist to Johns Hopkins Hospital, Baltimore.

RICHES, Sir Eric William (C)
Riches Diathermy Forceps, Bladder Syringe: Urological instruments.

He trained at the Middlesex (MB 1925), where he became Consultant Urologist, and later Emeritus Urological Surgeon. He was also on the staffs of the

Royal Masonic and Sts John and Elizabeth Hospitals, London, was Hunterian★ Professor at the Royal College of Surgeons from 1938 to 1942, and in 1942 won the Jacksonian Prize. He was consultant Urologist to the Army in the Second World War, won the Military Cross, and was President of the Medical Society of London and the Hunterian Society, and Vice-President of the Royal College of Surgeons.

RICHTER, August Gottlieb (1742–1812)
Richter's Hernia: Hernia constricting only part of the gut wall. D. 1777.

Surgeon in Göttingen, Germany.

RICKETTS, Howard Taylor (1871–1910)
Rickettsia: Pleomorphic micro-organisms causing varieties of typhus.

Chicago pathologist; he was the first to demonstrate (in 1906) the transmission of Rocky Mountain Spotted Fever by the bite of a wood-tick.

RIEDEL, Bernhard Moritz Carl Ludwig (1846–1916)
1. *Riedel's Lobe*: Accessory right lobe of liver. D. 1888.
2. *Riedel's Thyroiditis*: Struma fibrosa; painful enlargement of the thyroid, sometimes associated with retro-peritoneal fibrosis, and possibly a collagen disorder. D. 1896.

P. of Surgery, Jena.

RINGER, Sydney (1835–1910)
Ringer's Solution: Containing sodium, potassium and calcium chlorides. D. 1880.

P. of Medicine, University College London. He also wrote extensively on body temperature as a guide to diagnosis and prognosis in tuberculosis.

RINNE, Friedrich Heinrich Adolf (1819–1868)
Rinne's Test: Hearing test comparing bone and air conduction of the vibrations of a tuning-fork: 'negative' (i.e. bone better than air) in conductive deafness. D. 1855.

Aural surgeon, Göttingen, Germany.

ROBERTSON, Douglas Moray Cooper Lamb Argyll (1837–1909)

Argyll Robertson Pupil: Tabetic pupil which accommodates, but does not react to, light. D. 1869. (He acknowledged the previous descriptions by Romberg★ in 1839, and by Trousseau★.)

Born in Edinburgh, where his father was President of the College of Surgeons in 1848, he studied there and at St Andrews (MD 1857). He studied ophthalmology under von Graefe (who founded the specialty) in Berlin and returned to Edinburgh as Assistant Eye Surgeon to the Royal Infirmary in 1868, becoming Full Ophthalmic Surgeon (the first in Scotland) 2 years later, remaining there until 1897. He demonstrated the action of eserine in constricting the pupil, extracting the chemical from the Calabar bean. He described an operation for ectropion in 1883; like his father became President of the (by then Royal) College of Surgeons of Edinburgh, in 1886; and was Surgeon-Oculist to Queen Victoria and Edward VII in Scotland. An accomplished golfer, he won the Gold Medal at the Royal and Ancient Club (St Andrews) five times. He retired to a farm in Jersey in 1900. On a trip around the world with his wife in 1894 he befriended an Indian Prince, the Thakar of Gondal, and while visiting him again in 1909, Robertson died.

ROBIN, Pierre (1867–1950)

Pierre Robin Syndrome: Micrognathia, macroglossia and cleft palate. D. 1929.

French dentist and stomatologist to the Hospitals of Paris.

von ROENTGEN, Wilhelm Conrad (1845–1923)

1. *Roentgen Rays*: X-rays. D. 1895.
2. *Roentgenographs*: Radiographs.
3. *Roentgen*: International Unit of X- or γ-radiation.

Born of a Dutch mother and German father, who were cousins (Roentgen was colour-blind), he studied at Utrecht and Zürich; his doctoral thesis was on 'The Study of Gases'. He was P. of Physics successively at Strasbourg, Giessen, Würzburg and Munich, and in 1888 became Director of the Physics Laboratory at the U. of Würzburg. Here he discovered X-rays by chance when he noticed that some crystals lying on a table fluoresced as he passed an electric current through a nearby vacuum tube. He announced his discovery at the Medical Society of Würzburg in 1895; the first radiograph was of Mrs Roentgen's hand with a ring on her finger. He wrote only three papers on X-rays, and made no money out of his discovery: he won the 1901 Nobel★ Prize in Physics, but gave the money to the U. of Würzburg.

ROLANDO, Luigi (1773–1831)
1. *Fissure of Rolando*: Central sulcus in the cerebral cortex. D. 1809. (Named for him in 1839 by François Leuret.)
2. *Substance of Rolando*: Substantia gelatinosa. D. 1809.

Born in Turin, he became personal physician to the King of Savoy and Piedmont, following him into exile in Sardinia after Napoleon Bonaparte's invasion. There he became P. of Theoretical and Practical Medicine in Sassari, where he performed many animal experiments on the cerebrum and cerebellum, and illustrated his writings with his own engravings. He later returned to Turin as P. of Anatomy, and died there.

ROMANOWSKY, Dmitri Leonidovitch (1861–1921)
Romanowsky Stain: Archetypal eosin/methylene blue contrast stain for blood films and malarial parasites. D. 1891.

Born in Pskoff, Russia, he studied in St Petersburg (MD 1891) and became P. of Internal Medicine there. He died at Kislowdsk in the Caucasus.

von ROMBERG, Moritz Heinrich (1795–1873)
1. *Romberg's Sign (Rombergism)*: Inability to balance with eyes closed and feet together, classically due to loss of joint position sense in tabes dorsalis. D. 1846.
2. *Howship–Romberg Sign*: See *Howship*.

Born in Saxony, he studied in Berlin, qualifying with an MD thesis on achondroplasia at 22. After a visit to Vienna, he returned to Berlin, becoming P. of Medicine, Director of the University Hospital (1840), and also P. of Special Pathology and Therapy (1845). He translated Bell's★ *The Nervous System of the Human Body* into German in 1831, himself wrote a major neurology textbook (1840–1846), and was world-famous as a pioneer neurologist. He was in charge of cholera hospitals in 1831 and 1837 during the Berlin cholera epidemics. He was Eduard Henoch's* uncle. He died in Berlin of heart disease at 78.

RORSCHACH, Hermann (1884–1922)
Rorschach Test: Projective type of personality test using ink-blots. D. 1921.

German-born psychiatrist in Bern, Switzerland.

ROSENBACH, Anton Julius Friedrich (1842–1923)
Erysipeloid of Rosenbach: Skin infection caused by *Erysipelothrix rhusiopathiae*. D. 1887.

Born in Grohnde (Hanover), he studied in Heidelberg, Göttingen, Vienna and Paris, then was a pathologist in Wiesbaden, then P. of Surgery in Göttingen. He did much work on surgical bacteriology, doing his early experiments in his house as he had no laboratory.

ROSENMUELLER, Johann Christian (1771–1820)
Fossa of Rosenmueller: Pharyngeal recess. D. 1805.

P. of Anatomy and Surgery, Leipzig (1802–1820). He made many contributions to embryology.

ROTHERA, Arthur Cecil Hamel (1880–1915)
Rothera Test: Sodium nitroprusside reaction to detect acetone bodies in urine.

Biochemist in Melbourne, Australia.

ROTOR, Arthro B.
Rotor's Syndrome: Chronic familial non-haemolytic jaundice. D. 1948.

Physician, Philippines.

ROUS, Francis Peyton (1879–1970)
Rous Sarcoma: Transmissible fibrosarcoma of hens induced by a virus. D. 1910.

He studied at Johns Hopkins U. (MD 1905), was Instructor in Pathology at the U. of Michigan (1906–1908), and then became a member of the active staff of the Rockfeller Institute for Medical Research until 1945, when he became a member emeritus. He was elected to the National Academy of Sciences in 1927 and won the Nobel Prize in 1966. In 1915 he and Turner pioneered a blood testing and storage solution which was the basis for setting up bloodbanks.

ROUX, Jean Charles (1857–1934)
Roux-en-Y loop: Upper intestinal anastomosis using jejunal conduit. D. 1908.

P. of Surgery, Paris.

ROVSING, Niels Thorkild (1862–1927)
1. *Rovsing's Operation*: Removal of cysts from polycystic kidneys.
2. *Rovsing's Sign*: Pressure in the left iliac fossa causes pain in the right iliac fossa in acute appendicitis. D. 1907.

P. of Surgery, Copenhagen.

RUFFINI, Angelo (1864–1929)
Ruffini's Corpuscles: Sensory nerve endings in the subcutaneous tissues of the fingers. D. 1893.

After studying in Bologna, he worked in Florence and Siena, becoming Assistant at the Histological Institute, Bologna, in 1894, and in 1912 P. of Histology.

RUSSELL, Patrick (1728–1805)
Russell's Viper Venom: Venom of *Vipera russelli*, which has haemostatic properties, acting *in vitro* as an intrinsic thromboplastin.

Physician in Aleppo, Syria.

RUSSELL, R. Hamilton (1860–1933)
Hamilton Russell Traction: Balanced skeletal traction for femoral fractures, designed to relax muscle spasm. D. 1924.

He was Lord Lister's★ house-surgeon, and emigrated to Australia in 1890, where he introduced antisepsis widely. He became surgeon to the Alfred Hospital, Melbourne, and founded the Australasian College of Surgeons, and was its first Director-General. He described an operation for hypospadias (1900) and wrote on the technique for inguinal hernia repair. He reduced his own Colles fracture sustained in the Outback. He was killed in a car crash.

RYLE, John Alfred (1889–1950)
Ryle's Tube: Naso-gastric tube. D. 1921.

The son of a Brighton doctor, he studied at Guy's, winning the Gold Medal in medicine. After service with the RAMC in the First World War, he returned to Guy's as lecturer, where he designed a small-bore rubber tube for studying gastric juice, after his wife, who was one of his subjects, was unable to swallow the large one with a brass end he had used previously. He had a great interest in the natural history of untreated disease, and gave up a large private practice in London at 46 to be Regius P. of Physic at Cambridge, in 1935. He was Consultant Adviser to the Ministry of Health in the Second World War, and in 1943 became the first P. of Social Medicine at Oxford. He was a great idealist and advocate of democratic medicine, and of the National Health Service.

S

SABIN, Albert Bruce (b. 1906)
Sabin Vaccine: Oral polio vaccine: preparation of virus particles of attenuated virulence.

Born in Russia, he came to America as a child and studied at New York U. In 1934 he worked at the Lister★ Institute in London, and in 1937, while working as a bacteriologist, proved the existence of *Toxoplasma* in North America. He is now Emeritus Distinguished Service P. of Research Pediatrics, U. of Cincinatti College of Medicine, Ohio, and Distinguished Research P. of Biomedicine, Medical U. of South Carolina, Charleston.

SACHS, Bernard (Barney) (1858–1944)
Tay–Sachs Disease: See *Tay*. D. 1887.

Sachs was born in Baltimore, his parents having eloped from Bavaria and emigrated clandestinely to America. He spent 2 years in Germany during his childhood, and studied at Harvard (BA 1878), then at Strasbourg under Waldeyer★, von Recklinghausen★ and Kussmaul★; Berlin under Westphal★ and Virchow★; Vienna under Meynert★ and Freud★; Paris under Charcot★; and London under Hughlings Jackson★. He returned to New York in 1884 as Instructor in Neurology at the Polyclinic, and also worked at Mount Sinai, Bellevue and Montefiori Hospitals. He wrote 194 papers, was President of the First International Congress of Neurology in Bern in 1931, and President of the New York Academy of Medicine. He lost all his savings in the Wall Street crash, but lived to be 87, a great philanthropist and art expert, and the Mayor of New York, Fiorello La Guadria, came to his funeral.

SACKS, Benjamin (b. 1896)
Libman–Sacks Disease: See *Libman*.

New York physician.

SAINT, Charles Frederick Morris
Saint's Triad: Gallstones, hiatus hernia and diverticulosis.

P. of Surgery, Cape Town.

SALK, Jonas Edward (b. 1914)
Salk Vaccine: Polio vaccine of formalin-killed organisms.

Born in New York, He studied at the City College of New York and New York U., becoming P. of Preventive Medicine. U. of Pittsburgh School of Medicine, Pennsylvania, and then Fellow and Founding Director of the Salk Institute for Biological Studies at San Diego, California.

SALMON, Daniel Elmer (1850–1914)
Salmonella: Bacterial genus of Gram★-negative rods, usually mobile, and non–lactose-fermenters, which includes the organisms responsible for typhoid and paratyphoid. D. 1886.

Born in New Jersey, he studied at Cornell U. (New York) and at Alfort Veterinary College in France. He practised as a veterinary surgeon at Newark, New Jersey from 1872, and in 1883 set up a veterinary division in the US Department of Agriculture in Washington. He then became the first Director (1884) of the Bureau of Animal Industry of the Department of Agriculture, and in 1905 was appointed Head of the Veterinary Department of the U. of Montevideo in Uruguay. In 1910 he took charge of the production of anti-hog cholera serum in Butte, Montana, and died there of pneumonia.

SALTER, Robert (C)
Salter Operation: 'Shelf' procedure for acetabular reconstruction in congenital dislocation of the hip.

Senior Orthopaedic Surgeon, Hospital for Sick Children, Toronto, Canada.

SANTORINI, Giovanni Domenico (1681–1737)
Duct of Santorini: Accessory duct of the pancreas. D.
1724.

Born in Venice, the son of a pharmacist, he studied in
Bologna, Padua and Pisa, where he graduated in
1701. From 1703, aged 22, to 1728, he was P. of
Anatomy and Medicine in Venice, where he
published an anatomical textbook (1724) which he
dedicated to Peter the Great of Russia.

SAVAGE, Paul Thwaites (C)
Savage's Decompressor: Suction tube for per-operative
intestinal decompression.

Studied at the London Hospital, where he qualified in
1939, later becoming Consultant Surgeon to the
Whittington Hospital, London.

SCARPA, Antonio (1747–1832)
1. *Scarpa's Fascia*: Deep layer of the superficial fascia
of the abdominal wall. D. 1809.
2. *Scarpa's Triangle*: Femoral triangle.

He studied at Bologna and Padua, where he acted as
amanuensis to Morgagni★, the then P. of Anatomy,
who was almost blind. In 1772 he became P. of
Surgery in Modena, in 1783 P. of Anatomy in Padua,
and in 1791 a Foreign FRS.

SCHANZ, Alfred (1868–1931)
1. *Schanz Screws*: Threaded bone screws.
2. *Schanz Operation*: Angulation osteotomy for late
irreducible congenital hip dislocation, or old
un-united femoral neck fracture. D. 1907.

P. of Orthopaedic Surgery, Dresden.

SCHEUERMANN, Holger Werfel (1877–1960)
Scheuermann's Disease: Osteochondrosis of thoracic
vertebrae; 'adolescent kyphosis'. D. 1920.

The son of a Copenhagen doctor, he trained as a
radiologist and as an orthopaedic surgeon. His
description of the disease was given in his doctoral
thesis, but this was refused, and he was eventually
awarded an honorary doctorate at the age of 80. He
became Director of the radiological departments of
the Military Hospital and Sundbyhospital,
Copenhagen, and was the best-known radiologist in
Denmark.

SCHICK, Béla (1877–1967)
Schick Test: Intradermal test for immunity to
diphtheria. D. 1908.

Born in Boglar, Hungary, and educated in Graz,
Austria, he was assistant to Escherich★ and von
Pirquet★ at the Children's Clinic in Graz, and in 1918
became P. of Paediatrics in Vienna. In 1923 he was
appointed Director of the Children's Department at
Mount Sinai Hospital, New York.

SCHIFF, Ugo Josef (1834–1915)
Schiff's Reagent: A solution of decolorised fuschin
which turns blue in the presence of aldehydes; a
constituent of the periodic acid–Schiff (PAS) stain. D.
1866.

Born in Frankfurt, he studied chemistry and worked
in Florence with his brother Moritz (1823–1896), a
pioneer neurophysiologist.

SCHILLING, Robert Frederick (b. 1919)
Schilling Test: For Vitamin B_{12} absorption, using
radioactive B_{12}.

Born in Adell, Wisconsin, he trained at the U. of
Wisconsin, was Commonwealth Research Fund
Fellow at the London Hospital in 1959, and returned
as P. of Medicine at the U. of Wisconsin, Madison.

SCHLATTER, Carl (1864–1934)
Osgood–Schlatter's Disease: See *Osgood*. D. 1903.

P. of Surgery, Zürich. An operation for total
gastrectomy (D. 1897) also bears his name.

SCHLEMM, Friedrich S. (1795–1858)
Canal of Schlemm: Sinus venosus sclerae, at junction of
cornea and sclera. D. 1830.

Born in Hanover, he was from 1833 until his death P.
of Anatomy in Berlin.

SCHMIDT, Henry D. (1823–1888)
Schmidt–Lantermann clefts: Microscopic incisures in the
medullary sheath of peripheral nerves. D. 1874. (D.
1877 by Lantermann.)

Pathologist, Charity Hospital, New Orleans.

SCHMORL, Christian Georg (1861–1932)
Schmorl's Nodes: Prolapses of the nucleus pulposus of

the intervertebral disc through the cartilage plate into the spongy bone of the vertebral body. D. 1926.

P. of Pathology, Dresden. Some methods of staining bone also bear his name.

SCHÖNLEIN, Johann Lukas (1793–1864)
Henoch–Schönlein Purpura: See *Henoch*. D. 1832.

Born in Bamberg, Bavaria (also the birthplace of von Wassermann*), he taught medicine and pathology in Würzburg, Zürich and Berlin (1839–1859); Virchow* was among his pupils.

SCHÜLLER, Artur (1874–1958)
Hand–Schüller–Christian Disease: See *Hand*. D. 1915.

Neurologist in Vienna. He performed cordotomy for pain relief experimentally in a monkey in 1910.

SCHWANN, Theodor (1810–1882)
1. *Schwann Cell*: Myelin-secreting cell of the neurilemmal sheath of nerves. D. 1839.
2. *Schwannoma*: Neurilemmoma; tumour of Schwann cells.

Born near Dusseldorf, the son of a bookseller, he was at a Jesuit College in Cologne, and studied medicine in Bonn. He then worked in Würzburg and Berlin, where he was a pupil of, and for 5 years Assistant to, Müller*, and was a colleague and lifelong friend of Henlé*. He however failed to get an academic post in Germany, and so became P. of Anatomy in Louvain, Belgium, in 1839, and from 1848 to 1880 was P. of Comparative Anatomy and Physiology at Liège. He was the first to show that fermentation involved living organisms (in 1878 Pasteur* wrote to him: 'For twenty years I have been travelling along some of the paths opened up by you'). He also discovered pepsin (in 1835), demonstrated that bile is essential to digestion, and was one of the first to recognise the cellular basis of living organisms. A tiny, genial man, and a devout Catholic, he did very little original scientific work after the age of 30, and died a bachelor, on a visit to his brother in Cologne.

SENGSTAKEN, Robert William (b. 1923)
Sengstaken Tube: Inflatable tube used to arrest bleeding from oesophageal varices.

Surgeon, Garden City, New Jersey.

SERTOLI, Enrico (1842–1910)
Sertoli Cells: Supporting and nutritive cells in tubules of testis. D. 1865.

P. of Experimental Physiology, Milan.

SEVER, James Warren (1878–1964)
Sever's Disease: Calcaneal apophysitis.

Orthopaedic Surgeon to the Children's Hospital, Boston, USA. He also described operations for obstetrical paralysis and for recurrent dislocation of the shoulder.

SHARPEY, William (1802–1880)
Sharpey's Fibres: Connective tissue strands running from periosteum into bone.

Born in Arbroath, Scotland, he studied at University College, London, and became P. of Anatomy in Edinburgh, and then P. at University College, London, succeeding Quain. He remained there from 1836 to 1874, and died at Hastings. He was one of the first (in 1830) to describe ciliary motion.

SHEEHAN, Harold Leeming (b. 1900)
Sheehan's Syndrome: Post-partum pituitary necrosis. D. 1937.

He studied in Manchester, winning the gold Medal for his MD thesis, and became successively Lecturer in Pathology there, then Director of Research at Glasgow Royal Maternity Hospital, and P. of Pathology, Liverpool, where he is retired. He is a Fellow of the Royal Colleges of Physicians, Obstetricians and Gynaecologists, and Pathologists.

SHENTON, Edward Warren Hine (1872–1955)
Shenton's Line: Regular arcade traced on a radiograph connecting the undersurface of the femoral neck in a smooth line to the undersurface of the superior pubic ramus. D. 1911.

Consultant Radiologist to Guy's Hospital, London and to St Bartholemew's Hospital, Rochester, Kent (the oldest hospital in England). Author of *Disease in Bone*.

SHERMAN, H. M. O'Neill (1854–1921)
Sherman Plates and Screws: Stainless-steel implants for internal fixation of fractures.

Chief Surgeon to the Carnegie Illinois Steel Trust,

who set up accident services for industry in America based on those of Robert Jones★, which Sherman had studied in England during the First World War.

SHERREN, James (1872–1946)
1. *Oschner–Sherren Regime*: See *Oschner*. D. 1905.
2. *Sherren's Triangle*: Area of skin hyperaesthesia in acute appendicitis, from umbilicus to highest point of iliac crest to right pubic tubercle. D. 1903.

Born in Weymouth, the son of a printer and publisher, he went to sea at 13, served behind the mast in four-masted sailing schooners, and obtained his master's certificate. After giving the anaesthetic for the ship's doctor in an operation at sea he decided to become a doctor himself, was on the staff of the London Hospital, and, like his colleague there, Treves★, was a master mariner.

SHIGA, Kiyoshi (1870–1957)
Shigella: Genus of bacteria causing dysentery. D. 1891.

Born in Sendai, Japan he studied in Tokyo from 1892 to 1896, and worked with Ehrlich★ from 1900 to 1903. From 1904 to 1920 he was at the Institute for Infectious Diseases in Tokyo, and then Dean of the Medical Faculty at Keijo Imperial U.

SHOPE, Richard Edwin (Sr) (b. 1902)
Shope Papilloma: Transmissible tumour in rabbits. D. 1932.

Pathologist, Philadelphia. (His son, Richard Edwin Jr (b. 1926) is P. of Veterinary Medicine and Microbiology, U. of Minnesota.)

SHRAPNELL, Henry Jones (1761–1841)
Shrapnell's Membrane: Pars flaccida of tympanic membrane. D. 1832.

Born in Berkeley, Gloucestershire, he qualified MRCS in 1814 and became Surgeon to the Royal South Gloucestershire Regiment of Light Infantry Militia. In 1822 he married Maria Marklove, a Ward of Edward Jenner (of vaccination fame), and settled in London as surgeon and anatomist.

SHWARTZMANN, Gregory (1896–1965)
Shwartzmann Phenomenon: Severe hypersensitivity reaction to serial injection of typhoid cultures (endotoxin) into rabbits. D. 1928.

Russian-born bacteriologist who emigrated to the USA.

SHY, G. Milton (1919–1967)
Shy–Drager Syndrome: Neurological disorder with postural hypotension. D. 1960.

Neurologist, National Institute for Neurological Diseases and Blindness, Bethesda, Maryland.

SIBSON, Francis (1814–1876)
Sibson's Fascia: Covering the apical pleura with attachment to the 1st rib. D. 1844.

Born in Maryport, Cumberland, he became P. of Medicine at St Mary's Hospital, London, and died on holiday in Geneva.

SILVESTER, Henry Robert (1829–1908)
Silvester Method: Manual technique of artificial respiration. D. 1858.

English physician.

SIMMONDS, Franklin Adin (C)
Simmonds' Test: With the patient kneeling, squeezing of the calf produces plantar-flexion of the foot only if the Achilles tendon is intact.

He studied at Cambridge and St Thomas's (MB 1935), became Orthopaedic Surgeon to the Rowley Bristow Hospital, Pyrford, Surrey, and is now retired in Surrey.

SIMMONDS, Morris (1855–1925)
Simmonds' Disease: Panhypopituitarism; 'pituitary cachexia'. D. 1914.

Born in St Thomas, Virgin Islands (then a Danish possession), his family moved to Hamburg, Germany, when he was 6. He studied in Tübingen, Leipzig, Munich and Kiel. Remembered as a generous and honest man, he went into general practice in Hamburg, and was also a pathologist, becoming Secretary of the German Pathological Society, and in 1919 Professor (honoris causa) at the U. of Hamburg.

SIMS, James Marion (1813–1883)
1. *Sims' Speculum*: Vaginal speculum (the original instrument was a bent spoon). D. 1852.

2. *Sims' Position*: Left lateral position for gynaecological examination,

After studying at Jefferson Medical College, Philadelphia, he practised surgery in Montgomery, Alabama, and later New York, where in 1855 he set up the State Hospital for Women. While in Alabama he was the first surgeon successfully to close a vesico-vaginal fistula: he perfected this operation which in due course made him the most famous gynaecologist in the world.

SINDING LARSEN. See *Larsen*

SISTRUNK, Walter (1880–1933)
Sistrunk's Operation: Excision of thyroglossal fistula. D. 1920.

Surgeon to the Mayo* Clinic, Rochester, Minnesota.

SIWE, Sturre August (b. 1897)
Letterer–Siwe Disease: See *Letterer*. D. 1933. (D. 1924 by Letterer.)

P. of Paediatrics, Lund, Sweden.

SJÖGREN, Henrik Samuel Conrad (b. 1899)
Sjögren's Syndrome: Rheumatoid arthritis with xerostomia and kerato-conjunctivitis sicca. Sometimes described as Mikulicz* disease with generalised arthritis. D. 1933.

He studied at the Carolinska Institute, Stockholm, and in 1935 became Head of the Eye Clinic, Jönköping, Sweden, and in 1961, P. of Ophthalmology (honoris causa) at Göteborg, for his pioneer work on corneal transplantation. Now retired, he lives in Lund. (The syndrome is sometimes ascribed to Tage Sjögren (1859–1939), a Swedish physician.)

SKENE, Alexander Johnston Chalmers (1838–1900)
Skene's Tubules: Female paraurethral glands. D. 1880.

Born in Aberdeen, he moved to America, qualified at the U. of Michigan, and became P. of Gynaecology at the Long Island College Hospital, Brooklyn, New York.

VAN SLYKE, Donald Dexter (1883–1971)
Van Slyke Apparatus: For estimation of oxygen and carbon dioxide content in blood. D. 1918.

Born in Geneva, New York, where his father was
chemist to the New York Agricultural
Experimental Station, he studied organic chemistry
at the U. of Michigan, published his first paper
with his father in 1907, and was from 1907 to 1914
at the Rockefeller Institute, New York. From 1914
to 1949 he was chemist to the Hospital of the
Rockefeller Institute. He described the concept of
'urea clearance' in 1921 and in the same year was
elected to the National Academy of Science. In
1936 he held a Charles Mickle Fellowship at the U.
of Toronto. His last appointment was as Director
of Biology and Medicine at the Brookhaven
National Laboratory.

SMITH, Robert William (1807–1873)
Smith's Fracture: Fracture of the distal radius, with
volar and proximal displacement, and dorsal
displacement of the distal ulna. Sometimes called a
reversed Colles★ fracture. D. 1847.

He had a flourishing private practice in Dublin,
which he gave up to become P. of Surgery at Trinity
College, succeeding Colles★, whose post-mortem he
performed. He founded the Pathological Society of
Dublin, described Madelung's★ deformity before
Madelung, and von Recklinghausen's★ disease of
bone (in 1849) before von Recklinghausen. In 1849 he
also wrote a book on neuromata which was larger
than a dinner-table, and was at the time the largest
book ever published in Ireland.

SMITH, Sir Thomas (1833–1909)
Tom Smith's Arthritis: Septic arthritis of infancy.

Born in Kent, he studied at Barts, where he was later
on the surgical staff, and was also surgeon to Great
Ormond Street Children's Hospital. He described
xanthomatosis of bone in 1865 and suggested blood
transfusion as a treatment for purpura in 1873.
He never wrote a textbook, saying: 'It's the men
who don't get the cases who write the books about
them'.

SMITH-PETERSEN, Marius Nygaard (1886–1953)
1. *Smith-Petersen Approach*: Anterior subperiosteal
approach to the hip. D. 1917.
2. *Smith-Petersen Nail*: One of the original devices for
internal fixation of femoral neck fractures. D. 1931.

3. *Smith-Petersen Cup*: Vitallium mould hip arthroplasty. D. 1939.

Born in Grimstad, Norway, where his family had owned a fleet of windjammers, he came to America at 17, speaking no English. His mother gave violin lessons to put him through university in Wisconsin; he became Cushing's★ registrar in Boston, and trained in orthopaedics at Massachusetts General, and from 1935 to 1946 was P. of Orthopaedic Surgery at Harvard. His work on mould arthroplasty started in 1918 when he saw a perfect foreign-body cyst in a boy's back from which he had removed a piece of glass; the idea of the trifin nail came to him during a sleepless overnight train journey.

SNELLEN, Hermann (1834–1908)
Snellen Chart: Eye-testing chart composed of test-types of varying size. D. 1862.

Ophthalmologist in Utrecht, Holland.

SOMOGYI, Michael (1883–1971)
Somogyi Units: Measure of serum amylase activity estimated by the Somogyi method. D. 1938.

Emeritus Biochemist, Jewish Hospital, St Louis, Missouri.

SONNE, Carl Olaf (1882–1948)
Sonne Dysentery: Bacterial dysentery due to *Shigella*★ *sonnei*. D. 1915.

Physician and bacteriologist in Copenhagen.

SOUTHEY, Reginald (1835–1899)
Southey's Tubes: Fine cannulae for draining subcutaneous fluid from the limbs in dropsy. D. 1877.

The son of the Physician-in-Ordinary to King George IV, he was born in Harley Street, educated at Westminster and Oxford, and studied medicine at Barts, then in Berlin, Prague and Vienna. He contracted TB and convalesced in South America, returning to become Assistant Physician at Barts (1865), and Full Physician in 1870. From 1883 to 1898 he was Commissioner in Lunacy. He had a lifelong fascination with watches and clocks.

SOUTTAR, Sir Henry Sessions (1875–1964)
Souttar's Tube: Silver tube passed down oesophagus

to relieve dysphagia in inoperable carcinoma of oesophagus. D. 1924.

Surgeon to The London Hospital.

SPENCER WELLS, Sir Thomas (1818–1897)
Spencer Wells Forceps: Self-retaining haemostat. D. 1879.

Born in St Albans, the son of a builder, he studied at Leeds General Infirmary, Trinity College, Dublin, and St Thomas's Hospital, London, qualifying MRCS in 1841, and FRCS by election in 1844. He did postgraduate study in Paris, accompanied the Marquis of Northampton to Egypt, and was a naval surgeon in Malta for 6 years, before settling in Brook Street, London, at first as an ophthalmologist. In 1854 he became obstetric surgeon to the Samaritan Hospital; he worked in Turkey during the Crimean War; and in 1858 he performed the first successful oophorectomy. He also resurrected the operation of splenectomy for trauma and for haemopoietic disease. He demanded absolute silence during operations. In 1882 he was elected President of the Royal College of Surgeons, and the following year was made a baronet. He became enormously successful and bought as his home Golders Hill Park, a famous house in Hampstead.

van der SPIEGEL, Adrian (1578–1625)
Spigelian (sic) Hernia: Hernia through the Spigelian fascia, or linea semilunaris: the aponeurosis between transversus and rectus abdominis.

P. of Anatomy and Surgery, Padua.

SPRENGEL, Otto Gerhard Karl (1852–1915)
Sprengel's Shoulder: Congenital elevation of the scapula. D. 1891.

Born in Dresden; he became Surgical Director of the Grossherzoliche Hospital, Brunswick.

STANFORD
Stanford–Binet Test: Stanford University, California psychologists' modification of the Binet–Simon Test to suit conditions in America.

STANNIUS, Herman Friedrich (1808–1883)
Stannius Ligature: Ligature isolating sinus venosus

from auricle in experimental preparation of frog's heart.

Physiologist at Rostock.

STARLING, Ernest Henry (1866–1927)
1. *Starling's Hypothesis*: Fluid transfer across a capillary wall depends on hydrostatic and osmotic pressures on either side, and the properties of the membrane.
2. *Starling's Law*: 'The Law of the Heart': The energy of cardiac contraction is proportional to the initial length of the cardiac muscle fibres. D. 1915.

Born in London, he studied at Guy's, eventually becoming Head of the Physiology Department there, and in 1899 Jodrell P. of Physiology at University College, London. Here he discovered secretin with W. M. Bayliss in 1902. In 1899 he was elected FRS, and won the Gold Medal in 1913. He was made CMG in 1918, and gave the Harveian★ Oration at the Royal College of Physicians in 1923. He died on board ship at Kingston, Jamaica.

STARR, Albert (b. 1926)
Starr Valve: Ball-and-socket prosthetic aortic valve. Designed with M. L. Edwards (b. 1906), hence sometimes known as Starr–Edwards valve.

Born in New York, he studied at Columbia U., and is now P. of Cardio-pulmonary Surgery, U. of Oregon Medical School, Portland, Oregon.

STEELL, Graham (1851–1942)
Graham Steell Murmur: Diastolic murmur at left sternal edge in pulmonary regurgitation. D. 1888.

Physician in Manchester.

STEIN, Irving F. (Sr) (b. 1887)
Stein–Leventhal Syndrome: Obesity, hirsutism, amenorrhoea and polycystic ovaries. D. 1935.

Gynaecologist in Chicago. His son Irving F. (Jr) is P. of Surgery at Northwestern U. Medical School, Chicago.

STEINDLER, Arthur (1878–1959)
Steindler Release: Operation for pes cavus. D. 1917.

P. of Orthopaedic Surgery, Iowa U. College of Medicine; President of the American Orthopaedic

Association in 1933. He also described a technique for wrist fusion and a regime for scoliosis treatment.

STEINMANN, Fritz (1872–1932)
Steinmann Pin: Stainless-steel pin for skeletal traction. D. 1907.

P. of Surgery, Bern, Switzerland.

STENSEN, Niels (1638–1686)
Stensen's Duct: Parotid duct. D. 1661.

Son of the Court Goldsmith to King Christian IV of Denmark, he was born in Copenhagen and studied there under Bartholin★ and in Leyden (where de Graaf★ was a fellow-student) under Sylvius★. As a student in Copenhagen he fought for the defence of the city when besieged by the King of Sweden. He described the parotid duct at 23, then travelled widely in Europe, studied the structure of biological tissues and of crystals, and is sometimes known as 'The Father of Geology'. In 1672 he was appointed P. of Anatomy in Copenhagen by King Christian V, and made many contributions to anatomy; he described Peyer's★ patches before Peyer and Fallot's★ tetralogy before Fallot. In 1667 he had become a Catholic and in 1674 abandoned his scientific work. In 1677 he was appointed Titular Bishop of Titiopolis by Pope Innocent XII (whose personal physician his close friend Malpighi★ later became). He spoke nine languages, and preached in three on a single day. He lived 9 years in Germany, proselytising and subjecting himself to great hardships, and died in Schwerin; he is buried in Florence. He was the great-uncle of Jacob Winslow★.

von STERNBERG, Karl (1872–1935)
Reed–Sternberg Cells: See *Reed*. D. 1898 (D. 1906 by Reed.)

Pathologist in Vienna.

STEVENS, Albert Mason (1884–1945)
Stevens–Johnson Syndrome: A form of bullous erythema multiforme sometimes associated with reaction to drugs. D. 1922.

New York paediatrician.

STIEDA, Alfred (1869–1945)
Pellegrini–Stieda Disease: See Pellegrini. D. 1908.

P. of Surgery, Königsberg.

STILL, Sir George Frederick (1868–1941)
Still's Disease: Juvenile polyarthritis with
splenomegaly and lymphadenopathy. D. 1896 (in his
MD thesis, while still a registrar).

The son of a customs surveyor, he obtained a First in
Classics at Cambridge, studied medicine at Guy's,
and was the greatest paediatrician of his day. He was
physician to King's College and Great Ormond Street
Hospitals, London, then P. of Paediatrics (the first
such post in Britain) at King's. In 1937 he was
knighted and made Physician to the King. He was
also Physician to Dr Barnardo's Homes and to the
Society for Waifs and Strays, though he himself never
married. He lived with his mother, and was a
sensitive poet and classical scholar.

STOKES, William (1804–1878)
1. *Stokes–Adams Attacks*: Syncope in complete heart
block.
2. *Cheyne–Stokes Respiration*: See *Cheyne*. D. 1854.
(D. 1818 by Cheyne.)

The son of a Dublin physician, who took him on
archaeological expeditions in the Irish hills, he studied
in Edinburgh and a year after qualifying, in 1815, he
obtained the MD and was elected Physician to the
Meath Hospital, Dublin, in place of his father, who
resigned. In 1840 he succeeded his father as Regius P.
of Physic. An enthusiastic art-lover, he insisted that
medical students should have a prior arts degree.
Stokes, together with Graves★, Cheyne★, Corrigan★,
Adams★ and Colles★ were leaders of the 'Dublin
School' of medicine in the early nineteenth century.

STOKES, Sir William (1839–1900)
Stokes–Gritti (or Gritti–Stokes) Operation: See *Gritti*.
D. 1868. (D. 1857 by Gritti.)

Dublin surgeon.

von STRÜMPELL, Ernst Adolf Gustav Gottfried
(1853–1925)
Marie–Strümpell Arthritis: See *Marie*. D. 1884. (D.
1898 by Marie.)

Born in Kurland, he spent his childhood in Estonia,
where his father was P. of Philosophy at Dorpat. An
accomplished violinist at the age of 6, he studied
psychology in Prague, then medicine in Dorpat
(under Stieda★) and Leipzig (under Thiersch★,

Crédé★ and Ludwig★). He became P. of Medicine
and Director of the polyclinic in Heidelberg in 1883,
then Chief of Internal Medicine in Erlangen (1886)
and Breslau (1903), and finally succeeded
Curschmann★ as P. of Internal Medicine at Leipzig.

STRUTHERS, Sir John (1823–1899)
Ligament of Struthers: Fibrous band, sometimes
ossified, on medial aspect of distal humerus. D. 1848.

Born in Dunfermline, Scotland, the son of a flax
merchant, he graduated from Edinburgh in 1845 and
from 1846 to 1863 was an extramural teacher there. In
1863 he became P. of Anatomy at Aberdeen, and
studied the anatomy of whales.

STURGE, William Allen (1850–1919)
Sturge–Weber Syndrome: Congenital angiomatosis of
leptomeninges, with port-wine stain of face. D. 1879.

London physician.

SUDECK, Paul Hermann Martin (1866–1945)
    1. *Sudeck's Atrophy*: Severe osteoporosis with
    stiffness and soft-tissue changes after fracture. D.
    1900.
    2. *Sudeck's Critical Point*: Site of anastomoses between
    lowest sigmoid branch of marginal artery and upper
    rectal branch of superior rectal artery, supplying the
    pelvic colon.

After studying in Tübingen, Kiel and Würzburg, he
became in 1923 P. of Surgery, Hamburg.

SULKOWITCH, Hirsh Wolf (b. 1906)
Sulkowitch Test: Test for urinary calcium in suspected
hyperparathyroidism, using Sulkowitch's reagent
(oxalic acid, ammonium oxalate, glacial acetic acid
and distilled water). D. 1937.

Urologist, Boston, USA.

SYDENHAM, Thomas (1624–1689)
Sydenham's Chorea: 'St Vitus' Dance'; a CNS disorder
which may occur after rheumatic fever. D. 1686.

He studied at Oxford, was a Captain in Cromwell's
army in the Civil War, and despite having only
studied medicine for a few months he was created
BM by the Chancellor of Oxford U., also a
parliamentarian. He later studied at Montpellier, then

set up in practice in London, becoming the most celebrated physician of his time; he was variously dubbed 'The Father of English Clinical Medicine', and 'The English Hippocrates'. He suffered from gout and gave one of the best descriptions of the condition (1683). 'It makes life worse than death', he wrote, 'and finally brings death as a relief.'

SYLVIUS, Franciscus (latinised version of François de la Böe) (1614–1672)
1. *Aqueduct of Sylvius*: The cerebral aqueduct connecting the third and fourth ventricles. D. 1660.
2. *Sylvian Fissure*: Lateral cerebral fissure, on the inferior and lateral surfaces of the hemisphere. D. 1660.

He was born in Frankfurt, and after travelling extensively in Europe, settled in Amsterdam, becoming in 1658 P. of Practical Medicine in Leyden, where he died. De Graaf★ and Stensen★ were among his students there. The Aqueduct and Fissure had both been described 20 years earlier in a publication edited by Caspar Bartholin★; the Aqueduct is sometimes ascribed to Jacobus Sylvius (Jacques Dubois) (1478–1555), a French anatomist and teacher of Vesalius★.

SYME, James (1799–1870)
Syme's Amputation: Through distal tibia, immediately proximal to the joint. D. 1842 as an alternative to below-knee amputation.

The son of a lawyer, he was born in Edinburgh and studied there, being appointed Superintendent of the local fever hospital in 1820, while still a medical student; he qualified MRCS in 1821. At about this time he discovered the process of waterproofing fabrics by treatment with india-rubber dissolved in naphtha, which was patented in 1823 by Macintosh★. At first he assisted his cousin Robert Liston (1794–1847) in running an anatomy school and in private surgical practice, until they fell out and Syme opened his own private hospital, Minto House. His teaching was so successful that the envious Edinburgh Royal Infirmary refused his application to join its staff. He eventually succeeded James Russell as P. of Surgery at Edinburgh, but only after agreeing to pay him a pension to persuade him to retire, at 81. He then succeeded Liston (who had just performed the first operation under anaesthesia outside America) as P. of Surgery at UCH in London, but after a few months returned to Edinburgh, where Joseph Lister★ became, successively, his dresser, his assistant and finally his son-in-law, and Syme was one of the first to adopt antisepsis (in 1868) (as he had been one of the first to make use of anaesthesia, in 1847).

SYMMERS, Douglas (1879–1952)
Brill–Symmers Disease: See *Brill*. D. 1927. (D. 1925 by Brill.)

American physician.

T

TAKAYASHU, Mikito (1860–1938)
Takayashu's 'Pulseless' Disease: An obliterative arteritis affecting especially the carotid and subclavian arteries of young Asiatic women. D. 1908.

Japanese surgeon who studied in Tokyo, Breslau, and St Thomas's Hospital, London, taking the Conjoint in 1896. He later became P. of Ophthalmology at the Medical College, Kanazawa, Japan.

TANNER, Norman Cecil (C)
Tanner Slide: Relaxing incision in rectus sheath for inguinal herniorrhaphy.

He studied at Bristol (MB 1929), won the Markham–Skerritt Prize in Bristol in 1943, the Jacksonian Prize of the Royal College of Surgeons in 1948, and was Hunterian★ Professor in 1960. In 1954 he was visiting P. of Surgery at Ein Shamus U., Cairo, and in 1960 at the Royal North Shore Hospital, Sydney, and is now Honorary Consulting Surgeon to the Charing Cross and St James's Hospitals, London.

TAWARA, Sunao (1873–1952)
Node of Tawara: Atrioventricular node. D. 1906 (also called Aschoff's★ Node).

Japanese pathologist.

TAY, Warren (1843–1927)
Tay–Sachs Disease: Amaurotic familial idiocy; excessive ganglioside deposition leading to mental and physical deterioration, described amongst Jewish children in New York. D. 1881. (D. 1887 by Sachs.)

London ophthalmologist.

TAYLOR, Charles Fayette (1827–1899)
  Taylor Brace: Orthosis for spinal tuberculosis (Pott's★
  Disease).

New York surgeon.

THIERSCH, Karl (1822–1895)
  1. *Thiersch Graft*: Split-thickness skin graft. D. 1874.
  2. *Thiersch Operation*: Silver wire suture to retain
  rectal prolapse.

Born in Munich, he studied in Berlin, Paris, Vienna
and Munich, and became P. of Surgery at Erlangen,
then in Leipzig (1857–1885). In 1870 he was an Army
Surgeon in the Franco-Prussian War.

THOMAS, Hugh Owen (1834–1891)
  1. *Thomas Splint*: Metal resting splint for the
  treatment of femoral shaft fractures. D. 1875.
  2. *Thomas's Test*: For fixed flexion deformity of hip,
  by flexion of sound hip after eliminating lumbar
  lordosis.
  3. *Thomas's Test of Function*: Progressively increasing
  mobilisation during recovery from infective joint
  disease.
  4. *Thomas's Wrench*: Instrument for forcible
  correction of foot deformity.

'The Father of Orthopaedic Surgery' came from a
long line of Anglesey bone-setters; he was born there
and brought up in the country on account of his
delicate health. He studied medicine at Edinburgh
and University College, London, qualifying MRCS
in 1857. He set up as a bone-setter in Liverpool, but
never held a hospital appointment. He was renowned
for his treatment of joint disease by rest – 'enforced,
uninterrupted, and prolonged' – the splint having
been intended originally to rest a tuberculous knee.
He offered his splint to the French Army in the 1870s
but was refused; his nephew by marriage, and great
disciple, Robert Jones★ popularised its use in the
First World War, thereby reducing the mortality
of a compound femoral fracture from 80% in
1916 to 7.3% in 1918. A brilliant and original man,
Thomas was, however, intolerant in manner and
polemical in his writings; a chain-smoker, he always
had a naval 2nd mate's discharge cap tilted down
over a deformed eyelid, the result of an accident as a
student.

THOMPSON, Frederick R. (C)
Thompson's Prosthesis: Vitallium hip
hemiarthroplasty. D. 1952.

Director of Orthopaedic Surgery, St Luke's Hospital,
New York.

TIETZE, Alexander (1864–1927)
Tietze's Disease: Costo-chondritis of the
costo-chondral junction. D. 1921.

Chief Surgeon, Allerheiligen Hospital, Breslau.

TILLAUX, Paul Jules (1834–1904)
Tillaux Fracture: Involving distal tibial articular
surface, the fracture-line running up to the lateral
cortex. D. 1890. (D. 1822 by Astley Cooper★ and
1872 by Gosselin★.)

P. of Surgery, U. of Paris (at the same time as
Guyon★ was P. of Surgical Pathology). His fracture
was originally drawn on a piece of paper and found
and published after his death by Chaput★.

TINEL, Jules (1879–1952)
Tinel Test: Distal tingling on percussion of divided
nerve ends indicates the presence of regenerating
axons. D. 1915.

A fifth-generation doctor, his father was P. of
Anatomy at Rouen, where Tinel was born. He
studied in Paris, wrote a large book on the autonomic
nervous system, and constructed medical apparatus
out of Meccano. He became Physician and
Neurologist to the Hôpital Beaujou in Paris, and gave
the first account of paroxysmal hypertension in
phaeochromocytoma. A brave Resistance fighter
during the Second World War, his family were
interned by the Germans, and one son was executed
by the Gestapo.

TISELIUS, Arne Wilhelm Kaurin (1902–1971)
Tiselius Apparatus: For protein electrophoresis. D.
1930 in his doctoral thesis.

Born in Stockholm, of a family of scientists and
biologists, he studied physical chemistry at the U. of
Uppsala, and was a Rockefeller Fellow at Princeton in
1934–1935. In 1938 he was appointed to a personal
Chair of Biochemistry at Uppsala, and in 1947
became Vice-President of the Nobel★ Foundation,

winning the 1948 Nobel Chemistry Prize. He was a foreign FRS, and a great naturalist and ornithologist. He died of a coronary in Stockholm at a scientific meeting.

TODD, Robert Bentley (1809–1860)
Todd's Paralysis: Transient post-ictal paralysis. D. 1856.

Born in Ireland, he became a noted London physician, and close friend of Thomas Addison★. The mental strain of appearing for the prosecution in the famous murder trial of Thomas Smethurst, MB, contributed to his sudden death at 50, after travelling to Vevey in Switzerland to recuperate. Depression and alcohol also played a part, however, as confirmed by the cirrhosis found at his own post-mortem, and his enthusiastic teaching to medical students of alcohol as a panacea.

TOLDT, Karl (1840–1920)
Fascia of Toldt: Fascial layer behind body of pancreas.

Born in Brunneck in the Austrian Tyrol, he became P. of Anatomy in Prague, and later in Vienna, where he died.

TOOTH, Howard Henry (1856–1926)
Charcot–Marie–Tooth Disease: See *Charcot*. D. 1886.

London physician and neurologist. He described the disease later in the same year, but independently of Charcot and Marie, in his Cambridge MD thesis.

TOREK Franz (1861–1938)
Keetley–Torek Operation: See *Keetley*. D. 1931.

Surgeon to Lenox Hill Hospital, New York. In 1913 he reported the first successful resection of the thoracic oesophagus for carcinoma.

TOUTON, Karl (b. 1858)
Touton Giant Cell: Large lipoid-containing multinucleate cells in xanthoma and histiocytosis X.

German dermatologist.

TREITZ, Wenzel (1819–1872)
Ligament of Treitz: Suspensory ligament of the duodenum. D. 1853.

Austrian physician, born in Bohemia, who became P.

of Pathological Anatomy in Cracow and then P. of
Pathology in Prague, where he died.

TRENAUNAY, Paul (b. 1875)
Klippel–Trenaunay Syndrome: See *Klippel*.

Paris physician.

TRENDELENBURG, Friedrich (1844–1924)
1. *Trendelenburg Position*: Head–down operating
position. D. 1890.
2. *Trendelenburg Operation (1)*: Emergency
pulmonary embolectomy. D. 1908. (His original
three cases all died).
3. *Trendelenburg Operation (2)*: Ligation of venous
tributaries at fossa ovalis. D. 1890. (D. 1846 by
Brodie★.)
4. *Brodie–Trendelenburg Test*: See *Brodie*. D. 1890. (D.
1846 by Brodie.)
5. *Trendelenburg Test*: For effectiveness of hip
abductor mechanism. D. 1895.
6. *Trendelenburg Gait*: Dipping gait in the absence of
effective hip abductors.

He studied in Glasgow and Berlin (MD 1866); was
Langenbeck's★ Assistant from 1868 to 1874, and was
then P. of Surgery successively at Rostock, Bonn and
Leipzig (where Wilms★ was his Assistant). A noted
medical historian, he was also a pioneer of
endotracheal anaesthesia with tracheotomy (1869).
Kirschner★ was one of his pupils, and demonstrated a
successful case of pulmonary embolectomy to him at
the age of 80, just before he died, of cancer of the jaw.

TRETHOWAN, W. H. (1882–1934)
Trethowan's Line: Drawn along the upper border of
the femoral neck on a hip radiograph: it normally
enters the head, but fails to do so in the case of a
slipped upper femoral epiphysis.

He studied at Guy's, and in 1912 became its first
orthopaedic surgeon. In the First World War he
worked at Shepherd's Bush with Robert Jones★, and
afterwards was on the staffs of the Royal National
Orthopaedic Hospital, and Queen Mary's Children's
Hospital, Carshalton. He had one of the largest
private practices in London, wrote little, but was an
enthusiastic organ-player, and had an organ installed
in the billiard-room of his Hampstead house.

TREVES, Sir Frederick (1853–1923)
Bloodless Fold of Treves: The ileo–caecal fold. D. 1885.
(An intestinal clamp also bears his name.)

He was born in Dorchester, and studied at and was
Demonstrator in Anatomy to the London Hospital
from 1881 to 1884, when he was appointed Surgeon.
He served in the Boer War, and on June 24th 1902,
with Lord Lister★, he operated on King Edward VII
in the Buhl Room at Buckingham Palace for an
appendix abscess, 2 days before the Coronation was
due; it was delayed for 6 weeks. Tragically, though,
his daughter died of a perforated appendix. He wrote
a description of the case of John Merrick, who had
neurofibromatosis and became referred to as 'The
Elephant Man': this has recently formed the basis of a
successful play and film. He was also an expert
seaman and master mariner: his surgical practice
became so successful he retired at 55. He died of
peritonitis.

TROISIER, Charles Émile (1844–1919)
Troisier's Sign: Enlargement of Troisier's node
(supraclavicular lymph-node) in gastric malignancy.
D. 1886.

P. of Pathology, Paris.

TROLARD, Paulin (1842–1910)
Vein of Trolard: Intracerebral vein. D. 1868.

Paris physician who described the vein in his thesis.

TROUSSEAU, Armand (1801–1867)
1. *Trousseau's Sign (1)*: Spontaneous
thrombophlebitis migrans as a sign of visceral cancer.
(He noted this sign in himself as confirmation of his
suspicion of his own gastric carcinoma.)
2. *Trousseau's Sign (2)*: 'Main d'accoucheur'
(carpopedal spasm) in response to tourniquet-induced
ischaemia in hypocalcaemic tetany. D. 1862.

Physician to the Hôpital Necker, Hôpital St Antoine
and the Hôtel-Dieu, Paris. A compelling teacher, his
lectures prompted Lasègue★ to change his studies
from philosophy to medicine. He coined the term
'aphasia', wrote a classic thesis on laryngology, and
gave an early description of haemochromatosis
(1865).

TUBBS, Oswald Sydney (C)
Tubbs Dilator: Adjustable transventricular mitral valve dilator.

He studied at Cambridge and at Barts (MB 1932), was Hunterian★ Professor of the Royal College of Surgeons in 1943, President of the Thoracic Society, and of the Society of Thoracic Surgeons of Great Britain, and Consultant Cardiothoracic Surgeon to Barts and the Brompton Hospital, London. He is now retired in Essex.

TURNER, George Grey (1877–1951)
Grey Turner's Sign: Skin discolouration in the loin in acute haemorrhagic pancreatitis. D. 1920.

He was Surgeon to the Royal Victoria Infirmary, Newcastle-on-Tyne for 30 years, and then the first Director of Surgery at the Postgraduate Medical School, London.

TURNER, Henry Hubert (b. 1892)
Turner's Syndrome: Infantilism, gonadal agenesis, webbed neck and cubitus valgus, with XO genotype. D. 1938. (A clinical description had been given by Morgagni★ in 1768.)

Clinical P. of Medicine, Oklahoma U., USA.

TWORT, Frederick William (1877–1950)
Twort d'Herelle Phenomenon: Bacteriophage activity; transmissible bacterial lysis. D. 1915. (D. 1917 by d'Herelle.)

Born in Camberley, Surrey, the son of a doctor, he qualified at St Thomas's in 1900, and became clinical assistant there, and in 1902 became Demonstrator in Bacteriology at The London Hospital. In 1909 he became Superintendent of the Brown Institution, an animal dispensary, and was the first to cultivate the causative organism of Johne's★ Disease of cattle. Elected FRS in 1929, he was almost obsessive in his disapproval of the 'nationalisation' of scientific research.

TYNDALL, John (1820–1893)
1. *Tyndall's Light*: Light reflected or dispersed by particles suspended in a gas or liquid.
2. *Tyndallisation*: Fractional sterilisation. D. 1877.

Born at Leighlin Bridge, Co. Carlow, Ireland, he worked in the Ordnance Survey, taught mathematics at Queenswood College in 1847, and in 1848 studied chemistry under Bunsen★ at Marburg. After further study in Berlin he returned to England in 1851, was elected FRS the following year, and was awarded the Royal Society's Rumford Medal in 1864. In 1853 he became P. of Natural Philosophy at the Royal Institution and succeeded Michael Faraday as Superintendent in 1867, a post he held for 20 years. He was one of the first to climb the Matterhorn, and also experimentally confirmed Pasteur's★ findings of the impossibility of spontaneous generation. He wrote of *Penicillium* in 1877, 52 years before Sir Alexander Fleming's discovery of the mould's antibiotic properties. His experiments on heat sterilisation were performed in the Royal Institution and in the Joddrell Laboratories in the Royal Gardens at Kew. He died of accidental poisoning and is buried in Haslemere.

TYSON, Edward (1651–1708)
Tyson's Glands: Bilateral sebaceous glands on either side of the fraenum which secrete smegma, and may become infected in gonorrhoea.

Born in Bristol, he studied at both Oxford and Cambridge, becoming Master of Anatomy at the Barber-Surgeons Company of London. He was a great classical scholar and bibliophile, and died in London.

V

VALSALVA, Antonio Maria (1666–1723)
Valsalva's Manoeuvre: Forced expiration against a closed glottis which raises intra–abdominal pressure, produces discharge in the auditory canal in cases of chronic otitis media. D. 1704.

Born in Imola, Italy, he studied in Bologna, graduating in 1687, and succeeded his teacher Malpighi★ as P. of Anatomy there. He performed hundreds of dissections of the ear, was the first to divide it into external, middle, and internal parts, and named the Eustachian★ tube. Morgagni★ was among his students. He died in Bologna.

VAN DEN BERGH, A. A. Hijmans (1869–1943)
Van Den Bergh Reaction: Test for bilirubin by

comparison of normal with test diazotised serum or plasma. D. 1913.

Physician in Utrecht, Holland.

VAN DE GRAAFF, Robert Jemison (1901–1967)
Van de Graaff Generator: High-voltage electrostatic generator.

Born in Tuscaloosa, Alabama, he studied engineering at the U. of Alabama and worked for the Alabama Power Company, before studying at the Sorbonne in Paris, where Marie Curie's★ lectures stimulated his interest in atomic physics. He was in Oxford as a Rhodes Scholar in 1925–1928, and at Princeton, New Jersey in 1929–1931, then at the Massachusetts Institute of Technology, where he developed a 2-megavolt generator. After the Second World War he was Director of the High Voltage Energy Corporation.

VAQUEZ, Louis Henri (1860–1936)
Osler–Vaquez Disease: See *Osler*.

Paris physician; he was one of the first to make the clinical diagnosis of a phaeochromocytoma (1926).

VEILLON, Adrien (1864–1931)
Veillonella: Genus of anaerobic cocci found as gut and respiratory tract commensals.

Bacteriologist in Paris.

VELPEAU, Alfred-Armand-Louis Marie (1795–1867)
Velpeau's Bandage: Supporting bandage. D. 1839.

P. of Clinical Surgery, Paris, and surgeon to Hôpital de la Charité. The bandage was originally introduced for the treatment of fractures of the clavicle. Velpeau also wrote a standard work on diseases of the breast.

VENABLE, Charles Scott (b. 1877)
Venable Plates and Screws: Implants for internal fixation of fractures.

Surgeon, San Antonio, Texas. He introduced Vitallium to orthopaedics in 1937 to avoid the effects of electrolysis on bone when other metals were used.

VERBRUGGE, Jean (1896–1964)
Verbrugge Clamp: Bone-holding clamp.

Born in Belgium, he worked in a field hospital in France in the First World War, and qualified in Brussels in 1921, having spent some months at Barts in London as a medical student. He then worked at the Mayo★ Clinic, and with Putti★ in Bologna and Leriche★ in Strasbourg, before settling in Antwerp as an orthopaedic surgeon. He was President of the Belgian Orthopaedic Society in 1939/1940 and 1962, and P. of Orthopaedics and Physiotherapy in Ghent from 1946. He was also an Olympic fencer, and played the violin in a chamber orchestra.

VESALIUS, Andreas (1514–1564)
1. *Foramen of Vesalius*: Small inconstant opening in the greater wing of the sphenoid, medial and anterior to the foramen ovale, which transmits a vein which connects the veins of the face with the cavernous sinus. D. 1543.
2. *Os Vesalii*: Accessory ossicle at the base of the 5th metatarsal.

Born in Brussels, the son of the Apothecary to Emperor Maximilian and his English wife, he studied philosophy at Louvain and medicine in Montpellier and Paris. Becoming bored with the texts of Galen★, he went to North Italy, as more dissection was being done there, and performed dissections in Bologna, Pisa, Padua, and then Basle. His researches undermined many long-established teachings of Galen and Aristotle. From 1535 to 1542 he was P. of Anatomy at Padua, and later held the same Chair in Bologna and Pisa. Fallopio★ was his favourite pupil. In 1543, at the age of 29, he published in Basle *De Humani Corporis Fabrica*, a landmark in the history of science, and one of the great books of all time. The following year he became Court Physician in Madrid, and was physician to Charles V and Philip II of Spain, and Surgeon to the Army of Charles V. Convicted by the Inquisition for post-mortem work, he was condemned to a pilgrimage to the Holy Land, and fell ill on the return voyage, being put ashore on the Island of Zante, in Greece, where he died. He was buried there by a goldsmith who erected his tomb.

VICQ d'AZYR, Felix (1748–1794)
Bundle of Vicq d'Azyr: Mamillo-thalamic tract in brain. D. 1781.

Physician and comparative anatomist in Paris. He was Secretary to the Académie de Medicine and the

French Academy (succeeding Buffon), and also
Physician to the Queen.

VIDUS VIDIUS
Vidian Canal: See *Guido Guidi*.

VINCENT, Jean-Hyacinthe (1862–1950)
Vincent's Angina: Brawny swelling due to acute
infection of face with *Borrelia*★ *vincentii* organisms in
symbiosis with *Fusiformis fusiformis*. D. 1898.

Born in Bordeaux, he was a brilliant student there
and in Paris, and in 1897 became P. of Forensic
Medicine, and in 1901, P. of Bacteriology and
Epidemiology, at the Val-de-Grâce Military
Hospital, Paris. He set up bacteriological laboratories
in Marseilles and Algiers, and was a pioneer of
anti-typhoid vaccination during the First World War.
He became a general in 1917, and retired from the
Army in 1924, becoming *ad hominem* P. at the Collège
de France in 1925. He was awarded the highest
French civil and military honours on his death-bed:
the Lègion d'Honneur, and the Medaille Militaire.

VINSON, Porter Paisley (1890–1959)
Paterson–Brown Kelly–Plummer–Vinson Syndrome: See
Paterson: D. 1919. (D. 1912 by Plummer; 1919 by
Paterson and Kelly.)

Surgeon to the Mayo★ Clinic.

VIRCHOW, Rudolf Ludwig Karl (1821–1902)
1. *Virchow's Node*: Enlarged supraclavicular
lymph-node containing tumour tissue. D. 1860.
2. *Virchow's Triad*: The factors predisposing to
vascular thrombosis: changes in the vessel wall, in the
local pattern of blood flow, and in the constituents of
the blood. D. 1856.

Born in Schievelbein in Pomerania, he studied in
Berlin under Müller★, and Schönlein★; among his
fellow students were Henle★, Schwann★ and von
Helmholtz★. At 26, after having had two papers
rejected for publication, he founded his own journal:
*Archives for Pathological Anatomy and Physiology and
Clinical Medicine* (called *Virchow's Archiv* after his
death). He was politically active during the 1848
revolution in Germany and was dismissed from his
post at the Charité Hospital in Berlin because of
allegations of agitation among the work-force. He

became P. of Pathological Anatomy at Würzburg, and there laid down the basis of the cellular theory. In 1856 he became P. of Pathological Anatomy in Berlin and became one of Europe's leading medical scientists; he gave the first description of leukaemia, described the first bone cyst (1877) and described rickets as a nutritional disorder (though the priority for this is due to Broca★). In later life he opposed Bismarck as an enthusiastic liberal politician: always an impetuous man, he died at 81 after breaking his hip jumping off a moving tram.

VOGES, Otto (b. 1867)
Voges–Proskauer Reaction: Test for acetyl-methyl carbinol to distinguish *E. coli* from typhoid group of organisms. D. 1898.

Physician in Berlin.

VOLKMANN, Alfred Wilhelm (1800–1877)
Volkmann's Canals: Blood vessels passing into bone from periosteum. D. (by his son, though discovered by A. W. Volkmann) 1863.

Born in Leipzig, he became P. of Physiology and Anatomy in Dorpat, then in Halle, where he died. His son was Richard von Volkmann★.

von VOLKMANN, Richard (1830–1889)
1. *Volkmann's Contracture*: Ischaemic contracture of forearm flexor musculature. D. 1872.
2. *Volkmann's Spoon*: Double-ended curette, originally designed for curetting tuberculous abscesses.

He studied in Berlin (MD 1854), became P. of Surgery at Halle at 26, and introduced Listerian★ antisepsis, of which he was a strong proponent. At his operations the wound was irrigated with carbolic solution poured by assistants from watering-cans. In 1878 he performed the first excision of the rectum for cancer. Under the pseudonym Richard Leander, he also wrote poems and fairy stories.

W

WALDENSTRÖM, Jan (b. 1906)
Waldenström's Syndrome: Chronic macroglobulinaemia with purpura. D. 1948.

Swedish physician.

WALDENSTRÖM, Johann Henning (b. 1877)
Calvé–Legg–Perthes–Waldenström Disease: See *Perthes*.
D. 1920. (D. 1910 by Calvé, Legg and Perthes.)

Orthopaedic surgeon, Stockholm.

von WALDEYER-HARTZ, Heinrich Wilhelm
Gottfried (1836–1921)
1. *Waldeyer's Ring*: Tonsillar ring of adenoid tissue
comprising the lymphatic drainage of the neck. D.
1884.
2. *Waldeyer's Fascia*: Fascia of the rectum. D. 1899.

Born in Hehlen, he became P. of Pathological
Anatomy in Breslau (where Weigert★ was his
Assistant), P. of Anatomy in Strasbourg, then
Director of the Anatomical Institute in Berlin, where
he died. He did much research on embryology and
the sex glands, and named the basic cell of the central
nervous system, the neuron, enunciating the neuron
theory in 1891.

WALLACE, Alexander Burns, CBE (b. 1903)
Wallace's Rule of Nines: Guide to aid estimation of
proportion of body surface affected by burns. D.
1950.

He studied in Edinburgh and McGill U., Montreal,
was demonstrator in Surgery at McGill, and
subsequently Plastic Surgeon to the Royal Edinburgh
Sick Children's Hospital, and Reader in Plastic
Surgery, U. of Edinburgh.

WALLER, Augustus Volney (1816–1870)
Wallerian Degeneration: Pathological change
undergone by severed peripheral nerves. D. 1850.

Born on a farm in Kent, he spent his childhood in the
South of France, then returned to England at 14, but
studied medicine in Paris (MD 1840), and again
returned thereafter to practise in Kensington from
1842 to 1851. He studied degeneration in the severed
nerves of frog's tongues, and eventually gave up
medical practice in favour of physiology, working in
Bonn and Paris. In 1856 he developed rheumatic
fever, retired to Switzerland, and died in Geneva of a
coronary.

WANGENSTEEN, Owen Harding (1898–1980)
Wangensteen Tube: Naso-gastric tube under suction.
D. 1932.

Born in Lake Park, Minnesota, he studied at the U. of Minnesota, and from 1927 to 1928 was Assistant P. at de Quervain's★ Surgical Clinic in Bern, Switzerland. Prior to his death he was Emeritus Regent's P. of Surgery at the U. of Minnesota Medical Centre, Minneapolis, and Director of Surgery at the U. Hospital, with honorary doctorates from Paris and Athens.

WARTHIN, Aldred Scott (1866–1931)
Warthin's Tumour: Adenolymphoma of the parotid. D. 1929.

Born in Indiana, he became P. of Pathology, U. of Michigan.

WARFARIN
Warfarin: A coumarin derivative oral anticoagulant, named for the *W*isconsin *A*lumni *R*esearch *F*oundation, where it was developed.

von WASSERMANN, August Paul (1866–1925)
Wassermann Reaction: Complement-fixation test for the diagnosis of syphilis. D. 1906.

Born in Bamberg, Bavaria (also the birth-place of Schönlein★), he studied in Strasbourg and Vienna, was a pupil of Robert Koch★ in Berlin, and worked at his Institute, becoming in 1907 Director of the Department of Therapeutics and Serum Research at the U. of Berlin, and in 1913 Director of the Kaiser Wilhelm Institute for Experimental Therapy, Berlin. He was made a noble in 1910.

WATERHOUSE, Rupert (1873–1958)
Waterhouse–Friderichsen Syndrome: Bilateral adrenal cortical haemorrhages in meningococcal septicaemia. D. 1911. (D. 1918 by Friderichsen, and in 1901 by Sir Ernest Gordon Graham Little, a London physician (b. 1867).)

Physician to the Royal United Hospital, Bath.

WATSON-JONES, Sir Reginald (1902–1972)
Watson-Jones Bone Levers and other orthopaedic instruments.

He trained at Liverpool, where on the advice of Robert Jones★ he was put in charge of the new

Orthopaedic Department and Fracture Clinic at the
Liverpool Royal Infirmary, at the age of 24. In 1928
he was appointed to the County Orthopaedic
Hospital at Gobowen, Oswestry, where he trained
numerous orthopaedic surgeons and wrote a classic
text on fracture treatment. He was Civilian
Consultant in Orthopaedic Surgery to the RAF in the
Second World War, was on the Council of the Royal
College of Surgeons from 1943 to 1959, and its
Vice-President from 1952 to 1954. He was President
of the British Orthopaedic Association in 1952, and
Editor of the British edition of the *Journal of Bone and
Joint Surgery*, from its inception in 1948 until his
death. He was Orthopaedic Surgeon to King George
VI and Queen Elizabeth II, and was knighted in 1945.

WEBER, Frederick Parkes (1863–1962)
  1. *Osler–Rendu–Weber Syndrome*: See *Osler*. D. 1907.
  2. *Sturge–Weber Syndrome*: See *Sturge*. D. 1922. (D.
  1879 by Sturge.) Also called Weber–Dmitri Disease.

London physician.

WEBER, Friedrich Eugen (1832–1891)
  Weber Test: Hearing test in which a middle-C tuning
  fork is placed on the forehead: if the vibration is
  perceived in the middle the test is negative.

German otologist. (The test is also ascribed to Ernst
Heinrich Weber (1795–1878), P. of Anatomy and
Physiology at Leipzig.)

WEEKS, John Elmer (1853–1949)
  Koch–Weeks Bacillus: See *Koch*. D. 1886.

New York ophthalmologist.

WEGENER, F. (C)
  Wegener's Granulomatosis: Acute midline necrotising
  granulomas related to periarteritis nodosa. D. 1936.
  (Also called Klinger's Disease.)

German pathologist.

WEIGERT, Karl (1845–1904)
  Weigert's Stain: He described numerous stains, for
  bacteria, nuclei, and various specialised tissues
  (notably myelin), and introduced haematoxylin in
  1904.

Born in Muensterberg, Silesia, a cousin of Paul
Ehrlich★, he studied medicine in Breslau, Berlin and
Vienna. His teachers included Haidenhain★ and
Waldeyer★, and he became Assistant to the latter in
Breslau in 1868. He was a military surgeon during the
Franco-Prussian War (1870–1871), then worked as
pathologist in Breslau (as Assistant to Cohnheim),
Leipzig (as Professor) and Frankfurt (as Chief of
Pathology at the Senckenberg Institute for
Pathological Anatomy) from 1885 to 1904, where he
worked with Ehrlich★ and Edinger★. A patient,
honest, and hard-working man, he discouraged
visitors, never achieved his ambition of becoming
Ordinarius, or Full Professor, and died suddenly of a
coronary.

WEIL, Edmund (1880–1922)
Weil–Felix Reaction: Agglutination of *Proteus* bacteria
by serum from patients with typhus, due to presence
of a shared antigen. D. 1916.

Viennese physician who worked in Prague.

WEIL, H. Adolph (1848–1916)
Weil's Disease: Leptospirosis icterohaemorrhagiae. D.
1886.

Born in Heidelberg, he became Director of the
Medical Clinic at Dorpat, Estonia, and also practised
at Wiesbaden and other spas, as he himself had
developed TB of the larynx. He retired to Italy.

WEISS, Konrad (1898–1942)
Mallory–Weiss Syndrome: See *Mallory*.

American physician (internal medicine).

WEITBRECHT, Josias (1702–1747)
Ligament of Weitbrecht: Oblique radio-ulnar ligament.

Born in Schorndorf, Germany, he became Prosector
of Anatomy in 1725, and subsequently P. of
Anatomy, in St Petersburg, Russia, where he died.

WELCH, William Henry (1850–1934)
Clostridium welchii: Bacterial species causing gas
gangrene. D. 1892.

A fourth-generation doctor born in Norfolk,
Connecticut, he studied at Yale, New York and in
Europe (in Strasbourg, Breslau, Berlin and Leipzig),

and in 1879 became P. of Pathology at Bellevue Medical College, New York. In 1884 he became P. of Pathology at Johns Hopkins Hospital, Baltimore, and in 1893 Dean of the newly opened Medical School there. In 1916 he became Director of the School of Hygiene and Public Health in Baltimore, and in 1926 P. of the History of Medicine at Johns Hopkins U., and he travelled through Europe collecting old medical books. He described a method of performing a post-mortem by eviscerating the abdomen *per rectum* to avoid mutilation of the cadaver with incisions.

WENCKEBACH, Marel Frederik (1864–1940)
Wenckebach Phenomenon: Progressive lengthening of the P–R interval of the ECG in second–degree atrioventricular block until the P wave occurs without a ventricular response.

Dutch–born physician who practised in Vienna.

WERNICKE, Karl (1848–1904)
Wernicke's Encephalopathy: Mental deterioration in thiamine deficiency. D. 1875.

Born in Tarnowitz, Upper Silesia, the son of a civil servant, he studied in Breslau, then under Meynert★ in Vienna, and then became Assistant to Westphal★ in Berlin. He continued there as a private psychiatrist and neurologist, then becoming P. of Neurology and Psychiatry in Breslau, then Halle. He was killed in an accident riding his bicycle through the forest in Thuringia.

WERTHEIM, Ernst (1864–1920)
Wertheim's Operation: Radical hysterectomy. D. 1900.

He studied in Graz and Vienna, and became Assistant in Gynaecology in Prague. He was then Director of the gynaecological and obstetrical clinic in Vienna, and became world-famous for his operations for uterine cancer. He was the first to show the importance of gonococcal disease in women.

WESTERGREN, Alf (b. 1891)
Westergren Method: For estimating erythrocyte sedimentation rate. D. 1921.

Swedish physician.

WESTPHAL, Karl Friedrich Otto (1833–1890)
Edinger–Westphal Nucleus: See *Edinger*. D. 1885.

Born in Berlin, he practised there as neurologist

and psychiatrist, becoming Director of the Brain Institute, then P. of Psychiatry. Wernicke* was his Assistant. He died in Berlin; his son Alexander Karl Otto Westphal (1863–1941) was also a neurologist and psychiatrist, and was P. of Neurology in Heidelberg, then Berlin.

WETZEL, Norman Carl (b. 1897)
Wetzel's Grid: Chart for the evaluation of physical fitness, in terms of physique, development and basal metabolic rate. D. 1941.

Paediatrician, Cleveland, Ohio.

WHARTON, Thomas (1614–1673)
1. *Wharton's Duct*: Duct of the submandibular salivary gland.
2. *Wharton's Jelly*: Intercellular material of the umbilical cord. D. 1656.

Born in Winston-on-Tees, Co. Durham, he studied at Pembroke College, Oxford, and Trinity College, Cambridge, and was granted an MD in Oxford by General Fairfax in 1647. He was tutor to the illegitimate son of the Duke of Sutherland, was elected FRCP in 1650, and in 1657 became Physician to St Thomas's Hospital, London. With his friend Francis Glisson* he remained in London during the Plague. A skilled anatomist, he named the thyroid gland: his own name is mentioned by his friend Izaak Walton in *The Compleat Angler*. He died in Aldersgate, in the City of London.

WHEATSTONE, Sir Charles (1802–1875)
Wheatstone Bridge: Electrical apparatus for the accurate measurement of resistance.

Born near Gloucester, he became P. of Experimental Physics at King's College, London, at the age of 32, and 2 years later was elected FRS. He disliked lecturing, but investigated acoustics, binocular vision, and wave form and resonance, and took out a patent to develop the electric telegraph commercially.

WHIPPLE, Alan Oldfather (1881–1963)
1. *Whipple's Operation*: Radical pancreatico-duodenectomy. D. 1935.
2. *Whipple's Triad* (Diagnostic of insulinoma of the pancreas): (1) Hypoglycaemic attacks in fasting state;

(2) Blood sugar below 45 mg/100 ml; (3) Symptoms relieved by glucose. D. 1935.

P. of Surgery, Columbia U., New York.

WHIPPLE, George Hoyt (1878–1976)
Whipple's Disease: Intestinal lipodystrophy. D. 1907.

The son and grandson of New England country doctors, he studied at Yale, where he was a keen athlete; to support himself through medical school at Johns Hopkins he taught at a military academy and worked on lake steamers in New Hampshire. He became Lecturer, then Associate P. of Pathology (1914) at Johns Hopkins, then in 1920 P. of Research Medicine at the U. of California Medical School, and in 1921 P. of Pathology and Dean of the Medical School at Rochester, New York. He shared the 1934 Nobel★ Prize with G. R. Minot and W. P. Murphy of Harvard, for discoveries of the value of liver treatment in anaemia. He coined the term 'thalassaemia' for Mediterranean anaemia (also called Cooley's★ anaemia).

WHITE, Paul Dudley (1886–1973)
Wolff–Parkinson–White Syndrome: See *Wolff*.

Boston cardiologist.

WHITFIELD, Arthur (1867–1947)
Whitfield's Ointment: Benzoic and salicylic acids in lanolin. D. 1907.

Dermatologist to King's College Hospital, London.

WHITNALL, Samuel Ernest (1876–1950)
Whitnall's Tubercle: Prominence on the zygomatic bone. D. 1911.

Born in Eccles, he first taught at Oxford, then became P. of Anatomy at McGill U., Montreal (1919–1934) and then at Bristol (1935–1941).

WICKHAM, Louis-Frédéric (1861–1913)
Wickham's Striae: Network of lines on the papules of lichen planus.

Paris dermatologist.

WIDAL, Georges Fernand Isidore (1862–1929)
Widal Reaction: Test for typhoid by agglutination of *Salmonella*★ *typhi* by serial dilutions of patient's serum. D. 1896. (The reaction had in fact been

discovered a few months earlier by H. E. Durham, an English bacteriologist.)

Widal was born in Dellys, Algeria, studied in Paris (MD 1889) and became successively P. of Internal Pathology, and P. of Clinical Medicine, in the U. of Paris. A well-known teacher, clinician and research worker, he held clinics at the Hôpital Cochin; he is buried in Montmartre.

von WILLEBRAND, E. A. (1870–1949)
von Willebrand's Disease: Clotting factor VIII deficiency with capillary and platelet abnormalities. D. 1926.

Physician at Helsingfors, Sweden.

WILLIS, Thomas (1621–1675)
Circle of Willis: Circulus arteriosus; the anastomotic arterial system at the base of the brain. D. 1664.

Born in Great Bedwyn, Wiltshire, the son of a farmer, his family moved to Oxford in 1631 when his mother died. There, at Christ Church College, he studied theology and medicine; during the Civil War he was in the Royalist Oxford University Legion. In 1646 he qualified BM, and in 1660, as a reward for his Royalist sympathies, was awarded the DM degree, and made Sedleian P. of Natural Philosophy. He was a founder of the Royal Society in 1662, and became an honorary FRCP in 1664. Physician, anatomist, teacher and writer, he was the leader of the 'iatrochemical' school in medicine, and had a flourishing private practice both in Oxford and in London, where he moved in 1667 at the insistence of Gilbert Sheldon, the Archbishop of Canterbury. His pupils included Richard Lower★ (who performed the first human blood transfusion) and the architect Christopher Wren, who helped to illustrate his most famous book, *Cerebri Anatome* (1664). As a schoolboy he used to give away his lunch to the poor, and he was always known for his charitable works. Willis was the first to describe myasthenia gravis (1671), paracusis, whooping cough (1684), and the intercostal, spinal and spinal accessory nerves. He was the first to record the sweet taste of diabetic urine (1670), he named puerperal fever, and coined the terms 'reflex', and 'neurology'. He died of pleurisy in St Martin's Lane, London, and is buried in

Westminster Abbey, together with Lister* and John Hunter*.

WILMS, Max (1867–1918)
Wilms Tumour: Nephroblastoma of kidney. D. 1899.

Born in Aachen, the son of a lawyer, he studied in Berlin and Bonn (MD 1890). He was Assistant at the Pathological Institute, Cologne, where he wrote on the pathology of mixed tumours; then became Surgical Assistant to Trendelenburg* at Leipzig, and subsequently Professor (1904). In 1907 he became P of Surgery in Basle and in 1910, in Heidelberg.

WILSON, Clifford (b. 1906)
Kimmelstiel–Wilson Disease of Kidneys: See *Kimmelstiel*. D. 1936.

After studying at Oxford and The London Hospital (BM 1933), he was Research Fellow at Harvard (1934–1935), Major in the RAMC, and later Emeritus P. of Medicine, London U. He is now retired in Hampshire.

WILSON, Samuel Alexander Kinnier (1878–1937)
1. *Wilson's Disease*: Hepatolenticular degeneration; an autosomal recessive trait in which copper is deposited in various organs, pathognomonically in Descemet's* membrane of the cornea, producing Kayser*–Fleischer* rings. D. 1912, in his Edinburgh MD thesis, which won the Gold Medal.
2. *Wilson's Sign*: Positive glabellar tap in early Parkinson's* Disease.

Born in Cedarville, New Jersey, the son of an Irish clergyman, he returned with his family to Scotland as a child, and studied medicine in Edinburgh (MB 1903). After working as house-physician at the Edinburgh Royal Infirmary he studied neurology under Marie* and Babinski* in Paris, and in Leipzig, and from 1904 spent the rest of his career as neurologist at the National Hospital for Nervous Diseases, at Queen Square, London, where Gowers*, Hughlings Jackson* and Horsley* were among his colleagues. A large, dominating man, he once asked a patient with an ususual neurological disorder to: 'See to it that I get your brain when you die'. A dramatic lecturer, he spoke fluent French and German, and made many contributions to neurology: he died of cancer at 59.

WIMSHURST, James (1822–1903)
Wimshurst Machine: Instrument generating static electricity.

English engineer.

WINSLOW, Jacob Benignus (1669–1760)
1. *Foramen of Winslow*: Epiploic foramen; opening into the lesser sac of peritoneum. D. 1732.
2. *Winslow's Ligament*: Oblique popliteal ligament of the knee-joint.

Born in Odense, Denmark, the eldest of 13 children, he was a great-nephew of Niels Stensen★. He went to Paris in 1698 studying theology at first, until a 'travelling scholarship' from the King of Denmark enabled him to study medicine, and he qualified MD in 1705. He became a Catholic and was disinherited by his Lutheran family, and so never returned to Denmark. Instead he remained in Paris, where he was recognised as one of the greatest teachers of anatomy in Europe, up to the time of his death there at the age of 90. It was not until 1743, however, when he was 74, that the U. of Paris made him P. of Anatomy, Physic and Surgery.

WINTROBE, Maxwell Myer (b. 1901)
Wintrobe Method: For haematocrit determination. D. 1933.

Born in Halifax, Nova Scotia, he studied at the U. of Manitoba, Winnipeg, Canada, and at Tulane U., New Orleans. He practised internal medicine in both places, and at Johns Hopkins Hospital, Baltimore, and is now Distinguished P. of Internal Medicine, U. of Utah School of Medicine, Salt Lake City.

WIRSUNG, Johann Georg (1600–1643)
Duct of Wirsung: Pancreatic duct. D. 1642.

Born in Augsburg, Bavaria, he became in 1629 Prosector of Anatomy, and later P. of Anatomy, at Padua, and was murdered there one night in 1643 while entering his house.

WISKOTT, Arthur
Wiskott–Aldrich Syndrome: Eczema, thrombocytopenia and susceptibility to infection, now believed to predispose to the development of lymphoma. D. 1937. (D. 1954 by Aldrich.)

German-born paediatrician who emigrated to the USA.

WOLFE, John Reisberg (1824–1904)
Wolfe Graft: Full-thickness skin graft. D. 1875.

Austrian ophthalmologist who settled in Glasgow; he described repair of an eyelid by a post-auricular graft in 1873.

WOLFF, Julius (1836–1902)
Wolff's Law: The trabecular pattern in lamellar bone is laid down in accordance with lines of transmitted force; i.e. changes in bone function are associated with alterations in internal architecture. D. 1884.

Born in Prussia, he studied with Langenbeck★, and in 1890 became P. of Orthopaedic Surgery, Berlin, where he died, and was succeeded in the chair by Albert Hoffa★.

WOLFF, Kaspar Friedrich (1733–1794)
Wolffian Duct: Mesonephric duct of embryo; the primordial male genital duct, which becomes the epididymis and vas deferens. D. 1759.

Born in Berlin, he studied there and in Halle, became an Army Surgeon, but failed to become a P. in Germany. In 1759 he became P. of Anatomy and Physiology in St Petersburg, and is remembered as a founder of modern embryology, who introduced the concept of the germ layers.

WOLFF, Louis (b. 1898)
Wolff–Parkinson–White Syndrome: Physiological bundle branch block with short P–R interval and prolonged QRS time on ECG. D. 1930.

Boston cardiologist.

WOOD, Robert Williams (1868–1955)
Wood's Light: Ultraviolet radiation of wavelength 365 nm from a mercury-vapour source which is passed through a nickel-oxide filter, used in the diagnosis of fungal infections of the scalp, and to detect porphyrins.

Born in Concord, Massachusetts, he studied at Harvard and in Berlin, taught physics at the U. of Wisconsin from 1897 to 1901, and then became P. of Experimental Physics at Johns Hopkins U.,

Baltimore. A talented artist, musician and writer, he published a book of satirical poetry. He was elected a foreign FRS, and won the Rumford Medal in 1938.

WORM, Ole (Olaus) (1588–1654)
Wormian Bones: Bones formed by intersecting skull sutures. So named by Thomas Bartholin Primus, whose father, Caspar Bartholin Primus, was Worm's brother-in-law.

Born in Butland, he studied anatomy and theology in Germany, Italy, France, and Basle (Switzerland). In 1613 he was appointed P. of Greek and Philosophy in Copenhagen, and in 1624 succeeded Caspar Bartholin Primus (grandfather of Caspar Bartholin Secundus★) as P. of Anatomy. He died in Copenhagen.

WRISBERG, Heinrich August (1739–1808)
1. *Cartilage of Wrisberg*: Cuneiform cartilage of the larynx. D. 1785.
2. *Ligament of Wrisberg*: Attaching the posterior aspect of the lateral meniscus to the inner side of the medial femoral condyle, behind the posterior cruciate ligament in the knee joint. D. 1764.

Anatomist and gynaecologist, born in St Andreasburg, who was P. of Anatomy in Göttingen from 1764 until his death.

WUCHERER, Otto (1820–1873)
Wuchereria: Genus of filarial nematodes of which one species, *bancroftii*★, is the causative organism of elephantiasis.

German physician who worked in Brazil.

Y

YERSIN, Alexandre Émil Jean (1863–1943)
Yersinia pseudotuberculosis: Gram★-negative bacterium implicated in mesenteric lymphadenitis in man. This bacterial genus was formerly called *Pasteurella*★.

Born near Lausanne, Switzerland, he was a pupil of Pasteur in Paris, and with Emile Roux (1853–1933) he was the first to demonstrate diphtheria toxin (1888). He became a surgeon in the French Colonial Army, and was Director of the Pasteur Institute at Nha-Trang in Annam (now Vietnam). He discovered the plague bacillus independently in Hong

Kong in 1894, and in 1895 developed an anti-plague serum with Calmette★.

YOUNG, Hugh Hampton (1870–1945)
Young's Prostatectomy: Prostatectomy by perineal approach. D. 1905.

P. of Urology, Johns Hopkins School of Medicine, Baltimore.

YOUNG, Thomas (1773–1829)
1. *Young–Helmholtz Theory of Colour Vision*: There are three types of cone receptor, responding to red, green and violet light. D. 1801. (D. 1852 by von Helmholtz.)
2. *Young's Rule*: Paediatric drug dosage =
$$\frac{\text{Age} \times \text{adult dose}}{\text{Age} + 12}.\ \text{D. 1813.}$$

'The father of physiological optics' was born in Milverton, Somerset, and was a child prodigy, with a phenomenal memory and grasp of languages and mechanics. By the age of 17 he had mastered Newton's *Principia* and *Optics*. In 1793 he studied medicine at Barts, and the following year, aged 21, was elected FRS for a paper on the action of the ciliary muscle in accommodation. He then studied in Edinburgh, Göttingen, and Emmanuel College, Cambridge (1797–1799), and in 1801, having been left £10,000 and a London house by an uncle, he became P. of Natural Philosophy at the Royal Institution. He was a failure as a lecturer, however, and resigned in 1803, became Physician to St Thomas's Hospital in 1811, and in 1817 Secretary to the Commission on Weights and Measures. An eminent philologist, as well as physicist, mathematician and physician, he was Foreign Secretary of the Royal Society, and worked on Egyptian hieroglyphics, including the decoding of the Rosetta Stone.

Z

ZAHN, Friedrich Wilhelm (1845–1904)
Lines of Zahn: Alternating layers of fibrin and platelets in ante-mortem thrombus.

Swiss pathologist.

ZEIS, Eduard (1807–1868)
Glands of Zeis: Ciliary glands (sebaceous glands of eyelids). Suppurative inflammation of these leads to a hordoleum, or stye.

P. of Surgery, Marburg, Germany. He coined the term 'plastic surgery' in 1863.

von ZENKER, Friedrich Albert (1825–1898)
Zenker's Degeneration: Fragmentation of eosinophilic leucocytes.

Pathologist in Munich. He described fat embolism.

ZIEHL, Franz Heinrich Paul (1857–1926)
Ziehl–Neelsen Stain: Carbol-fuschin stain for acid-fast bacilli.

Born in Wismar, Germany, he became Assistant in the medical clinic in Heidelberg (1882–1886) and later a neurologist in Lübeck.

ZINN, Johan Gottfried (1727–1759)
Zonule of Zinn: Part of the hyaloid membrane adjacent to the margins of the lens. D. 1753.

P. of Medicine and Director of the Botanical Gardens, Göttingen.

ZOLLINGER, Robert Milton (b. 1903)
Zollinger–Ellison Syndrome: Recurrent peptic ulceration associated with gastrin-producing islet-cell tumour of the pancreas. D. 1955.

P. of Surgery, Ohio State U., Columbus, Ohio.

ZONDEK, Bernhardt (1891–1966)
Aschheim–Zondek Pregnancy Test: See *Aschheim*.

P. of Gynaecology, Berlin, who later became P. of Obstetrics and Gynaecology at the Hebrew University, Jerusalem.

ZUCKERKANDL, Emil (1849–1910)
Fascia of Zuckerkandl: Retrorenal fascia.

Born in Raab, Austria, he became P. of Anatomy first in Graz, then in Vienna, where he died. He made an especial study of rhinology.

Bibliography

American Men and Women of Science (14th edition) (1979).
   Ed. Jacques Cattell Press. New York: R. R.
   Bowker.

Bailey, H. and Bishop, W. J. (1959). *Notable Names in
   Medicine and Surgery.* (3rd edition). London:
   H. K. Lewis.

Birch, C. A. (1979). *Names We Remember.* Beckenham:
   Ravenswood Publications.

Bradley, W. G. (1974). *Disorders of Peripheral Nerves.*
   Oxford: Blackwell Scientific Publications.

Bulloch, W. (1938). *The History of Bacteriology.* London:
   Oxford University Press.

Butterworth's Medical Dictionary (2nd edition). Ed.
   Macdonald Critchley. London: Butterworths.

Castiglioni, A. (1947). *A History of Medicine.* New
   York: Alfred Knopf.

Clain, A. (Ed.) (1973). *Hamilton Bailey's Demonstrations
   of Physical Signs in Clinical Surgery.* Bristol:
   Wright.

Cole, F. J. (1944). *A History of Comparative Anatomy.*
   London: Macmillan.

Cope, Z. (1959). *The History of the Royal College of
   Surgeons of England.* London: Anthony Blond.

Dobson, Jessie (1962). *Anatomical Eponyms.* Edinburgh:
   Livingstone.

Dobson, Jessie (1973). In: Last, R. J. (Ed.) *Anatomy,
   Regional and Applied* (5th edition). Edinburgh:
   Livingstone.

Dorland's Illustrated Medical Dictionary (25th edition).
   (1974). Philadelphia: W. B. Saunders.

Durham, R. H. (1969). *Encyclopedia of Medical
   Syndromes.* Philadelphia: J. B. Lippincott.

Foster, W. D. (1961). *A Short History of Clinical
   Pathology.* Edinburgh: Livingstone.

Garrison, F. H. (1929). *An Introduction to the History of*

Medicine (4th edition). Philadelphia: W. B. Saunders.

Glendinning, L. (1942). *Source Book of Medical History*. New York: Paul B. Hoeber.

Gould's Medical Dictionary (1979) (4th edition). New York: McGraw-Hill.

Haymaker, W. and Schiller, F. (1970). *The Founders of Neurology* (2nd edition). Springfield: Charles C. Thomas.

Jablonski, S. (1969). *Illustrated Dictionary of Eponymic Syndromes and Diseases and Their Synonyms*. Philadelphia, W. B. Saunders.

Kelly, E. C. (1948). *Encyclopaedia of Medical Sources*. Baltimore: Williams and Wilkins.

Long, E. R. (1962). *A History of American Pathology*. Springfield: Charles C. Thomas.

Magalini, S. (1971). *Dictionary of Medical Syndromes*. Philadelphia: J. B. Lippincott.

McGraw-Hill Modern Men of Science (1966). New York: McGraw-Hill.

Peel, J. (1976). *The Lives of the Fellows of the Royal College of Obstetricians and Gynaecologists 1929–1969*. London: Heinemann Medical Books.

Rains, A. J. Harding, and Capper, W. M. (1968). *Bailey and Love's Short Practice of Surgery* (14th edition). London: H. K. Lewis.

Rang, M. (1966). *Anthology of Orthopaedics*. Edinburgh: Churchill Livingstone.

Schultz, R. J. (1972). *The Language of Fractures*. Baltimore: Williams and Wilkins.

Singer, C. and Underwood, E. A. (1962). *A Short History of Medicine* (2nd edition). Oxford: Clarendon Press.

Skinner, H. A. (1970). *The Origin of Medical Terms*. New York: Hafner Publishing Company.

The Medical Directory (1980). Edinburgh: Churchill Livingstone.

Trail, R. R. (ed.) (1968). *Munk's Roll. Lives of the Fellows of the Royal College of Physicians of London*, vol. 5. London: Royal College of Physicians.

Williams, T. I. (Ed.) (1974). *A Biographical Dictionary of Scientists* (2nd edition). London: A. & C. Black.

Examiner (showing candidate a urinary catheter with an elbow-like bend in it):

    'This is a Coudé catheter; tell me, who *was* Coudé?'

Over-confident candidate (who has not read this book):

    'Oh, he was a nineteenth-century French urologist, Sir.'

Examiner (holding up a urinary catheter with *two* elbow-like bends in it):

    'And who was Bi-coudé?'

(Fr. *coude* = elbow)